CITY LITERACIES

'This is a remarkably timed, different, humane and richly detailed study. The epilogue is moving and very neatly summarises the present state of things. The whole book should be widely read.'
  Margaret Meek Spencer, *Institute of Education, University of London*

' . . . an illuminating interweaving of social, historical, educational and personal literacy histories. It is well written, clear and focused.'
  Dinah Volk, *College of Education, Cleveland State University*

City Literacies explores the lives and literacies of different generations of people living in two contrasting areas of London, Spitalfields and The City, at the end of the twentieth century. It contrasts these two 'square miles' of London, which outwardly symbolise the huge difference between poverty and wealth existing in Britain at this time. The book presents a study of living, learning and reading as it has taken place in public settings – including the school classroom, clubs, places of worship, theatres – and in the home. Over fifty people recount their memories of learning to read in different contexts and circumstances.

Eve Gregory and Ann Williams contextualise the participants' stories and go far to dispel the deep-seated myths surrounding the teaching and learning of reading and writing in urban, multicultural areas. The result is both poignant and highly significant to the study of literacy.

Eve Gregory is Professor of Language and Culture in Education at Goldsmiths College, University of London and **Ann Williams** is Research Fellow at Goldsmiths College and King's College, London.

LITERACIES
Series Editor: David Barton
Lancaster University

Literacy practices are changing rapidly in contemporary society in response to broad social, economic and technological changes: in education, the workplace, the media and in everyday life. This series reflects the burgeoning research and scholarship in the field of literacy studies and its increasingly interdisciplinary nature. The series aims to provide a home for books on reading and writing which consider literacy as a social practice and which situate it within broader institutional contexts. The books develop and draw together work in this field; they aim to be accessible, interdisciplinary and international in scope, and to cover a wide range of social and institutional contexts.

Titles in the series:

SITUATED LITERACIES
Reading and writing in context
Edited by David Barton, Mary Hamilton and Roz Ivanič

GLOBAL LITERACIES AND THE WORLD WIDE WEB
Edited by Gail E. Hawisher and Cynthia L. Selfe

MULTILITERACIES
Literacy learning and the design of social futures
Edited by Bill Cope and Mary Kalantzis

Editorial Board:

CITY LITERACIES

Learning to read across generations and cultures

Eve Gregory and Ann Williams

London and New York

3607229903

First published 2000
by Routledge
11 New Fetter Lane, London EC4P 4EE

Simultaneously published in the USA and Canada
by Routledge
29 West 35th Street, New York, NY 10001

Routledge is an imprint of the Taylor & Francis Group

Typeset in Baskerville by Keystroke, Jacaranda Lodge, Wolverhampton.
Printed and bound in Great Britain by TJ International Ltd,
Padstow, Cornwall.

British Library Cataloguing in Publication Data
A catalogue record for this book is available from the British Library

Library of Congress Cataloging in Publication Data
Gregory, Eve.
City literacies : learning to read across generations and cultures /
Eve Gregory & Ann Williams.
p. cm. – (Literacies)
ISBN 0–415–19115–7 – ISBN 0–415–19116–5 (pbk.)
1. Literacy–Social aspects–England–London–Case studies. 2. Multicultural
education–England–London–Case studies. I. Williams, Ann. II. Title. III. Series.
LC156.G72 L654 2000
302.2'244'094212–dc21   00–024989

ISBN 0–415–19115–7 (hbk)
ISBN 0–415–19116–5 (pbk)

To our parents, who taught us to value the past

CONTENTS

FIGURES

TABLES

PLATES

ACKNOWLEDGEMENTS

This book is the result of many years (for one of us, a lifetime) of living in, loving or learning about Spitalfields and the City of London. During these years, we have met countless people who have both explicitly and implicitly contributed to this book. Some of these contributors have long disappeared: the Jewish stallholders in Wentworth Street, the butchers and their shops lining Aldgate High Street and the housekeepers' children running through the City or in the Tower of London. They have now been replaced by children rushing to or from their Qur'anic classes and the Imam calling people to prayer. All these people have contributed to the spirit of the book and we remain grateful without being able to name individuals. Others can be named. We are particularly grateful to all the present pupils and their families and the staff of both Canon Barnett and Sir John Cass School, particularly Rani Shamas, Gerry Lochran, Sandra Murphy and Bill Green. Invaluable information on Jewish history in the East End of London has been provided by the Springboard Educational Trust, particularly by A. Shapiro, and on the history of the area generally by C. Lloyd of Bancroft Road Library, and T. Budgen and A. Prescott of Toynbee Hall. A number of earlier papers have been published relating to this work and we should like to thank Margaret Meek, Brian Street, Dinah Volk, Susi Long, David Barton, Nasima Rashid, William Bright, Karen Jones, Marilyn Martin-Jones, Jane Mace, Jenny Cook-Gumperz, Viv Edwards, Ali Asghar, Geoffrey Walford, Alexander Massey, Eddie Williams, Karl Kimmig, Joy Stanton, Constant Leung, Arturo Tosi, as well as members of the intercollegiate research group on language and culture held at University College, London for helpful suggestions on these. We should like to thank Paul Stanton, Claudine Kirsch and Joe Williams, whose photos show the vitality of the area today. We owe an enormous debt of gratitude to all those who gave so freely of their time to share their memories with us, to read and correct our work – and on some occasions even continue the writing where we left off! Particularly, we wish to thank R. Barnes, M. Adelman, S. Rowbotham, A. Levy, A. Shapiro, E. Duller, N. Isaacson, G. Morgan, G. North, L. Cohen, R. Hussey, T. Hussey, C. Miller, J. Abel, R. Gregory, C. Searle, R. Shamas, A. Hossain, R. Mortuza, A. Ahmed,

H. Begum and R. Islam. Finally, we should like to express our gratitude to all those who made the work possible through their financial assistance. Particularly, we should like to thank the Leverhulme Trust for enabling work for Part II of the book to take place through the award of a Research Fellowship to Eve Gregory in 1997, to the Economic and Social Research Council in 1994–5 (*Family Literacy History and Children's Reading Strategies at Home and at School* R000 221186; and *Siblings as Mediators of Literacy in Two East London Communities* R000 222487) for assisting work leading to Part III of the book, and the Paul Hamlyn Foundation and Goldsmiths College, without whose early support and financial assistance the work could never have been started.

PROLOGUE

I love Spitalfields . . . there's nowhere in London that I love more than Spitalfields . . . But it's not because we have a big Bangladeshi community residing here, not because of that. It's also because I like the idiosyncrasies of Spitalfields, that it's got a lot of history. Not just the recent history of Bangladeshi immigrants but the history prior to that. I love that sort of energy that we have here . . . Spitalfields is almost quaint . . . It's not because it has curry houses . . . I never step into those . . . It's something that you just love, that you are part of the architecture of Spitalfields and I love it . . .

(Tahmin, born in 1975)

This book will appeal to all those fascinated by the lives and literacies of different generations living in two square miles of London, which have possibly experienced more social and cultural changes during the twentieth century than any other neighbourhood in Britain. One of the square miles is Spitalfields; the other is the City of London which lies directly to its west. Within these neighbourhoods, we have chosen to focus on two adjacent schools; one in the City and one just over the border in Spitalfields. All the participants whose stories follow, have attended, taught in, cleaned, managed or had other close links with the schools and the work taking place in their classrooms. The book presents an intergenerational study of living, learning and reading as it has taken place throughout the twentieth century in homes, clubs, churches, synagogues, mosques, theatres, and, of course, the school classrooms. Over fifty people have participated in the book, telling their memories of learning to read in different contexts and circumstances and of the role of reading in transforming their lives. The origins of those whose voices are heard span the world: from Cockney London to Ireland, from Bangladesh to Africa. The oldest participant in the study is 91 years old, the youngest, a 3-year-old child who has recently started nursery in one of the two schools.

Spitalfields and the City of London outwardly symbolise the huge contrasts between poverty and wealth existing in Britain at the end of the twentieth century. The City is a bubble of gleaming glass skyscrapers, banks, offices and wine and sandwich bars where people work, entertain or rush to eat, but do not now live. The clientele is white and predominantly male. In contrast, the neighbourhood of Spitalfields presents a higgledy-piggledy architecture: gloomy Victorian tenements and the worst of high-rise, mid-twentieth-century-built flats alongside bright sari shops, tastefully renovated eighteenth-century Huguenot houses and, during the last few years of the century, the scrubbed and beautiful old Victorian warehouses which are suddenly emerging from years of grime and obscurity. From Monday to Friday, at least, business people live in expensive studio conversions in the same street as the council flats of their first- and second-generation Bangladeshi-British neighbours. The area has long been multicultural and multilingual; just a stone's throw from the old London docks, it has traditionally been the first port of call for immigrants arriving in Britain. The experiences and progress of these children, therefore, may well reflect the way in which the host society generally, and the school particularly, welcomes newcomers into its midst.

The two schools have remained largely untouched by the white business world on their doorstep. Their children now come from very similar backgrounds: one receives almost all its pupils from Bangladeshi-British families; the other, approximately 80 per cent of its roll, a number which, at the end of the twentieth century, was rising. They have not always been so similar, nor have their children always been from Asia, as we shall see in the following chapters. Their clientele does not mean that they share the same traditions; the City school has followed the traditions of a Church of England Foundation school, while its neighbour has changed its cultural traditions to fit that of each new majority group in the neighbourhood.

City Literacies was born primarily out of the wish to dispel deep-seated myths concerning the teaching and learning of reading in urban, multi-cultural areas. The first of these myths equates economic poverty with poor literacy skills. This book, however, is about success not failure. It aims to celebrate the diversity, scope and importance of literacy activities in the lives of children living and learning in a neighbourhood which throughout the century has been home to some of the poorest residents of Britain. This celebration is not just for children's success in mastering the reading and writing demanded in the classrooms they attended, but for their out-of-school literacy activities which usually remained invisible to both the school and society's eyes.

A second myth equates early reading success with a particular type of parenting. During the second half of the twentieth century, parents in Britain have been advised to read stories to their infants on a regular basis and in a relaxed, enjoyable fashion in order to secure early reading success. Children unfamiliar with this practice are said to be more likely to find learning to read in school difficult. In this book, however, we see successful reading by many who did not have access to what is now recognised as 'good' literature and whose parents did not participate in this practice. We see how young children in each generation have been introduced to a wealth of different access points to literacy by mediators or 'guiding lights'[1] who have inspired them to become lifelong readers. Parents by no means play a passive role. However, most provide *different* opportunities for learning from those officially recognised. A number of families in this book remember particular teachers, others speak of grandparents or siblings, yet others of drama teachers or even army officers who influenced their literacy development later in life.

A third myth associates a mismatch between the language and learning styles used in the home and those demanded by school with difficulty and early reading failure. Children who do not speak English at home are often regarded as having general language 'problems'; the main concern of the school has long been to attempt to replace the home language without any recognition of the skills and possible advantages it may bring. Likewise, attendance at community-language or religious classes has often been viewed as detrimental or, at best, as providing no preparation at all for the main-stream school. This book highlights ways in which children syncretise or blend home, community and school language and learning styles to enhance both home learning and official school achievement. In each chapter, we see how, out of expediency, religious, language and cultural practices are constantly changing as the learners blend new and old.

Finally, the myth of the 'correct method' of teaching reading has become particularly powerful in Britain during the final years of the twentieth century. Early years teachers are told repeatedly that children are likely to fail to learn to read unless a particular approach to teaching initial literacy is taken. Yet the memories of both families and teachers in this book reveal a wealth of successful teaching methods. Many children experienced an array of methods in different contexts; for example, letter naming in school, chanting and blending sounds in their religious classes and reciting whole chunks of text at choir or drama classes. Rather than the teachers' method of teaching reading being significant for success, it was their whole approach to teaching about learning itself which was absolutely decisive. A common factor dividing memorable and successful teachers from others was their energy, knowledge and commitment to their work as well as their respect for the individual child.

To our US readers, we should like to emphasise the relevance of this book to those interested in language and literacy education. There are similarities and differences between the two contexts. In many large US cities, neighbourhoods like Spitalfields have been repeatedly transformed through waves of immigration. While the specifics of government educational reports and policies have inevitably been different from those in Britain, broader trends have been remarkably similar.

Our four myths also have a strong hold on educational thought in the United States. The first two myths equating poverty with poor literacy skills as well as 'inadequate' parenting are particular to countries on both sides of the Atlantic. In spite of the positive features of TV programmes such as *Headstart* and *Sesame Street*,[2] they are based on the premise that children from economically disadvantaged homes are deficient in language and literacy skills. Both advice to parents and 'good-parenting' programmes in the USA stress the importance of storyreading to children. This message is promoted in a whole range of formats, including training programmes and packs for parents and messages from schools.

The third myth of language 'mismatch' also prevails although more programmes have been established to minimise this through bilingual, multicultural and Afro-centric programmes, all of which are lacking in the British context. Despite these efforts at creating continuity, the emphasis is still on a mismatch as responsible for children's problems. Most efforts to diminish this mismatch concentrate on imposing the school culture on the home, although a whole series of research projects on both sides of the Atlantic have shown that this process is far more complex than previously imagined.[3] The fourth myth promoting the importance of a 'correct method' of teaching initial literacy is also prevalent in the USA. In the same way as in Britain, different methods have been ascendant in the American context and different proponents have each claimed that their way is the 'natural' one for early reading success.

This book gives a voice to generations of readers growing up, living and working throughout the twentieth – and twenty-first – centuries in London's East End. They tell us what was really significant about reading and learning to read for their lives; not what they did not do or what they should have done according to official sources. At the beginning of the twenty-first century, it is important that we hear from those who lived in the area themselves and do not simply listen to the latest report on poor reading standards in the East End. Spanning almost a hundred years, the people in this book speak up for all those learning to read successfully in economically disadvantaged areas. For it is the community and all those who lived and worked there who are the true authors. Their words reveal a breadth and depth of knowledge, a wealth of experiences and a love and respect for reading, which no one else can convey.

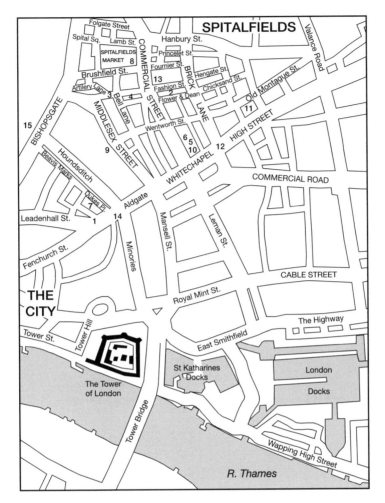

1   Aldgate Pump
2   Flower and Dean Walk
3   Jews' Free School, Bell Lane
4   East End Soup Kitchen, Brune Street
5   Toynbee Hall
6   Canon Barnett School
7   Sir John Cass Foundation School
8   Spitalfields Market
9   Petticoat Land (Middlesex Street)
10 Site of Bloom's restaurant
11 Black Iron Yard
12 Whitechapel Library & Whitechapel Art Gallery
13 Christchurch, Spitalfields
14 St. Botolph's Church
15 Liverpool Street Station

Map of the Spitalfields Area of London

INTRODUCTION: POVERTY AND ILLITERACY – THE DEFICIT MYTH

I just think, if you're working class, you're expected to be a low achiever. And if you show no initiative, then you're going to be left behind. And that's still true today, I think.

(Linda, born in 1953)

Myths do not prevail without reason. If the aim of this book is to challenge assumptions that economic poverty equates with low literacy skills, we need first to unravel their origins, to examine how they developed and to analyse why, at first sight, such notions appear convincing. Why is poverty generally held to be synonymous with low reading standards in Britain? Why should social and economic disadvantage result in problems of early literacy learning in school? What 'counts' as successful early reading in Britain today and who determines this? The first part of this chapter unpicks different threads in the argument linking poverty with cognitive, cultural and linguistic deficit and outlines an alternative paradigm for early literacy success that will be illustrated through the families in this book.

The second part of the chapter introduces the Spitalfields study itself. We outline the theoretical framework which underpins and informs our work, to assist all those who, after reading the book, feel they want to conduct a similar study in their own community. We go on to explain how the research is rooted in our own reading histories, how we have set about getting to know families across different generations, how we have observed, interviewed and worked with teachers, families and children in homes, communities and classrooms and how we have analysed our findings during different phases of the work. Our argument throughout the book is that teachers in every school will discover a similar wealth of literacy traditions and 'funds of knowledge'.[1] It is the teacher's awareness of this wealth that best exposes as groundless the deficit myth.

1

The myth of poverty and learning difficulty

R: *Like when they used to say, 'Bob, read out page one, Harry, read out page two. We won't ask Raymond, he's thick.' And they said that, you know.*

E: *They said it in the class?*

R: *Oh yes. I do remember that. Yes, they said it. And then I went around and said, 'They won't ask me to read, I'm thick.' And I liked it. They gave me this label and I accepted it.*

(Raymond, Linda's brother, born in 1947)[2]

As the lives of the characters in this book unfold, readers will notice a crucial difference between the generations. Whereas those born before World War II see leaving school at a young age and a lack of examination passes as inevitable, the post-war generation blame themselves for not taking advantage of education to the full.[3] Only the young Bangladeshi-British women who have a university education speak out and blame their teachers and the school. It is certainly true that poverty in London's East End during the first half of the century meant that children left school early. Most of the older people in the book who completed their formal education before World War II left school at the age of 14 in order to help their families. But it was recognised by all that *poverty itself* was to blame for this. The priority was to contribute to feeding and clothing younger siblings and there was no stigma attached to finding any kind of manual labour in order to do this. This picture was reflected in official education reports of the time. As late as 1931, the Hadow Report put forward the reason for general low achievement as that of poverty itself, since the child from a 'poor home' had 'little opportunities for reading' (para. 48). No suggestion was made that intellectual, cultural or linguistic deficit might bear any responsibility. But by the 1960s, after compulsory schooling had been extended first to 15, then 16, after comprehensive education and Educational Priority Areas (EPAs) were attempting to ensure greater equality of opportunity and children in poor areas were still leaving school early, the locus of blame had changed. It was argued that it was not poverty as such that was responsible for children dropping out of school early; rather, it was what poverty brought with it in terms of cognitive, intellectual or linguistic deficiency. What was the evidence underpinning such a major shift in argument?

During the 1950s and 1960s, interest in educational research was centred upon the investigation into children's intelligence (IQ) and the extent to which it might be either genetically or environmentally determined. In 1955, a large-scale study carried out across London by Burt claimed a correlation between poverty and backwardness as well as between 'giftedness' and the more economically favoured, and argued strongly for intelligence being genetically determined. The numbers of children involved, as well as the array of standardised tests used, looked impressive. However, these findings were refuted shortly afterwards in a similar large-scale study conducted by Cullen in 1964 who found no relationship between IQ scores and social class but a definite relationship in terms of poor school *performance*. Hence the crucial question which has preoccupied educationists in Britain from the 1960s onwards has been: how might poor school performance and particularly early literacy difficulties be explained?

Interest was still focused on children's IQ scores in the influential Plowden Report on children's primary education published in 1967. In this report, the committee argued not only that children's IQs were *environmentally* determined, but went on to claim that the poor school performance of lower-class children was due to a 'cognitive deficit', a defective attitude, a low level of imagination, a dislike of the abstract and a lack of curiosity, some-times referred to as a 'psychological poverty', which could have disastrous results: 'We do not know at what age and to what extent this process is reversible by suitable experience or treatment' (para. 70). Intelligence, therefore, was not viewed as innate or genetically determined, but the result of *primary socialisation*. Children's upbringing, rather than poverty itself, was said to result in an intellectual poverty which desperately needed early treatment if children were to have any chance of school success. A crucial part of a child's upbringing was, of course, the language used in the home. A prevailing argument during the 1960s and 1970s was that 'inadequate' language experiences at home were likely to lead to a low level of cognitive ability and poor school achievement.

The 'language–cognition' link was a vital turning point in the argument explaining the school learning difficulties of the poor. Compensatory projects during the 1960s were claiming that the lower-social-class child was entering school virtually without language.[4] By the time of the publication of the Plowden Report in 1967, the 'poor language = inferior cognition' argument was being claimed as conventional wisdom. Drawing upon research studies from psychology,[5] anthropology[6] and sociology,[7] the Plowden Committee claimed that, since language was recognised to be the symbolic representation of thought, and since the language of many lower-class children was proved to be restricted, this would be reflected in their intellectual growth. It went on to maintain that many lower-social-class children would be unable to have the breadth of vocabulary necessary even to begin formal reading instruction (para. 55).[8]

This 'language deficiency = cognitive weakness = school failure' argument rested upon one basic assumption: that linguistic forms used in speech directly reflected intellectual capacity and that cognitive ability could, therefore, be measured by testing spoken language. In other words, the Committee assumed that speech was synonymous with language and that language could be tested through speech. However, this assumption had been hotly contested by linguists and sociolinguists from the mid-1960s onwards. In 1965, the linguist Noam Chomsky had proposed a model in which language is seen as a system with two parts: competence (a universal grammar which is part of the biologically endowed human language faculty) and performance (the specific utterances of an individual's speech). Competence is concerned with the tacit knowledge of language structure; that is, the knowledge implicit in what an ideal speaker-listener would say and which belongs to being human. Performance is what is actually *said* given the psychological, social and contextual constraints in which speakers might find themselves. It is difficult to test a child's competence, however, without relying on his/her performance, i.e. speech. This dilemma led to underestimations of the language competence of working-class children in particular who, placed in an asymmetric context with a middle-class, adult interlocutor, did not display the same verbal skills as their middle-class counterparts. By altering the context to suit the child, linguists such as William Labov have demonstrated that all children share language skills. Nevertheless, even today, crude notions such as 'poverty = language deficit = low cognitive ability' can still be heard.

The myth of poverty and parental deficiency

Although my mother didn't have much and had to spend a lot of time – well, living in those conditions, you had to be meticulously clean – she still found time to take me to Madame Tussaud's. She took me to Hyde Park and we used to sit and listen to the band. She'd take me to Lyons Corner House and buy me a cup of tea and some pastries to teach me how to behave when you go out with other people . . . This is all education. This was an education from my mother that very few got, you know . . .

(Gloria, born in 1939)

During the 1970s, responsibility for children's educational success in Britain began to shift more noticeably to the parents and the family environment. The Bullock Report had been commissioned in 1975 as a result of concern over reading standards generally, but particularly over those of children from lower-social-class families where measures of assessment were indicating deterioration. Drawing particularly upon research in language development[9] and sociolinguistics,[10] the Report stressed the 'vitally important role' (5.1) played by parents in extending and elaborating a child's speech. Further, whether a child grew up in an 'educative' family would depend upon both the role relationships within the home (which, according to the Report, should be flexible rather than fixed) as well as the preparation for school given to the young child.

As far as literacy was concerned, the Bullock Report left little doubt as to the precise material which should be used and the form this preparation should take:

the best way to prepare the very young child for reading is to hold him [sic] on your lap and read aloud to him stories he likes, over and over again . . .

We believe that a priority need is . . . to help parents recognise the value of sharing the experience of books with their children.

(7.2)

This interest in one particular language activity signalled a change of focus in the deficit argument that was to prevail from the 1980s. Rather than suffering from generally 'restricted' language as claimed earlier in the Plowden Report, children were now considered 'disadvantaged' if they lacked a knowledge of language in one particular context, namely written narrative.

The 'narrative inexperience' argument was grounded in research by linguists and psychologists[11] into the different demands made by the written and spoken context. The Cox Report which first appeared in 1988 stated clearly that

Learning to read demands the existence of certain cognitive and linguistic development gained primarily through familiarity with written stories. Parents should read books with their children from their earliest days, read aloud to them and talk about the stories they have enjoyed together.

(2.3)

This view of what differentiated 'good' from 'poor' parenting gained momentum throughout the 1980s and has continued to the present time. It was enhanced by results from Gordon Wells's ten-year study of 128 children's literacy performance at ages 7 and 11 published in 1985 and 1987,[12] which claimed that, of all the factors in pre-school literacy investigated, only listening to written stories at home had a strong correlation with early school literacy success. This finding alone would have been uncontentious: schools were teaching reading using precisely the texts that such children would be familiar with from home. However, it went further to claim that the absence of storyreading in lower-social-class homes simply perpetuated the cycle of disadvantage and failure. Children in such homes, the reports claimed, 'urgently need the experience of books and the pleasure of being read to'.[13] This official view that 'babies need books', and that it is the duty of parents to provide them, has now become a commonly accepted belief in Britain. From supermarket hoardings to packets of detergent,[14] the image portrayed is of a mother sharing a storybook with her young child. As 'partnership in reading'[15] schemes are currently being replaced by 'home–school contracts',[16] which request parents to participate in officially sanctioned practices, those who cannot or choose not to fulfil these tasks are likely to be judged increasingly as inadequate by the school.

The myth of mismatch and learning difficulty

... at the age of 7, we were learning Hebrew grammar, which is far more complicated in many ways than English grammar, so when we were in the English school, adjectives and nouns and verbs and all this sort of thing was very natural to us, things that our non-Jewish friends would just be beginning to attempt to grapple with.

(Aumie, born in 1924)

The education world has not generally viewed bilingualism in this positive light. During the first three decades of the twentieth century, evidence from the IQ test performance of children speaking more than one language led researchers to claim that bilingualism resulted in intellectual deficiency and mental retardation.[17] Such evidence has since been strongly disputed in studies which demonstrated that bilingual children have a more highly developed linguistic and social awareness as well as a cognitive and intellectual flexibility which exceeds that of their monolingual peers.[18] Crucially, however, these advantages have been said only to occur when the child's first language is of high and not low prestige and when the bilingualism is 'additive' (added to the first language) and *not* subtractive (replacing the first language).

Throughout the twentieth century, children in east London have fallen into the net of 'subtractive bilingualism' since mainstream schooling has largely aimed to ignore the children's mother tongue, replacing it with English. However, in reality, our children step outside this paradigm in its simple form. Both Jewish and Bangladeshi-British groups have worked in unofficial contexts with at least three languages. During the first half of the century, many Jewish children successfully mastered learning to read the Talmud in Hebrew and Aramaic[19] in their religious classes; more recently, Bangladeshi-British children learn to read and write in standard Bengali and to 'read'[20] the Qur'an in classical Arabic. Insofar as the children have always acquired different literacies in a second or third language, their bilingualism should, then, be seen as 'additive'.[21] However, the lack of acknowledgement of these literacies by the school coupled with the fact that all the children's additional languages have been viewed as low status by the host society have rendered them 'subtractive' in the eyes of the education world.[22] Moreover, the children's 'unofficial' literacies have not necessarily been in the language or dialect spoken in the home, since this was English or 'Yinglish' (a mixture of English and Yiddish) for the Jewish children and Sylheti[23] for those of Bangladeshi-British origin.

The 'additive–subtractive, beneficial–detrimental' hypothesis is even more problematic when applied to east London children throughout the twentieth century. First, the bilinguality[24] of Jewish children during the first half of the twentieth century cannot be fairly compared with that of the

Bangladeshi-British children from the 1970s onwards. Only one of the Jewish participants in this study could remember being unable to speak English before starting school and most understood Yiddish more than they could speak it. Although their parents often spoke Yiddish to each other, the children were encouraged to speak English at home to both their siblings and parents. Second, Jewish children were learning only classical Hebrew, a language which was not spoken, in their religious classes; Bangladeshi-British children are similarly learning classical Arabic at their Qur'anic class but in addition are learning to become literate in standard Bengali, while at home they speak Sylheti, the unwritten dialect of the majority of the Bangladeshi-British population. Third, Jewish children entered classrooms in both our schools alongside monolingual English as well as non-Jewish peers, whereas our Bangladeshi-British group is learning in a class where not one of their classmates is a native-English speaker.

In spite of a shared participation in multiple worlds, there were other hugely different starting points between groups, which affected their bilinguality.[25] For the pre-war Jewish settlers in our study, Britain was a safe haven from the pogroms in eastern Europe. For them, as for their parents, there was no myth of return and this was reflected in their aim to see the school and the library as mediators of the English language, literature and culture. Britain was a land of opportunities, of work and of limited xenophobia and discrimination.[26] This contrasts with the future faced by our Bangladeshi-British group during the final years of the twentieth century. As the children of economic migrants, visibly very different from the host community and living in an area of high unemployment, their class often has no native-English speaker as a role model with the exception of the teacher.[27] Books come more from the school than the library, since the roads are now dangerous and racial attacks not unknown. Finally, although most of the younger adults of our Bangladeshi-British group see Britain as their home, those who were born and educated in Bangladesh, including some of the parents of our group of young children, still see an eventual return to Bangladesh as a possible and even desirable outcome and return frequently with their children to the homeland.

Thus we see that the notion of mismatch between home and school languages, as well as the 'subtractive–detrimental' hypothesis as reasons for difficulty or deficiency, has always been highly complex and controversial when applied to the different generations of bilingual British children in east London schools.

The myth of the 'correct way' to teach literacy

We used to do everything by rote. It would be put up on the board and we would repeat what the teacher said. "Cat", "dog", that kind of thing . . .

(Abby, born in 1917)

Abby still lives adjacent to the school she first entered at the age of 3. The walls of her flat are lined with books on every subject. She has read them all and describes how she loves reading. Yet most professionals in the education world would now frown at the way she was taught. Since the 1960s and 1970s, when concern for the reading standards of lower-social-class children was expressed in both the Plowden Report *Children and their Primary Schools* and the Bullock Report *A Language for Life* (DES 1967, 1975), officially sanctioned approaches for initial reading instruction in Britain have swung in different directions, often reflecting the research trends in psychology or linguistics that held sway at the time.

Before compulsory schooling in 1870, children often learned to read by constant repetition of passages from the Bible; Sunday school classes would reinforce a rote, word-by-word learning. This practice continued into the early twentieth century. Thus, Abby and Minnie, both in their eighties, remember learning to read by saying the letter names and the full word, which they would learn by rote from the blackboard. This was followed during the early decades of the twentieth century by the structuralist notion that reading is a code system;[28] the key to learning to read lies in breaking the code bound in the letters. Instruction, then, was focused on teaching children to break up words into individual sounds and blending strings of sounds into words. Most of our 40- to 60-year-old age group in this book remember being taught through phonics in this way.

During the 1960s, behaviourism and Gestalt theory were important in psychology; children were repeatedly exposed to 'flash cards' and praised each time a word was remembered. The influence of psychologists on reading came largely through 'whole word' or 'look-and-say' tuition. Shortly afterwards, work in cognitive psychology and psycholinguistics argued that children do not learn simply by copying the actions and language of adults.[29] Instead, they actively construct their own view of the world; like scientists, they constantly make hypotheses in order to predict what awaits them. Similarly, their knowledge of language and their experience enables them to predict what word is likely to come next in a sentence. Translated into literacy programmes, educationists maintained that children would be able to read more easily if texts were related to their own experience and language, i.e. were meaningful to them.[30] Consequently, the 'language experience' approach whereby children learned to read through composing their own personal texts became popular during the 1970s. Many of the parent generation now in their thirties remember using the 'Breakthrough to Literacy' materials, which promoted this approach.

By the late 1970s, however, and throughout the 1980s, research in linguistics was highlighting the importance of a knowledge of 'book language' rather than children's own personal texts in learning to read.[31] Children were still to learn to read through meaningful texts, as with the 'language experience' approach, but, crucially, it was the text of the book that was to be meaningful. It was thus assumed that texts of 'high quality' in terms of plot, use of language, illustrations and reputation of the author, would be unquestionably accessible and meaningful to all children and their families. Through listening to enjoyable texts read aloud by teachers in school and parents at home, children would learn through an 'apprenticeship' approach.[32] This was a method whereby they would master whole chunks of language before breaking these into individual words, letters and sounds. The young generation of Bangladeshi-British women in our study largely remembered learning to read in school (though not at home) through the repetition or 'shared reading'[33] of enjoyable texts.

Are methods of teaching reading in school still shadowing research trends as we begin a new century? The answer is both yes and no. A number of research studies now illustrate the wide range of literacy practices taking place among adults, which contrast with the accepted or 'legitimate' literacy taught in school (see particularly Baynham[34] and Barton and Hamilton[35]). These practices each require different skills which are learned in different ways using a variety of materials; for example, religious literacy may require a knowledge of prayers and hymns that is very different from the literacy attached to reading train timetables, tax returns or classical literacy. Most practices necessitate understanding the meaning as a prerequisite for reading, but some – for example, reading hymns – do not. This view of literacy has had some influence on the reading methods sanctioned in schools. Instead of a shift to any new approach, the last decade of the twentieth century saw a syncretism of most earlier methods. The 'interactionist' model[36] describes reading in terms of the *process* of how children synthesise information from four 'knowledge centres': the grapho-phonic (the earlier phonic method), the lexical (the look-and-say method), the syntactic and the semantic (the language-experience and the story approaches). Each can be seen as a *knowledge centre* providing different sets of clues or 'cues', which children draw upon as they learn to read:

- *the grapho-phonic knowledge centre* comprises *orthographic* and *phonological* knowledge, which sends out clues concerning the patterns of letters in words and the sounds they make, e.g. the arrangement of letters and sounds in the word 'splash' or 'fridge' are acceptable in English whereas the sequence of sounds and letters in 'sjcit' or 'ngisr' are not;
- *the lexical knowledge centre* sends out clues concerning the word and the relationships and associations between words, e.g. 'knife and fork' rather than 'knife and powder puff';
- *the syntactic knowledge centre* sends out clues concerning the structure of the language, e.g. 'Catching rats is as easy for ratcatchers as catching toves is for ____' ('tovecatchers');
- *the semantic knowledge centre* sends out clues concerning the meaning behind the words (within the culture or within the text), e.g. 'John tried

hard to persuade his father that, far from being the ____ report in the class, his was, in fact, the ____.' (Experience of life and the culture should tell the reader that 'worst' and 'best' could never be the other way round!).

Information from different knowledge centres constantly interacts, e.g. 'The shooting of the hunters was terrible' may be interpreted in two ways (that is, *the hunters were poor shooters* or *it is terrible that the hunters have been shot*) according to the context.

All these knowledge sources provide *simultaneous* input into a '*pattern synthesiser*' which keeps a running list of hypotheses or hunches about the nature of the input; each hypothesis is evaluated by the knowledge source and confirmed or disconfirmed. The procedure is continued until a decision is reached and the hypothesis deemed to be correct. The *interactionist model* of reading, then, paradoxically recognises all past conflicting methods as valid and valuable but only when used *in combination*.[37] It also implicitly recognises that reading requires discrete skills which ultimately interact, but that beginning readers are likely to have stronger and weaker cues. In other words, it recognises that lexical and grapho-phonic cues are on the same level as cues which demand understanding the meaning of a text – that is, the syntactic and semantic cues – and, for some children, may possibly precede them.

It is this model that is upheld by the literacy hour, part of the National Literacy Strategy[38] (one hour per day of class- and group-directed literacy work), compulsory in all state primary schools in Britain from 1998 but with one crucial difference. The literacy strategy assumes that children should be able to discuss texts before being able to read them, or, in other words, that understanding the meaning of the text must *precede* learning to read it. It also makes it clear that certain early reading texts count as valid reading material while others do not. Texts which count are those grounded in what is deemed to be 'quality literature' for children. The titles of these texts are published so that parents can practise them with their children. And so we come full circle, back to the responsibility of parents. Preparing their children for school requires parents to purchase these books and ensure that their children not only have a knowledge of the words but can talk meaningfully about them. In other words, parents need to know that there is a body of knowledge about important texts with which they should equip their children for school.[39]

Success through difference: an alternative model

Using the literacy experiences of families throughout the twentieth century as evidence, we propose an alternative model of early reading success. It is a model based on the belief that *contrasting* rather than *similar* home and school

10

strategies and practices provide a child with a larger treasure trove from which to draw for school learning. The key task for teachers is to tap into this knowledge and to teach children to become conscious of existing knowledge and skills, to enable children to compare and contrast different languages and literacy practices. It is a model that is particularly relevant for children whose families do not share the literacy practices of the teachers and the school and whose reading skills, therefore, risk remaining invisible. The argument put forward in this book is that *difference* complements mainstream school literacy rather than opposes it.

The model of *contrasting literacies*, which we put forward in this book, provides a new framework for interpreting early literacy learning, which synthesises perspectives that originate in different disciplines and research traditions and have generally been associated with *either* childhood *or* adult learning. The framework includes six main perspectives. The first perspective is drawn from the research of Street, Barton and Hamilton, Baynham, and others whose work has come to be known as the New Literacy Studies.[40] These studies challenge the notion of a 'great divide'[41] between literacy and orality, arguing that there is no single, monolithic, autonomous literacy: rather, there are 'literacies' or 'literacy practices' whose character and consequences are different in each context. Literacy practices are, then, aspects not just of culture but also of power structures.[42] Viewed in this way, school-sanctioned literacy to which Street refers, is just one of a multiplicity of literacies which take place in people's lives, in different languages, in different domains and for a variety of purposes. Hitherto, the New Literacy Studies have studied the social literacy of adults rather than young children.[43] *City Literacies* reveals a multiplicity of literacy practices in the lives of young children at home, in communities and classrooms both at the end of and throughout the twentieth century.

From the New Literacy Studies, we have extended Baynham's[44] use of the term 'mediator of literacy' to mean not just 'a person who makes his or her skill available to others, on a formal or informal basis, for them to accomplish specific literacy purposes', but also any resource for literacy learning. Mediators may, then, be teachers at out-of-school community language or religious classes, clubs or drama activities, but also institutions such as libraries, which enable children to make use of their facilities. They may also be 'guiding lights', a term used by Padmore[45] to refer to mediators who are especially inspiring, such as mentors, role models, grandparents[46] or siblings.[47] Thus childhood initiation into literacy is viewed as *a collaborative group activity* rather than a dyadic activity between parent (usually mother) and child.

Although the New Literacy Studies stress the importance of recognising a multiplicity of literacy practices in children's lives, it is clear that different literacies are going to be valued differently by the school. A second perspective informing the *contrasting literacies* model is that of the sociologist

Bourdieu[48] who stresses the power of the school as an institution in validating certain forms of 'cultural capital' while rejecting others. The participants in this study all show the power not just of 'cultural capital' but also of 'social' and 'economic' capital in determining a child's success in school. Although this is played out differently by each generation, we see the effects of a lack of one, two or all these types of capital on different families in and out of school.

The third perspective informing the model is drawn from Cole's work in cultural psychology which offers a 'cultural mediational model of reading' and stresses that 'successful adult efforts depend crucially upon their organising a "cultural medium for reading" which . . . must use artefacts (most notably but not only the text), must be proleptic, and must organise social relations to co-ordinate the child with the to-be-acquired system of mediation in an effective way'.[49] (By prolepsis, Cole means the way we all carry within us the heritage of our cultural past, which we use to interpret and learn about the present, 'the cultural past greets the new-born as its cultural future'. Bateson[50] personalises this relationship as follows: 'We come to every situation with stories, patterns of events that are built into us. Our learning happens within the experience of what important others did.') The intergenerational aspect of the Spitalfields study enables us to see how reading practices and skills are transmitted from one generation to the next. Stanley, in his eighties, recalls how his mother read the classics and instilled in him a love of classics; Tony and Linda, in their early forties, recall teaching their children to spell through singing; Linda's own daughter is now doing the same.

The next perspective draws upon the powerful metaphor of 'scaffolding'[51] used by Bruner and other scholars in their studies of early childhood. This metaphor describes how adults or older experts provide a 'scaffold' to assist the young child, which is slowly dismantled as the child becomes competent in a task. This interpretation of the learning process complements that promoted earlier by Vygotsky[52] who sees the adult, or more competent peer, as assisting the child across the 'zone of proximal development' (ZPD), which is the space between what the child is capable of alone or with adult assistance (in other words, what she or he will be capable of alone tomorrow). 'Scaffolding' will be seen very clearly at different times in the book, but most clearly when we consider the home reading practices of the Bangladeshi-British children. Examples of how scaffolding is used in British classrooms are provided by Edwards (1998).

A further perspective, and linked to the third, comes from comparative studies which show that, although 'scaffolding' takes place universally, its nature is likely to be different from one cultural group to another. Thus, although all caregivers have been shown to provide their offspring with 'finely-tuned scaffolding', the nature of the 'curriculum' is different.[53] Rogoff provides examples of this practice across different cultures and also changes the term 'scaffolding' to 'guided participation' in order to emphasise the active part played by infants in structuring their own learning.[54]

A final and important perspective informing the *contrasting literacies* model is that of *syncretism* as used by cultural anthropologists. This view states that young learners are not entrapped within any single early childhood literacy practice. The families in the study certainly reveal a complex heterogeneity of traditions, whereby reading practices from different domains are blended, resulting in a form of reinterpretation which is both new and dynamic. Duranti and Ochs refer to this type of blending as *syncretic literacy*, which merges not simply linguistic codes or texts but different activities.[55] They use the example of Samoan American children doing homework to show how Samoan and American traditions, languages, teaching and child-rearing strategies blend. In our study, we see how languages (particularly 'Yinglish') for the older generation and literacies (particularly home reading) between Bangladeshi-British siblings in our younger generation produce unique new blends.

The Spitalfields study

This book is the result of a longitudinal study that began in 1992 and is still continuing at the time of writing.[56] The study aims to uncover and examine the literacy practices of past and present generations of families who have had close links with two schools, one in Spitalfields and one just over the boundary in the City of London. Our questions were: How have children in Spitalfields and the City throughout the twentieth century set about learning to read in their homes, schools and communities? Can we discern patterns of successful early reading common to all four generations? How do parents view their role in their children's literacy education? How much do teachers know about children's home literacy practices? How do young children set about transferring learning strategies from home to school and vice versa, and how do teachers facilitate their task in doing this? The scope of the questions widened during different parts of the study to include not just reading but writing and literacy-related activities, such as the learning of music, speech choirs, and even elocution lessons.

Separate phases of the research have addressed different issues, as we attempted to piece together a complex jigsaw of the role of reading in the lives of families whose learning practices in many cases do not match those required by 'official' school demands. In phases one and two of the research (1992–6) we examined the literacy histories and current reading practices in seven Bangladeshi-British and six monolingual English families whose 5- and 6-year-old children attended the two neighbouring schools, and we attempted to trace strategies used by the children as they set about learning to read in different domains. In parallel, we carried out weekly observations in the classroom, and used our findings from homes and communities to devise teaching strategies that would build upon children's outside-school literacy knowledge. The question investigated during this phase was: What is the nature of reading practices taking place in the children's lives and how far do children transfer reading strategies from home to school and vice versa? The third phase of the research (1997–8) widened the scope of the work to investigate the reading histories and early reading memories of past generations of pupils and others who have had close links with one of the two schools. Ex-pupils range from young Bangladeshi-British women in their early twenties to people over 90 years old, some of whom still live close to the schools. Finally, although this book calls largely upon the first three phases of the project, insights are also drawn from a fourth phase of the work, which is currently taking place and focuses on the home and school literacy activities of young siblings from Bangladeshi-British and monolingual English-speaking families living in the Whitechapel area.

The nature of the questions we set out to examine has necessitated a combination of research approaches usually associated with different disciplines. We have used ethnographic methods, as developed by anthropologists,[57] including participant observation, interviews, life histories and the study of historical documents, in our aim to investigate the role, scope and nature of literacy in people's lives as well as in the histories and traditions of which these are a part. An essential part of our task as ethnographers has been to collect emic descriptions of 'reading' held by the families and teachers (descriptions which view a phenomenon from the *participants'* rather than the researchers' point of view) (see Anderson and Stokes[58] and Barton and Hamilton[59]). This task has been greatly assisted by our position as 'insiders' (former teachers who are very familiar with the area) as well as giving our work an 'ecological validity'.[60] Access to the families has also been facilitated by the fact that all those involved as researchers in the study had lived or worked in the schools or in the immediate area themselves: one had attended one of the schools as a child and is currently chair of governors of another school; another had taught in one of the schools; another lived in the area and taught in one of the schools; another was a mother with a young child in the school: another had been a social worker in the area for some years. Thus we were able to build up a relationship of trust with both families and teachers.[61]

Nevertheless, since the focus of interest in ethnographies is in providing what Geertz refers to as the 'cultural grammar'[62] of a group, this approach could not tackle all our questions since it could not enable us to investigate in detail the way in which individuals (teacher–child; parent–child; siblings, etc.) negotiated the reading task together. In other words, an ethnographic approach could not provide us with a method that would permit us to carry out a finely tuned analysis of individual or group reading activities or lessons, both of which were essential to trace negotiation between teacher and learner. For this, we turned to ethnomethodology and conversation analysis, as developed by phenomenologists and social interactionists such as Sacks, Schleghoff and Jefferson, Heap, and Baker and Freebody. Ethnomethodologists shift the focus of attention from the group to the individual, and meaning is attributed to a continuous process of negotiation during interactions. Instead of asking the ethnographic question 'what is happening here?', the question posed by ethnomethodologists is 'what are the structures constituting the activity of interest and how do discourse formats reveal how "knowledge" is produced?'. Instead of becoming an 'insider' as the ethnographer, the researcher stands outside the situation, collecting discrete segments of reading sessions for a moment-by-moment analysis. Thus, researchers using ethnography and ethnomethodology aim both to analyse and to reveal patterns, but of a different nature; ethnography uncovers patterns of events and interpretations of events while ethnomethodology is able to highlight patterns of discourse leading to shared understanding or the breakdown of communication.

In order to interpret the different kinds of data, a multi-layering approach[63] has been used in which the focus moves from an ethnographic analysis of the outer layer, or the social context, to a detailed ethnomethodological analysis of individual reading and literacy interactions or inner layer. This method of analysis distinguishes this study from others that have recently been conducted on the literacy practices in local neighbourhoods in Britain.[64]

The book demands no specialist knowledge of education or literacy teaching and should attract all those fascinated by the lives of past and present generations living in the City of London and Spitalfields. For those who wish to read further on areas covered by each chapter, more comprehensive reading is suggested in the Notes and the Bibliography. The three parts of the book can be read independently and each is likely to hold a particular interest for different readers. Part I will appeal especially to those with a general interest in the historical background of Spitalfields and education in the area. Thus, the first two chapters describe the outer layer of social and historical context within which the members of the study find themselves. Data for these chapters have been drawn largely from secondary historical sources and official education reports. Part II of the book will interest social historians, anthropologists, sociologists and anyone wanting to find out about the lives of Spitalfields residents throughout the century. In this part of the book, we enter the literacy memories of different generations of members of the study. Data for this part of the book were collected through extended semi-structured interviews, in which participants knew our themes of interest but were not limited in what they wished to say. Chapter 3 goes back in time to pre-war days and beyond, and reveals classrooms, teachers and teaching methods from the first decades of the twentieth century. In Chapter 4 we watch as the post-war generation break through education barriers which would have been impassable for their parents. Chapter 5 reveals insights from a group of young Bangladeshi-British women who have been highly successful in school and further education. The participants in Part II of the book, then, reflect the changing population of the area throughout the twentieth century. Chapter 3 focuses on the Jewish community in Spitalfields; Chapter 4 shifts to the English City group and Chapter 5 returns to Spitalfields nearly half a century later to find a group of young Bangladeshi-British women. The third and final part of the book should appeal particularly to teachers. It moves to the homes, communities and classrooms of those whose memories are short, since they are still in primary school. Chapters 6 and 7 reveal the remarkable scope of literacy learning of these young children. We are invited into their 'unofficial' literacies at home and in their communities as well as the 'official' world of school. In each domain, finely tuned analyses reveal the depth of their early learning as they work at being learners and teachers at home and at school.

Finally, readers may question why, throughout the book, there are more female than male participants. We make no apologies for this. Our response lies in the very purpose of ethnography, whose justification has been neatly summed up by Erikson: 'Ethnography makes visible the lives of people whose lives are not normally told.'[65] This is the case for most of our participants, but nowhere is it more pertinent than for our group of Bangladeshi-British women living and learning in Spitalfields today.

Part I

LIVING AND LEARNING EAST OF THE ALDGATE PUMP

1

PLACES AND PEOPLES

'What will save East London?' asked one of our university visitors of his master. 'The destruction of West London' was the answer and, insofar as he meant the abolition of the space which divides rich and poor, the answer was right. Not until the habits of the rich are changed and they are again content to breathe the same air and walk the same streets as the poor will East London be saved.
(Canon Barnett, founder of Toynbee Hall, the Universities' Settlement, Whitechapel, speaking at St John's College, Oxford, 17 November 1883)

The people who are the subject of our book grew up in the busy cosmopolitan district that lies on the eastern borders of the City of London, in the square mile or so that stretches from Spitalfields Market in the north, down to the Tower of London in the south. Part of the area falls within Portsoken Ward, one of the ancient City wards that came into existence in the tenth century when King Edgar (959–975) granted thirteen knights a rough patch of land between Aldgate and the river that had been left 'desolate and forsaken by its inhabitants'. The land continued to be held by their descendants until 1115 when 'all the lands and the soke[1] called the English Knighten Guild' were handed over to the Priory of Holy Trinity, Aldgate. The Prior acted as alderman for the ward until 1531, when the Priory was surrendered to Henry VIII, who donated it to Sir Thomas Audley who demolished it. Thereafter the people of Portsoken Ward were represented by a 'temporal man elected by the citizens'. On the northern edge of Portsoken Ward lies Spitalfields, where, in medieval times, the Hospital of St Mary's Spital provided 'one hundred and eighty beds, well furnished for the receipt of the poor',[2] until it too was surrendered to Henry VIII and demolished. Adjoining the hospital lay the tiny 'liberty' of Norton Folgate (now remembered in Folgate Street). 'Liberties' were autonomous areas held by both lay and religious orders, caring for their own poor and dealing with crime. Since they were outside the jurisdiction of the Guildhall they acquired a reputation for lawlessness, especially after the Dissolution when they fell into various hands, and were feared as breeding grounds for blackguards and the plague.[3]

In medieval times the area was sparsely populated. The earliest maps show houses and churches crowded within the walls of the City of London while outside the walls stretch gardens, orchards, fields with cattle, archery butts and shooting ranges. In 1319, Portsoken had only forty-four citizens liable to pay taxes and, by 1332, a mere twenty-three. Much of the land was church estates. Stow, writing in the 1590s remembers Hog Lane (now Middlesex Street or Petticoat Lane), down which pigs were driven to market, and which 'had on both sides fair hedge rows of elm trees with bridges and easy stiles to pass over into the pleasant fields, very commodious for the citizens therein to walk, shoot and otherwise recreate and refresh their dull spirits in the sweet and wholesome air'.[4] During Stow's lifetime however, the transformation from pleasant countryside to urban sprawl had already begun. The Hog Lane that he remembered from his childhood was, by the end of his life in 1605, 'made continual building throughout, of garden houses and small cottages: and the fields on either side . . . turned into garden plots, tenter[5] yards, bowling alleys and such like from Hounds Ditch in the west as far as White Chappell'.[6] Other stretches of open land were also disappearing, 'From Aldgate east(wards) lieth a large street replenished with buildings [now Whitechapel High Street] . . . this common field I say, being sometime the beauty of the city, on that part is so encroached upon by building of filthy cottages and with other purpressors, inclosures and laystalls,[7] that in some places there scarce remaineth sufficient highway for the meeting of carriages and the droves of cattle'.[8]

The development, which had started with small cottages and garden houses in Stow's lifetime, grew and spread during the following century, until by 1680 most of Wapping and Shadwell and some of Spitalfields had been filled in: 'In old districts like St Katharines, houses were wedged into a maze of courts and sometimes even put up on refuse tips'.[9] By the end of the seventeenth century, distinctions between east and west London were already becoming clear. Whereas 'in the City and West London, rich and poor lived in close proximity, East London had already acquired the working class complexion it has had ever since'.[10] The terrible plague and the Great Fire of the 1660s drove many citizens to take up residence outside the city walls, but much of the new building served to accommodate the waves of migrants who poured into London from other parts of Britain and from abroad from the seventeenth century onwards.

Learning to live with contrasts

Abby: *My parents were of Dutch descent. My great-grandmother was married in Spitalfields, so we go quite a long way back. My father held a City licence and you couldn't hold that unless you were born in the City.*

20

EG: *What is a City licence?*
Abby: *To trade. He used to trade in Billingsgate market, Petticoat Lane and Covent Garden.*

(Abby, born in 1917)

Throughout history, London's role as a centre of trade and commerce has attracted migrants. In medieval times, the wool trade drew Flemish, Italian and Hanseatic merchants to operate from the City and, as prosperity increased, English migrants flooded in 'from East Anglia, the South-East and the East Midlands either to buy their citizenship, take up an apprenticeship or labour for a wage'.[11] Wealthy aliens were used as a source of loans by medieval kings. The Jews who followed William the Conqueror to England were providers of funds to the court until the thirteenth century when, their assets exhausted, they were expelled from the country and replaced by rich Italian merchants. Although the latter were unpopular with Londoners, 'royal policy was to favour any group rich enough to pay for the king's protection'.[12]

From the mid-sixteenth century onwards, London grew rapidly and, in the 150 years from 1550 to 1700, the population increased from 50,000 (less than many other European capitals including Paris and Rome), to 575,000, making it 'the greatest city in Christendom'.[13] By 1680, two-thirds of English townsfolk lived in London. By this time however, the balance of population was shifting: the percentage of Londoners living outside the City boundary increased from 25 per cent in 1560 to 75 per cent in 1680. The population increase was not due to natural population growth, however. Baptism and burial records, which were kept by parish sextons from 1519 onwards (although none survived until 1563), show that death rates were high and christening rates low, especially in the plague years. Rather, the massive changes in population were due to immigration, as the seventeenth-century demographer, John Graunt,[14] pointed out, 'London is supplied with people from out of the country, whereby not only to repair the overplus difference of burials . . . but likewise to increase its inhabitants'.[15] Earle[16] conducted an analysis of 4,115 witnesses before church courts in the years from 1660 to 1725 and found that 58 per cent of those aged 15 to 24 were migrants; while in the age group 45 and over, the figure was nearer 80 per cent. Approximately 70 per cent of these migrants were from other parts of Britain: 33 per cent from neighbouring counties (i.e. within 60 miles of the capital); 30 per cent from more distant counties (i.e. 125 miles or more from London); and 10 per cent from Scotland or Ireland. Porter estimates that by 1700, 8,000 young people a year were arriving in the capital. Rapid population growth in rural areas meant that agriculture was unable to absorb the expanding workforce and young people 'quit their clean and healthy fields for a region of dirt, stink and noise'[17] in the hope of finding well-paid work. A contemporary writer Corbyn Morris maintained, 'Not above one in twenty of shop and alehouse keepers, journeymen and labourers were either born or served their apprenticeships in town'. Many of these newcomers to the capital settled in the East End.

The Huguenots: from riches to rags

My grandfather worked for the Great Eastern Railway . . . He would do a day's work and then come home and have a little sleep and, I always remember, a baked onion before he went out. That kept out the cold and he would do a night's fogging[18] for the extra money. I think he originated in Huntingdonshire. Now his mother was descended from the French Huguenots . . . My mother was from Bethnal Green and her parents were definitely descended from the Huguenots. My great-grandfather was a weaver . . .

(Eric, born in 1924)

London had always attracted the Scots, the Irish, who had settled in St Giles and in the East End, and Welsh cattle drovers, livestock dealers and dairyworkers. However, it was political and religious persecution that drove many Europeans to migrate to Britain.[19] The first group to settle in any numbers were the French Huguenots. Parish records show that by the sixteenth century there was already an indigenous silk industry in Whitechapel. In December 1594, for example, Elidal Tolly, silk weaver, and David Inglishe, twister, were buried in St Botolphe's churchyard.[20] It was in this district that exiles first settled after the Massacre of St Bartholomew in 1572 and the Sack of Antwerp in 1585. Indeed, the area adjoining St Botolphe's, Bishopsgate, had for some time been called Petty France, and Shakespeare had lodgings there with the French Mountjoy family.

The main influx of French textile workers, however, arrived following the revocation in 1685 of the Edict of Nantes, which had protected the rights of Protestants to worship. In 1688, a London relief committee claimed it had assisted 13,500 Huguenots and there must have been many more wealthy families who needed no assistance. Although the great majority were textile workers, the Huguenots also brought their skills to other industries: the manufacture of guns, watches, clocks, wigs, fans, shoes, paper, tapestry and glass. They settled in Spitalfields and by the end of the century, the orchards and gardens had become 'all town'. The master weavers built three- and four-storey houses in streets laid out on a grid system, between Bishopsgate and Brick Lane.[21] These grand houses stood in stark contrast to the dwellings of poorer workers who moved into new homes hastily and shoddily constructed in open ground east of Brick Lane. The whole area was now rapidly disappearing under bricks and mortar. Daniel Defoe, who remembered that 'the part now called Spittlefields-market was a field of grass with cows feeding on it', wrote in 1724 that the area was '320 acres of ground all close built and well-inhabited . . . above two hundred thousand inhabitants'.[22] By the year 1700 there were seven French churches in Spitalfields. French was the language of the area and even the parish scavengers spoke no English.

At that time, the clothing and textile trades were the biggest manufacturing employers in London. In the early eighteenth century, between 50,000 and 60,000 people are thought to have been employed as weavers, throwsters,[23] knitters, dyers and other workers in Spitalfields and the East End, and 15,000 looms were producing the rich silk and brocade cloths that were in great demand both in Britain and in Europe. It is said that both Mozart and Handel came to buy cloth in Spitalfields. The period of prosperity was relatively short however, as the textile industry was notoriously vulnerable to the demands of fashion and to competition from home and abroad. In addition, increasing numbers of poor migrants from Ireland began to move into the area, undercutting the wages and threatening the jobs of the skilled textile workers. Unemployment led to civil unrest and rioting. In 1736, mobs of two to three thousand militant silk weavers protesting against cheap Irish labour destroyed Irish pubs and houses in Brick Lane, Goodman's Fields and Rosemary Lane. In 1763, several thousand journeymen weavers assembled in Spitalfields, broke into the house of a master weaver, destroyed looms and silks, and then paraded an effigy of the master through the streets before hanging and burning it on a gibbet. The government attempted to remedy the situation by passing the Spitalfields Act (1773), which restricted entry to the trade and controlled wage levels, but the East End silk industry was waning. Textile manufacture was flourishing in areas where labour was cheap, such as Macclesfield, Manchester and Essex, and although the Spitalfields silk industry continued to employ some 50,000 people well into the nineteenth century, conditions were poor and the living precarious. The introduction of free trade in the early nineteenth century and, most disastrous of all, the invention of the power loom, finally brought about the collapse of the industry. By the 1830s, tens of thousands of weavers were unemployed. The politician Charles Greville wrote in 1832, '1,000 are crammed into the poor house, five or six in a bed; 6,000 receive parochial relief . . . The district is in a complete state of insolvency and hopeless poverty'.[24] The once prosperous area of Spitalfields was now inhabited mainly by the poor and destitute.

The Irish: famine and Fenians

I lived in Herbert House. We were the only Irish family there. All the rest were the Jewish stallholders . . . It used to be all swamps around here [Poplar]. The only building for miles was the London Hospital. Pity it isn't like that now. The children though – they would have killed one another for a ha'penny.

(Raymond, born 1946)

As the silk industry declined and the descendants of the Huguenot weavers became destitute or moved to textile-manufacturing areas in other parts of England, a new wave of migrants was moving into the East End. London had always had an Irish population. In 1780, about 20,000 Irish men and women were living in St Giles (known locally as Little Dublin) and in the East End, but it was in the mid-nineteenth century that immigration from Ireland reached its peak. Table 1 shows immigration figures for the years 1841 to 1891.

The famine of the mid-1840s drove starving agricultural workers to seek work and food outside Ireland. The census of 1851 identified 109,000 Irish-born Londoners. By the end of the century it has been estimated that 5 to 6 per cent of Londoners considered themselves to be Irish 'by birth, descent or cultural affiliation'.[25] The principal occupations of the Irish immigrants were as workers in the textile industry, as itinerant fruit and vegetable sellers and as dock labourers. Mayhew, describing East End street life in the mid-nineteenth century found that, of the coster-mongers[26] 'one half of the class is costermongers proper, that is to say the calling with them is hereditary, whilst the other half is composed of three eighths Irish, one eighth mechanics, tradesmen and Jews'.[27] The Irish were frequently accused of undercutting the wages of other workers. Mayhew suggests that, by virtue of the privations they had experienced in famine-ravaged Ireland, the Irish could live more frugally than the other new immigrant group, the Jews: 'often in his own country he had to subsist on a stolen turnip a day; he could lodge harder . . . or sleep in the open air, which is seldom done by a Jew, he could dispense with the use of shoes and stockings; he drank only water, or if he took tea or coffee, it was a meal . . . he worked longer hours and sold more oranges than his Hebrew competitor.'[28] Many Irish immigrants lived and traded in Rosemary Lane, now Royal Mint Street, which runs eastwards from the Tower. It was a street market 'as regards things placed on the ground' and was 'more Irish' than Petticoat Lane. 'There were some cheap lodging houses in the courts to which the poor Irish flocked; and as they were very frequently street sellers, on busy days the quarter abounded with them. At every step you heard the Erse tongue.'[29] Like the Huguenots before

Table 1 Migration into London 1841–91

	British	Irish	Foreign	Total
1841–51	256,000	46,000	26,000	328,000
1851–61	243,000	14,000	29,000	286,000
1861–71	288,000	7,000	36,000	331,000
1871–81	440,000	19,000	39,000	498,000
1881–91	334,000	20,000	48,000	402,000

Source: Inwood (1998: 142)

them, the Irish were soon to be replaced in Spitalfields by others fleeing hardships and privation.

The Jews: anglicising the aliens

My father was in the Russian army . . . he came to England in 1910. He'd served in the Russo-Japanese war as a cap-maker, making caps for the Russian army. He was born in Poland but Poland at that time was under the control of Russia . . . They came to Britain like so many thousands of other Jewish people because of the very unpleasant living conditions in Poland. Although I don't think they personally experienced any attacks in terms of a pogrom, there was the atmosphere of being subject to attack which was a very unpleasant form of living.

(Aumie, born 1924)

Table 1 indicates that, as conditions in Ireland improved slightly and the numbers of Irish immigrants decreased, the numbers of foreign immigrants increased considerably. Jewish families, fleeing pogroms and persecution in Poland and Russia, accounted for a large proportion of these newcomers. After their expulsion from Britain in the thirteenth century, Jews were finally permitted to resettle in 1656 and a number of Sephardic Jews from Spain and Portugal took up residence near Aldgate, where they established the Bevis Marks Synagogue in 1701. They tended to be well established and prosperous and some rose to influential positions in London's civic and financial life.

Later in the eighteenth century, however, a very different type of Jewish immigrant began to arrive in Britain. These were the Ashkenazi Jews from central and eastern Europe. In the course of the nineteenth century, London's Jewish population increased from about 25,000 in 1815 to approximately 140,000 by 1905. By 1881, between two and seven thousand Russian Jews a year were arriving in the East End and settling in Whitechapel and Spitalfields. Charles Booth, in his survey of east London, wrote, 'Formerly in Whitechapel, Commercial Street divided the Jewish haunts of Petticoat Lane and Goulston Street from the rougher English quarter lying in the east. Now the Jews have flowed across the line: Hanbury Street, Fashion Street, Pelham Street, and many alleys and lanes have fallen before them . . . they live and crowd together and work and meet their fate, independent of the great stream of London life surging around them'.[30] Mayhew, in his description of street life in the East End, confirmed the separate nature of their culture: 'I should briefly treat of Jews generally as an integral but distinct and peculiar part of street life . . . to the masses they were almost strangers except as men employed in the not-very-formidable occupation of collecting and vending old clothes.'[31] By the late nineteenth century, most of the Jews resident in Britain lived in the East End and Yiddish had replaced French and

25

Irish Gaelic as the local language: 'On the way to Spitalfields . . . buxom Jewish matrons sat on doorsteps watching the little dark children who tumbled at their feet. Young Hebrews smoked short pipes and talked their own lingo. Now and then a young girl with jet black hair and flashing eyes ran by carrying a loaf of German bread under her arm, singing a foreign song or yodelling. There was nothing English about the place, only foreign faces, foreign shops, foreign talk'.[32]

Barred from taking up conventional trades, the first Ashkenazim made their living by street selling and old-clothes dealing. Jewish boys sold 'oranges and lemons, sponges, combs, pocket books, pencils, sealing wax, paper, many-bladed pen-knives, razors, pocket mirrors and shaving boxes'.[33] Jewish girls, on the other hand, were 'not street traders in anything like the proportion which the females were found to bear to the males among the Irish street traders and the English costermongers . . . In tending a little stall or a basket with such things as cherries or strawberries the little Jewish girl differs from her street selling sisters in being a brisker trader'.[34] Many of the new migrants from eastern Europe however, had been craftsmen in their country of origin where they constituted 'an intermediate class between the landowning aristocracy and the peasants'.[35] On arrival in London, they found work as tailors, cigar and cigarette makers, cabinet-makers, boot and shoemakers and cap-makers in the main.

A life of 'sweating' in Spitalfields

There was no money coming in, and as we grew older I remember in Whitechapel, on the corner near to where Black Iron Yard used to be, where Blooms Restaurant is now . . . well when the bosses that owned the tailors' shops needed staff, they'd come along there on the pavement and that's where the people would collect, the men and the women, the felling hands[36] on the street. They were out of work and they'd go over and ask them and they'd say, 'Please Mr . . .' in Yiddish, 'Brauchen Sie ein Arbeiter?' which is, 'Do you need a worker?' So he'd say, 'What do you do?' Some worked the treadle sewing machine, another was a baster – he used to put the garment together and the other one used to machine it, and from there it would go on . . . But if they took them on, it was just only for a short period as long as they needed them, you know . . . They'd give them a shilling and soon kicked them out . . . and the conditions . . . Oh, my God, the conditions . . . I shall never forget the conditions of the factories . . . What conditions . . .

(Minnie, born 1908)

Many of the new arrivals from Russia found work in East End sweatshops. Under the 'sweating system' poor and needy workers, migrants, women and children, were used by manufacturers as a source of semi-skilled, cheap labour with which to bypass the apprenticeship rules and traditional wage

Plate 1 Huguenot shopfront in Artillery Lane

Plate 2 The East End Soup Kitchen for the Jewish poor, which was originally set up in Leman Street in 1854 and moved to Brune Street in 1902

rates of skilled artisans. During the Napoleonic Wars with France in the early nineteenth century, large quantities of military uniforms and footwear were required, and women and children were recruited by the clothing industry as a source of cheap labour. In spite of protests from skilled artisans, cheap labour continued to flood the market after the wars were over, until by the middle of the century even skilled tailors and shoemakers were forced to take up sweated work. The wholesalers meanwhile were making their fortunes. Beatrice Webb describes her encounter with a principal partner in a wholesale clothiers firm in 1887:

> J.G. was a haw hawy young man in 'masher'[37] clothes, with silver tipped cane and camellia in buttonhole. Said there had been a revolution in the tailoring trade and small tailors were being wiped out. It was now a trade in which capitalists invested money and worked on wholesale scale.[38]

The prosperous wholesalers made their profits by distributing work to subcontractors or garret masters who employed sweated workers to carry out the piecework. The latter 'typically worked more than eighty hours a week in the sweater's crowded garret, and paid most of their wages back to their employer in return for bread, butter and weak tea, and the right to sleep two or three to a bed in the workroom. Most were malnourished and many consumptive'.[39] In some cases, worker turned manufacturer and, having paid a deposit on a sewing machine and pressing equipment, set up workshops in one or two rooms in their home. Beatrice Webb describes a typical sweatshop in Whitechapel in her diary for 1887:

> Four rooms and a kitchen, 12s, one room let 3s. Street deserted during daytime with public houses at each corner. A small backyard. Three rooms on groundfloor, two used as workshop; two machinists, Polish Jews; the master (Mr Moses) acts as presser. In back room, mistress and first hand, a Scottish woman, and two girls learning the trade. Coats turned out at 1s 2d each, trimmings and thread supplied by the sweater. Buttonholes 4½d a dozen by a woman outside. Evidently these people work tremendously hard; women working for ten to twelve hours without looking round and master working up to two o'clock and often beginning at five the next morning.[40]

The trade was seasonal and not only the workers but frequently the garret masters were without work. As Minnie so graphically describes on page 26, these conditions continued well into the twentieth century.

Plate 3
Bangladeshi-
British shop
with its original
Huguenot
doorway

Plate 4 Sclater Street signs from the eighteenth to the twentieth century

Plate 5 Huguenot weavers' houses in Fournier Street

Plate 6 Fabric wholesaler in Brick Lane

Plate 7 New houses in Flower and
Dean Walk – home to some of our
families. The arch is all that
remains of the old Rothschild
Buildings which stood on this site

Plate 8 The London Jamme Masjid
on the corner of Fournier Street
and Brick Lane. Built in 1743 as a
Huguenot church, it became a
Methodist chapel in the early 1800s
and the Machzike Hadas
Synagogue in 1898. In 1975 it
opened as the largest mosque in
the East End

East and West: 'the dark continent within easy reach of the General Post Office'[41]

> The whole of East London is starving. The West End is mad, or bad, not to see that if things go on like this we must have a revolution. One fine day, the people about here will go desperate; and they will walk westwards, cutting throats and hurling brickbats, until they are shot down by the military.[42]

Sweating was only one of the hardships the residents of Spitalfields had to endure. Housing conditions were atrocious, sanitation was non-existent and poverty was everywhere. As the nineteenth century progressed, the conditions grew steadily worse:

> Population rise had never been more explosive, industry never more polluting, disruption, demolition and building more frenzied. Air, water and bug borne diseases multiplied and London was visited four times by Asiatic cholera. The teeming masses presented a pandemonium of misery.[43]

By the end of the century, Spitalfields with its 'vile dens, fever haunted and stenchful crowded courts' was said to be 'a scandal to the hub of the civilised world'.[44] Overcrowding was rife. In London as a whole, population density was 50 persons to the acre; in Whitechapel the number was 176 per acre; in Bell Lane, Spitalfields, the figure was 600. The desperate conditions were the result partly of the high numbers of migrants arriving every year but were aggravated by avaricious planners and builders who had 'caught on to the profitability accruing from the need to house the poor' and had built workshops and dwelling-houses in garden spaces which 'obstruct light and shut out air'.[45] In addition, thousands of Londoners had been displaced by the new railways and road systems. Between 1840 and 1900, 120,000 people lost their homes to railways and a further 100,000 were evicted for road construction. New homes for the displaced tenants were not built, with the result that demolition led to even worse overcrowding. In spite of the atrocious living conditions, life in Spitalfields was not cheap. Jack London found that nearly 50 per cent of workers paid from a quarter to half of their earnings for rent. It was not unusual to find examples such as the following: 'In Whitechapel a man and his wife and their three daughters aged sixteen, eight and four, and two sons aged ten and twelve years occupy a small room'.[46] Sub-letting was rife and beds were often let on a relay system. 'It is notorious', wrote London, 'that the houses of the poor are greater profit earners than the mansions of the rich'.[47]

While rich entrepreneurs were happy to exploit their wretched neighbours, however, other sections of society were beginning to voice their concerns over the conditions in the ghetto. 'Rookeries' in particular worried the middle classes who feared not only the diseases such as cholera and typhoid, which flourished in their insanitary alleys, nor the thousands of criminals and felons who sheltered in their narrow passages and courts, but that the impenetrable mass of tenements and lodging houses on their very doorstep might harbour insurgents. Mearns, in his 1883 pamphlet, 'The bitter cry of outcast London', shocked respectable citizens with his description of this 'terra incognita' in the midst of comfortable Victorian London:

> Few who will read these pages have any conception of what these pestilential human rookeries are, where tens of thousands are crowded together amidst horrors which call to mind what we have heard of the middle passage of a slave ship. To get into them you have to penetrate courts reeking with poisonous and malodorous gases arising from accumulations of sewage and refuse scattered in all directions and often flowing beneath your feet.

Just as in medieval Spitalfields when the liberty of North Folgate had been a refuge for outlaws and criminals, so the area's rookeries continued to harbour those who lived outside the law. Arthur Morrison, who wrote graphically about the 'the blackest pit in London', The Old Nichol on the northern edge of Spitalfields, reminds the reader that conditions continued very much the same as in medieval times:

> Jago Court was an unfailing sanctuary, a city of refuge, ever ready, ever secure. A runaway had only to make for the archway and once he was in Jago Court, the danger was over. Beyond the archway the police could not venture, except in large companies.[48]

Perhaps the most notorious rookery, however, was in Flower and Dean Street in the heart of Spitalfields. Plans had been afoot to destroy this particular rookery since the 1830s, and the construction of Commercial Street in the late 1830s had partially demolished many of the dreadful courts and alleys, but in 1875 this area 'fruitful of sickness, misery, pauperism and crime'[49] was still largely intact. An epidemic of typhus fever in the 1870s however, hastened the plans for a demolition scheme which would render 1,800 people homeless and large areas were cleared, although many of the worst buildings, the common lodging houses, remained. However, by 1900, enough space had been cleared to build several new blocks of dwellings, accommodating more than 700 families. Many of these were occupied by the Jewish migrants.

Housing the poor: philanthropic capitalism

The new dwellings were privately funded. Since the 1860s, philanthropic Victorians had been able to invest in companies providing housing for the deserving poor and still receive a 5 per cent return on their investment. Companies such as the Improved Industrial Dwellings Company (1863), William Austin's Artisans' and Labourers' and General Dwellings Company had been established. In 1884, the East End Dwellings Company built flats in Lolesworth Street and in 1885 the Rothschild 4 per cent Dwellings Company for Jewish Labourers built the Charlotte de Rothschild Dwellings on the site of the Flower and Dean Street rookery.

The aim of the new, somewhat barrack-like buildings was to house as many people as possible as cheaply as possible and the quality of the buildings varied considerably. In some cases little money was wasted on comforts and amenities. In Katharine Buildings near the Royal Mint, for example,

> all the rooms were decorated in the same dull dead-red distemper unpleasantly reminiscent of a butcher's shop. Within these uniform cell-like apartments were no labour saving appliances, not even a sink and water tap: on the landings between the galleries and the stairs were the sinks and taps (three sinks and six taps to sixty rooms); behind a tall wooden screen were placed sets of six closets on the trough system, sluiced every three hours.[50]

The Rothschild Buildings were luxurious in comparison: each two-, three- or four-roomed dwelling had its own WC and scullery. The tenants were mostly Jewish but there was a wide range of incomes and occupations:

> Furniture? . . . One orange box – it was covered with a nice piece of material. We had orange boxes for to eat on . . . We had three chairs. My younger sister . . . a boy wanted to take her back so she said, 'I can't bring a boy home. We've only got three legs on one chair. Where's he going to sit?[51]

In the same block, however, lived another family who 'were not rich, but according to some [they] were, as [they] had a piano in the front room. It was very nice'.[52]

Accounts of life in these new blocks speak of a community spirit and supportive neighbours:

> The community was very close. During the summer months people used to be out to all hours even the children. You had that sense of warmth, of friendliness among the people . . . They used to stay outside. There used to be talking, the kids used to have sing-songs. . . .[53]

Many remember their childhoods in such buildings with nostalgia. Bertha Sokoloff recalls her life in Brady Street Mansions:

> Slums, they may have been (and certainly College Buildings [adjacent to Toynbee Hall] was most deficient in amenities) but poor they were not. The playground of Brady Street Mansions was rigorously swept several times daily by the caretaker Mr Dickens, a man of military bearing, respected by child and tenant alike, and most of the flats were kept extremely clean by the occupants . . . We were not poor . . . there was a culture . . . a rich one.[54]

In these new dwellings even the smallest flats enabled tenants to have a secure home from which to work and make their way in the world. Many of the large numbers of children living in the Rothschild Buildings (in 1899 there were 665 children out of a total of 1,162 residents) attended Commercial Street (later Canon Barnett) School, went to poetry readings and concerts at Toynbee Hall and studied for their exams at the Whitechapel Reference Library. Their parents, the first-generation migrants, were ambitious and enterprising and many joined the struggle for fairer working and living conditions that was by then underway in the East End.

Fighting back: rebels and revolutionaries

Throughout the nineteenth century, workers in most industries had endured terrible conditions. There had been strikes of gas workers, building labourers, and dockers in the 1870s but these had achieved nothing: the gas workers' strike ended when their leader was imprisoned for a year. In the 1880s, however, the new socialist movement was able to provide the largely unorganised workforce with resources, leadership and publicity and this proved to be the catalyst for change. The first spark came from Annie Besant, a Fabian and member of the Social Democratic Federation, who, outraged by the miserable wages paid to young matchgirls 'who [had] their jaws eaten out of their heads by phosphorus in order that matches should be sold cheaper and shareholders should get a higher price for their invest-ment', published an article, 'White slavery in London',[55] exposing the terrible working conditions. The employers, Bryant and May, indignant at the exposure, called upon the matchgirls to sign a document refuting the allegations. When the women withheld their signatures, they were dismissed. Besant took up their cause, calling for a boycott of Bryant and May products, setting up a strike committee and appealing nationally for funds. Politicians, clergy and intellectuals from Toynbee Hall took up the fight 'till the whole country rang with the struggle'. The strike was over in a few weeks, wages were increased, fines and deductions abolished and the Matchmakers' Union was formed. It was to be the role model for unionisation.

The gas workers formed the National Union of Gasworkers and General Labour and won a decrease in the working day without going on strike. In 1889, the organiser of the gas workers went on to address the dockers, whose working conditions were execrable. The system whereby 'six hundred men might wait at the dock gates and less than twenty get engaged' was degrading and dehumanising: men fought like rats to be selected for two hours' work a day. The dockers came out on strike, Ben Tillett an ex-docker took over the leadership and the Port was immobilised from Tilbury to Rotherhithe. Once again, intellectuals and politicians supported the cause and donations poured in from as far afield as Australia. The first dockers' strike is often seen as a turning point in British labour relations: new trade unions were formed, membership soared and workers realised that they had the power to change the status quo.

The Jewish population of the East End participated in the struggle for better conditions. Many of the East End tailors were involved in the strikes of 1889 (2,000 strikers), 1891 (10,000 striking in the East End alone), 1896 (500 women on strike), 1906 (5,000 East End workers) and 1912 (10,000 East End tailors).[56] Bootmakers and bakers also took to the streets. The Jewish Workers' Circle was established, and, led by Morris Mindel who lived in Rothschild Buildings, supported strikers, provided benefits and organised education for workers. At its peak, membership rose to 3,000. 'It was a fine example of collective independence: class conscious, aware of the Jewish workers' cultural heritage and active in fighting its decay, eager to assume responsibility for their own means of livelihood and destiny.'[57]

The hard work and industry of the first migrants enabled their children and grandchildren to enter the professions, run businesses and own property and finally to leave Spitalfields. By the 1960s the Victorian dwellings, which had sheltered so many hopeful 'greeners',[58] were left for the next group of migrants.

The Bangladeshis: from Sylhet to Spitalfields

You know, people always ask immigrant communities whether they're going to stay or whether they're going to leave. I mean, leaving and moving are a natural part of a person's development. You know, you get people from all over the home counties after they complete university and no one ever poses that question to them, 'Are you going to leave?'.

(Tahmin, born 1975)

Bombing and displacement during World War II and increased prosperity amongst the Jewish population meant that, like others before them, they began to leave the East End with the result that, as we enter the twenty-first century, only a few pockets of elderly Jewish people still live in the area. The synagogues have closed down and, one by one, Jewish businesses have moved away, although some of the original shop names can still be seen. A small number of thriving concerns remain in Brick Lane in the form of two very popular bagel shops and a funeral parlour.

As the Jewish population moved out to the more comfortable suburbs of Hendon, Golders Green, Hampstead and Highgate, the narrow streets and cramped courts of Spitalfields began to receive the next group of migrants, the Bangladeshis. Although the numbers were very small in the first half of the century, a series of political and economic factors meant that the population increased very rapidly from the 1960s onwards until, in the 1980s, Bengali speakers constituted the largest minority-language group[59] within the Inner London Education Authority. The 1991 Census puts the number of people of Bangladeshi origin in Britain at 163,000 but community leaders suggest that the real figure is likely to be nearer 200,000.[60] At the time of the 1991 Census, 53 per cent of the Bangladeshi population in the UK was concentrated in Greater London, half of whom were living in the borough of Tower Hamlets. Within the borough, the majority of the Bangladeshi community lives in the Spitalfields and St Katharine's Wards. The former is one of the few wards in the country where the majority of the residents (61 per cent) are members of an ethnic minority.[61]

The British-Bangladeshis originate almost exclusively in Sylhet, a rural tea-growing area on the north-eastern border of Bangladesh. They speak Sylheti, an, (as yet), unwritten dialect of Bengali. It has been a question of some speculation among scholars as to why there should be such a clear 'zonal imbalance' in immigration from Bangladesh and why such a remote, landlocked, agricultural corner of the country as Sylhet should supply so many men and women, eager to exchange their peaceful rural lives to cross 'seven seas and thirteen rivers'[62] for a new life in a cramped, polluted inner-city borough. Alam[63] points to historical reasons and to the ancient landowning practices of Bengal.

The population of the area we now know as Bangladesh has long been divided into Ashrafs, a landowning upper class who claimed to be descended from Arab and Persian rulers, and the landless Atrafs, the lower class. Such divisions were maintained throughout the Mugal period and the British Raj. In the eighteenth century, a middle class of zemindars, (or tax farmers) was created, who collected tithes from the peasants who worked the land. The zemindar system was finally abolished in 1950, but sharecropping continued. At the time of Partition in 1947, Hindus fled the newly created Muslim East Pakistan (now Bangladesh) to occupy lands vacated by Muslims fleeing in the opposite direction from areas such as Assam. Returning Muslims could not claim lands in Sylhet or Comilla vacated by fleeing Hindus however, since all the land in East Pakistan already belonged to the zemindars. Thus they became 'refugees' in their own land, a large group of landless poor struggling to survive in an area that has a difficult climate and more uncultivable land than most other parts of the Indian subcontinent.

There has also been a long tradition of seafaring among Sylhetis, with certain seamen's villages in central Sylhet producing generations of sailors. From the nineteenth century onwards, Eade maintains that seamen had been recruited from many parts of the Bengal Delta such as Chittagong, Noakhali, Comilla, to work on merchant ships travelling all over the world.[64] While sailors could easily be recruited from those areas bordering the Delta, it is more difficult to explain why so many seafarers originate from the remote, rural and landlocked Sylhet. Alam[65] suggests that when the British began to develop the tea trade in Sylhet in the 1830s, Sylhetis were taken as labourers, porters and general workers down from the plantations to Calcutta. Once in the port, their contracts were terminated and they had to find alternative work. Many of them joined ships of the British Merchant Navy as cooks or boiler-room workers and, as they were not natural seafarers, Alam proposes, they often jumped ship and settled in ports across the world. These were the pioneers who paved the way for later migrants.

In the early days of the 1920s, most of the Bangladeshi seamen were sporadic visitors to London, staying only long enough to buy presents and goods to take home before rejoining their ships.

> I found Mr Munshi at 16 Elder Street. He was the first of our people, he came in 1922. At that time there were only five: Ayub Ali Master; Marufah Khan; Nana; Naim Ullah and Mr Munshi.[66]

The newcomers gathered at Mr Munshi's lodging house or at the Shah Jahal Restaurant, a coffee shop run by Ayub Ali Master at 76 Commercial Street. As the numbers of settlers began to grow, Mr Master, himself an ex-seaman, provided rooms, food and practical help with literacy and financial transactions. He became president of the UK Muslim League and set up the Indian Seamen's Welfare League. Newcomers found jobs in the sweatshops and in the small factories of the East End, or in West End hotels where they worked in the boiler rooms or kitchens: 'these days the Savoy kitchen is filled up with our people'.[67] The more adventurous travelled to industrial cities such as Birmingham to find work in factories.

In spite of these early pioneers, migration from Sylhet continued to be very slow until the 1950s when, in the post-war economic boom, the voucher system was introduced whereby workers from East Pakistan, as it was then, were invited to come and work in Britain to make up the labour deficit. Many poor and landless agricultural workers left their homeland to settle in Britain. Alam maintains, 'Without such "free vouchers" they would not normally have ventured to come to Britain even with their knowledge of some "Atmiya-Svajan" (one's own people) living in Britain.'[68] These first settlers, however, provided the first link with their compatriots back home and gradually a community began to form. Alam describes the stages in such 'chain migration':

1   arrival of lone immigrant;
2   he becomes a success, but loneliness leads him to contact friends or visit home. News of his success spreads and other men follow: some intermarriage with host community;
3   a small community grows up: dependants follow and immigration reaches mass scale;
4   the second generation reaches maturity and some internal conflicts and upward mobility occur;
5   the third generation reaches maturity.[69]

The early migrants worked in sweatshops and factories in the East End. Many found work in the catering trade. In the 1930s, there were two Indian restaurants in London, Veeraswamy's and Shafi's, but in 1938 the first Indian restaurant run by a Sylheti was opened in Windmill Street. Soon after, two men from Maulvi Bazar in Sylhet, Mosharaf Ali and Israel Miah, pioneers of the restaurant trade, opened the first of many successful restaurants, the Anglo-Asia in Brompton Road.

> By 1946 there were twenty restaurants in London and they began to spread all over the country until in 1960 there were 300 Indian restaurants in Britain and in 1980 over 3000, of which the vast majority are owned by families from Sylhet.[70]

Although the original aim of the early settlers was to send money back home to Sylhet, and eventually to retire there, the birth of subsequent generations of children together with changing political and economic events in Bangladesh have made this an impractical goal for many. As we shall see in Chapter 6 of this book, few second-generation Bangladeshis seem determined to return to Bangladesh. Rather, they see themselves as citizens of London or merely of a 'Muslim community':

> They say 'your home is where your heart is', but I don't know where my heart is and that makes it difficult you know. My heart used to be in the East End when I was younger. I know I used to say that I could never go back to Bangladesh and live there. Maybe to stay there for a couple of months but never live there.[71]

Eade proposes that we are now in a global age where 'home' for young people whose origins lie in Bangladesh might be in 'anywhere, in Bangladesh or the Middle East, where Sylheti migrants are found. It could be in a country which observes shariah law or in the English countryside, in the USA or Asia or anywhere 'as long as they feel comfortable'.[72] The important word here is 'comfortable'. Later in this book, a group of young British-Bangladeshi women discuss where they would choose to live. One of the group, Tahmin, is very precise about her choice of home:

Moving? I'd stay in London. I love London because it's so cosmopolitan. Spitalfields, if you like, is a condensed version of that . . . it has all the characteristics that I love . . . I think north London is quite nice . . . Muswell Hill has got a nice atmosphere to it . . .

(Tahmin)

For many migrants, the freedom to choose is closely linked with literacy and education, as we shall see later in the book.

2

SCHOOLING THE CITY

I was the second eldest child in a family of eight and when I was 5,
I went to Redmans Road School and I stayed there until the age of
14. When I left school, I went to work in a cabinet-maker's workshop
and, living at home with us was a schoolmaster, my uncle Mr D.R.
Isaacs, who taught at the Jews' Free School. When he saw me coming
home, dressed in dirty clothes and covered in sawdust, he felt very
sorry for me and spoke to my mother and my father and he said, 'This
is not good enough for him'. So he paid for me to go to the Davenant
Foundation in Whitechapel. And so I went there when I was fourteen
and a half and three years later I matriculated. I passed three A-
levels and obtained bursaries which enabled me to enrol at Goldsmiths
College in 1929.

(Ralph Barnes, born in London in 1910; teacher at the
Jews' Free School, Bell Lane, Spitalfields)

Every generation believes it provides the best schooling for its children,
but a glance back in time shows us that what 'counts' as valid teaching and
learning is very different from one generation and from one country to
another. This is particularly the case for initial literacy teaching. At this point
in time, there is a tendency to believe that the answer to successful literacy
teaching has only just been discovered, that it is simple and that it lies in the
transmission of a particular set of skills by teachers in classrooms. A glance
back to earlier times, however, reveals that we cannot disregard the past. The
aim of this chapter is to reveal the diversity and contrasts in literacy provision
in the two square miles we have studied and to show how these have been
shaped by the efforts of educational pioneers or literacy mediators in
children's lives. The chapter has two parts. The first provides a brief history
of schooling in and around the City of London, with particular reference
to the education of children of the poor. It introduces three schools, the two
project schools, Sir John Cass School and Canon Barnett School (formerly
Commercial Street School) and the Jews' Free School. The second part
examines some mediators of literacy outside the mainstream school that were

important in the lives of our participants: the library, Toynbee Hall, Jewish religious classes and the Qur'anic and Bengali language classes of the Bangladeshi-British community. Throughout the chapter, we see how the types of literacy skills mastered by children were not isolated but intimately linked with the purpose for which they were learned.

Education and religion have been closely bound together in London since medieval times when the Church dominated intellectual life in England. Early schools were run by the churches principally to teach boys to sing in services and little was taught except Latin. Three of the earliest and finest church schools in London were, according to Stow,[1] St Paul's, St Peter's at Westminster and St Saviour's at Bermondsey in Southwark.[2] There were later schools at St Mary Overie in Southwark and at Holy Trinity by Aldgate.[3] During the fourteenth and fifteenth centuries, as English gradually replaced Latin and French in the domains of commerce, government and the law, the need for literacy in English grew. Small elementary schools taught by scriveners or 'dames' sprang up around the city. There were also a number of private grammar schools, especially in Cornhill, but their reputation was poor: 'there is great numbers of learners and few teachers and as the learners are compelled to go to the same few teachers and to no other, the masters wax rich in money and the learners poor in cunning'.[4]

The sixteenth century was a time of expansion in education although, according to some historians, the proliferation of establishments ranging from ancient grammar schools to dame schools had the effect of exaggerating rather than reducing social inequalities.[5] In 1509, John Colet, Dean of St Paul's, reorganised St Paul's School, introducing a more humanistic curriculum which became the model for other London schools such as Merchant Taylors', Charterhouse and Christ's Hospital. City merchants collaborated with clerics in establishing parish grammar schools. The Reformation, however, was to have a damaging effect on education, and many grammar schools, starved of funds and the support of the clergy, were obliged to close. Stow fondly remembers the halcyon days, early in the century, when 'scholars of divers grammar schools' would 'repair unto the churchyard of St Bartholomew, the priory at Smithfield, where they would argue about the principles of grammar, till [they] were by some better scholar overcome and put down'. By the end of the century, however, Stow noted that the quality of debate had deteriorated to such an extent that the young scholars 'usually fell from words to blows with their satchels full of books, many times in great heaps, that troubled the streets and passengers'.[6] There was, nevertheless, a continuing interest in education in the population at large: in 1518, the Royal College of Physicians was established and later in the century one of the earliest adult education centres, Gresham College, which offered lectures in, among other things, music, law, rhetoric, physic and divinity, opened its doors to the public. The first London theatres – the Theatre, built by James Burbage, and the Curtain – were opened in

Shoreditch just to the north of Spitalfields in 1576 and 1577 respectively. By the early seventeenth century, it is estimated that 75 per cent of London's tradesmen and 50 per cent of craftsmen and shopkeepers could sign their name.[7] Female literacy lagged behind that of men but it has been suggested that it rose from approximately 10 per cent of the female population in 1650 to 50 per cent in 1690.[8]

Education in the eighteenth century 'has acquired a wretched reputation'.[9] During that century London experienced unprecedented growth in trade and industry. Migrants poured into the metropolis to seek their fortunes until, by 1750, 10 per cent of England's population lived in the capital, which seemed to dominate the commercial life of the whole country; 'the whole kingdom are employed . . . to supply the city of London with provisions; . . . corn, flesh, fish, butter, cheese, salt, fewel, timber etc. . . . cloths and everything necessary for building and furniture for their own use'.[10] The result of such expansion was a flourishing middle-class culture with 'a distinctly pragmatic tone' and a very practical attitude towards education. New practical and progressive schools sprang up 'to fit the sons of middling sort to staff the professions and the world of business'.[11] Meanwhile, the grammar schools, many of which had been established in pre-Reformation times to provide a scholarly education for poor children, were failing in their responsibilities: 'most endowments proved inadequate to sustain the expenses or escape the cupidity of those who controlled them'.[12]

The new wealth of the middle classes was put to some good use, however. Charitable foundations flourished in London as never before. Hospitals such as the Middlesex, the London Hospital, Guy's Hospital (funded by Thomas Guy, a bookseller who had made his fortune by printing Bibles), were built, along with three lying-in hospitals, a hospital for the insane, another for the treatment of venereal diseases, and the Foundling Hospital, which took in unwanted babies. It was in the field of education, however, that the most charitable impulses were to be seen. By 1704, there were fifty charity schools in the capital, and by 1711, the number had risen to over 100, with £10,000 per year being raised to fund them. The first Protestant charity school in England was established on Tower Hill in 1667, and after the death of its founder it was endowed by Sir Samuel Starling, Alderman of Portsoken Ward. It became known as the Starling School and was the model for Sir John Cass School.

There had been charitable attempts at educating the poor before the Starling School was established. In the late sixteenth century, increasing numbers of homeless children had prompted schemes for combining education and work. In one such scheme, 1,000 paupers were housed and 100 young children taught in two confiscated Royalist properties until the restoration of Charles II in 1660, when the properties were reclaimed and the children sent to Christ's Hospital School. During the seventeenth and eighteenth centuries, provision for the poor was the responsibility of the parish authorities and badly underfunded. Children especially were at risk. A parliamentary survey carried out in 1767 found that of 100 workhouse infants, only seven survived until age 3.[13] Children who did manage to survive the orphanage were put as unpaid workhouse apprentices to masters in unskilled trades, such as chimney sweeps and shoemakers. Many were sent to work in the new factories in the Midlands or the North; others were sent to sea, often a fate tantamount to death.

Sir John Cass School

It was against this background of poverty and poor educational provision that Sir John Cass, a wealthy and ambitious Tory politician, offered to found, fund and build a school for the poor of Portsoken Ward in the City. This was an innovatory gesture at the time, as charity schools were usually funded collaboratively. The new school, situated in the corner of St Botolph's church-yard, was a two-storey building with schoolrooms on the upper floor, and shops and burial vaults on the lower floor. The profits accruing from the latter would contribute to the upkeep of the school. The inaugural service held in March 1711, attended by sixty peers and forty members of the House of Commons, and conducted by Dr Sacheverell, a High Anglican and leading member of the Tory party and arguably the most famous man in London at the time, gives some idea of the status of Sir John Cass.[14]

Fifty boys and forty girls were to receive instruction in the beliefs and practices of the Church of England; in addition, boys were to learn reading, writing and arithmetic and girls to write, read, cast accounts and learn plain sewing. The pupils were to receive 'decent blue clothing, and proper books' and 'a sufficient dinner or meals meat in lieu thereof as much money as the trustees should think reasonable'.[15] On leaving school at age 14, each pupil would receive a suit of clothes to enable him or her to take up a position, which the school would help them to find, the boys as apprentices to local tradesmen and the girls in domestic service. This regime continued for over a hundred years: all pupils had to be resident in Portsoken Ward and produce a certificate stating that they had been baptised in the Anglican Church. During this period, however, the population in this part of London was changing: the number of people living in the City was declining rapidly and Portsoken Ward came to house 'mainly warehouses, shops and offices'. Many Jewish children moved into the parish. So, when in 1869 the main body of the school moved to new premises in Jewry Street, the old schoolrooms in Church Row were retained, as a part of the school where neither religious nor residence restrictions were imposed, and sixty or so Jewish children had their lessons in the Church Row premises. A Hebrew teacher was employed to give religious instruction. In 1898, the school in Jewry Street was demolished and a new school and institute built on the adjacent site. In 1908, the school moved to a new building, the site of the present primary school, in Dukes Place.

For most of the nineteenth century, the school curriculum which was of 'a plain English kind' remained unaltered.[16] Then in 1896, a Mr Farthing took over as headteacher. He was dismayed at the conditions in the school. He found it 'in an even more backward state' than he had expected. Reading in the school was 'fair', spelling 'moderate', arithmetic 'bad' and 'geography and grammar' would have to be reintroduced from scratch. He immediately reduced the four half days per week the boys spent on woodwork to two half days, and the girls' cookery lessons were reduced to one afternoon. Testing and termly examinations became part of the regime and homework took on a special importance: only pupils who had satisfactorily completed their homework were allowed library books. The 'object lesson', a familiar feature in Victorian education, was an important part of the curriculum. 'Coal, its origin and how it is obtained', 'Lamps and their dangers', are noted in the school logbooks. Although, as in other schools, the curriculum already included poetry 'learnt for recitation' by the whole class, as well as the geography of the British Isles, Europe, the United States, Asia and Africa, Mr Farthing felt that more breadth was needed. He therefore introduced history, and French along with 'the systematising of Reading of the First Class by study of a special author during each period'. French was dropped in 1906 when the London County Council decided that 'except in special circumstances such as in one or two schools where there are many German Jews, the instruction in foreign languages should be discontinued in ordinary graded schools'.[17] Under Mr Farthing's leadership, the curriculum was given a commercial bias and children were encouraged to remain at school until age 15 rather than the mandatory 14 so that they could apply for jobs with good City firms (see Eric, Chapter 3, p. 77 in this book). In short, unlike other charitable schools and in particular the medieval grammar schools, which had quickly been appropriated by the middle classes, Sir John Cass School remained true to the wishes of its founder and has continued to provide an excellent education for the people of the parish to the present day.

During World War I, the work of the school was disrupted by Zeppelin raids and many children were sent to the country. The headteacher wrote, 'Long periods of absence on the part of some, combined with serious nervous and mental disturbances on the part of many, have seriously affected the character of the work and made normal progress impossible'.[18] The central location of the school meant that it would suffer intolerable disruption when World War II began. In the event, preparations for evacuation were made and on Saturday 2 September 1939, 232 children and 26 adults set off for Aylesbury, where school commenced two weeks later. In May 1941, the Duke Street premises were severely damaged in an air raid. This did not prevent some parents from keeping their children in London and sending them to an emergency London County Council (LCC) school in Dukes Place. Many of the Cass pupils, teachers and the headteacher remained in Aylesbury for the duration of the war, however, and returned to London within a few weeks of the cessation of hostilities. On 30 August 1945 school reopened in Dukes Place. Robert and his parents, whom we meet in Chapter 4, were anxiously awaiting the reopening.

Sir John Cass School is a unique institution in many ways and its long and fascinating history is reflected in the way the older ex-pupils talk about the school. They recall the May Day celebrations when 'teachers would get up at the crack of dawn to go and buy flowers in Spitalfields Flower Market to decorate the Hall'; the Rifle Range in the north playground, and the award-winning shooting team. All ex-pupils remember Founder's Days, usually held in January or February, which celebrate a somewhat gruesome event that marked the first years of the school's life. In 1709, John Cass made a will, stating his intention to build a school. Nine years later, he made a second will and, it is said, died of a haemorrhage while in the act of signing. To this day, the pupils of Sir John Cass Primary School wear red feathers when they attend the Founder's Day service in St Botolph's Church, in memory of the blood-stained quill pen that marked the founder's death. Glynn, however, finds no mention of a haemorrhage in contemporary accounts and concludes that 'many years after the event, the death of Sir John Cass gained a touch of Victorian melodrama'.[19]

From charity to Board school

> It's a very cheering thing to come into London by any of these lines which run high and allow you to look down upon houses like these. Look at those big isolated clumps of buildings rising above the slates, like brick islands in a lead-coloured sea. The Board Schools, Lighthouses, . . . Beacons of the Future. Capsules with hundreds of bright little seeds in each, out of which will spring the wiser, better England of the future.
>
> (Sherlock Holmes on the Board schools)

It was during the nineteenth century that public opinion finally moved towards the view that there should be a national system of public education. This was prompted in part by the social unrest that followed the French Revolution, and by the fear that without a skilled workforce Britain would fall behind its industrial competitors. Progress was dogged, however, by disputes between the established Church and the nonconformists as to who should control education. Thus two groups were established to provide for elementary schooling: the British and Foreign School Association (founded 1808), run on a non-denominational basis, and the National Society for the Promotion of the Education of the Poor (founded 1809) which was run according to the principles of the established Church in England and Wales. Religious animosity continued to hinder reforms throughout the whole century. An early bid to introduce a national education system based on rate aid foundered. In 1861, a report produced by the Duke of Newcastle on the state of elementary education rejected free and compulsory education for all 'in view of the religious difficulties involved and upon general grounds of individualistic principle'. The findings of the Newcastle Commission revealed that, although one in seven children in England (2,500,000 children) were attending school, fewer than one in twenty were attending a school whose efficiency could be guaranteed through inspection and the provision of government grants. In London there were some 860 public day schools, 1,700 private schools, 700 or so Sunday schools and 100 evening schools. Standards were not high, however. J.S. Mill asserted that the education provided by both the National and the British and Foreign Schools was 'never good except by some rare accident and generally so bad as to be little more than nominal'.

In spite of the poor quality of the education offered, the number of people sending their children to school continued to grow. By the time the Elementary Education Act was passed in 1870, the majority of children attended a school of some description. Elementary education was still neither free nor compulsory, but the 1870 Act established local school boards, elected by ratepayers, whose role was to ascertain that provision was in place in their districts, and who were entitled to frame local laws rendering education compulsory and to pay school fees for the poor. London constituted a single school board with an area that covered seventeen square miles. A survey carried out in the 1870s by the newly appointed London School Board found that of the 681,000 children living in the London area, 97,307 (one in seven) were being educated at home or in schools with relatively high fees, 9,100 were in workhouses, orphanages or other institutions, and 176,000 (one in four) did not attend school because of parental neglect, ill health, or because they had to work. Of the remaining 400,000 who did attend, 250,000 were at schools run by the British and Foreign or the National Schools Associations (see above discussion) and the rest in cheap private schools, dame schools or ragged schools.[20]

The early years of the London Schools Board saw considerable increases in the number of schools and school places with the result that by 1904 when the London County Council took over education, there were 469 Board schools in London. Commercial Street School, later to be named Canon Barnett School, our project school, built in 1901, was one of these schools. At a time when poverty and destitution were matters of national concern, the Board schools were hailed by the social scientist Charles Booth as having a 'civilising' influence.

> Habits of cleanliness and of order have been formed; a higher standard of dress and of decency has been attained, and this reacts upon the homes.

Schoolmasters need no longer fear the tongue of the mother or the horsewhip of the indignant father.[21]

The Toynbee Record noted in 1889:

> The Board Schools which promised to devote themselves to the three R's are every day becoming more and more centres for the larger education which many had hoped for. The common sense of the community has recognised that in the future the schools will have to produce not merely clerks and labourers but devoted and intelligent citizens.

The Board schools were distinctive and well constructed. Beatrice Webb wrote:

> Among the public buildings of the Metropolis, the London Board schools occupy a conspicuous place. In every quarter the eye is arrested by their distinctive architecture, as they stand closest to where the need is greatest, each one like a tall sentinel at his post keeping watch over the interests of the generation that is to replace our own. . . . Taken as a whole they may be said fairly to represent the high water mark of public conscience in this country in its relation to the education of the children of the people.[22]

As so often in the field of education, the East End of London produced pioneers and visionaries. In 1888 Annie Besant (whose work inspired the Matchgirls' Strike, see Chapter 1, p. 35 in this book) was elected as the London School Board member for Tower Hamlets. In her campaigning speech she presented her aims for education, some of which are still being campaigned for today. She demanded

> free secular, compulsory, technical education for all . . . the opening of higher education to the poor . . . putting the board schools at the service of the public and throwing open the playgrounds to all children during the hours of daylight after school time and during the school holidays . . . power to provide free school meals as children who are hungry cannot profit from education.

On 30 January 1890, the Board passed the historic act, introduced as a resolution by Besant, declaring that schools receiving state grants should be free. This example set by the London School Board prompted an Act of Parliament the following year implementing free elementary education for all.

Contrasts and change: Canon Barnett School

Children used to come from other schools for their Jewish dinners. Boys used to come up and I think they used to have the first sitting. They always came up and then the others had theirs later. It was a Jewish kitchen, you see. Then, you see, it gradually changed. We had all races there at one time . . .

(Grace, cleaner and primary assistant from 1960 to 1990)

[The school now has a Moslem halal kitchen]

Commercial Street School, or Canon Barnett School as it was renamed in 1955, was opened at the turn of the century in 1901. Situated just behind Toynbee Hall, it was built on the site of Jack the Ripper's first murder which had taken place thirteen years earlier on Gunthorpe Street. It is a tall three-storey building, with its completion date, and 'Boys', 'Girls' and 'Infants' inscribed in stone above its three entrances. Built to accommodate 1,500 children, it has three halls, three staircases and two playgrounds. Grace, who joined the school as a cleaner in 1960, remembers her daily task:

I used to have to wash all those stairs from top to bottom. And then we had to get on our hands and knees and scrub and he [the old schoolkeeper] used to shout, and sometimes I'd kick the bucket down the stairs accidentally on purpose, you know, I'd just wipe it up. Most of the time, they didn't want washing . . . and he used to shout out, 'I can't hear those scrubbing brushes going . . . '
EG: *So he was quite a tyrant?*
Grace: *Oh yes.*

During World War II the school was caught by a bomb blast. It was empty, since the children had been evacuated to Oving, just outside Aylesbury, which also housed the Cass children. A row of shops in front of the school was demolished, leaving space for the school to enlarge its playground and build a new nursery wing. Apart from those changes, the structure of the school remained the same into the twenty-first century.

The school has seen extraordinary changes in its population throughout its lifetime. In the first years of its existence, it was reported that 40 per cent of the boys in standard one were unable to speak English. An old pupil interviewed by White[23] believed that 300 of the 304 girls in one year were Jewish. Attendance was good and punctuality was rewarded by 'bits of coloured ribbons and brooches' for the infants, a tea-party with the headmistress for the girls and a lantern show for the boys.[24] Hot milk was provided in winter for those children who needed it. Free clothing was also distributed to the very poorest: 'the Jewish Schools Boot Fund gave boots regularly to the school, and the Jewish Ladies Clothing Association handed out 857 articles of clothing there over a three year period'.[25]

During the 1920s and 1930s, when our oldest participants were pupils, one finds surnames such as Levy, Zimmermann, Flaum, Nasmanowitz, Isaacs, Rabin, Lazarus, Schlachtaub, Gertsky, Keltbrodt, Gertler, Cohen, Zussmann, Nussdorf and Goldstein in just one infant class. These children joined Odel French, Jacqueline Carmel, Lawrence Lancome and Marie-Antoinette Lal, whose parents were of Huguenot origin. Some twenty-five years later, in 1953, Letife Ali, the first Asian child started at age 6. The following year, four children came to the school from India; in 1957, eight Asian children were admitted; in 1958, eleven new arrivals came and in 1960, they were joined by forty-eight new pupils from India or Pakistan. At this time children were also leaving; in 1953, one child left for the USA; in 1956 two went to Israel, two to Cyprus and one to Egypt. By 1984, the transformation of the population was complete. Four children in the school were from India or Pakistan and all the remaining children were of Bangladeshi origin.

Parents' occupations have seen a similar transformation. One page of the logbook for 1937 reveals a remarkable variety of trades or occupations: stevedore, carpenter, photographer, asbestos worker, trenchman, managing director, importer, prison minister, accountant, embassy clerk, fishmonger, chief engineer, radio engineer, British transport worker, toolfitter, publican, taxi-driver, tobacconist, cook, foreman, porter, labourer, tailor, draughts-man, optician, office-cleaner and Indian police (an Englishman). The illness or unemployment of a father was given special mention in the school diary; red ink was used if the period of unemployment was longer than six months or if a baby was ill. It was so rare for a mother to work that this situation was also marked in red. By the mid-1990s, the occupations of fathers had shrunk to include only machinist, waiter, tailor, presser, spinner, sweet-maker or unemployed. Only by the end of the twentieth century do we find the first professional working mothers in the history of the school. We meet three of these mothers later, in Chapter 5 of this book.

The nature of Canon Barnett School, however, is not to be merely a passive recipient of all newcomers who move into its catchment area. Rather, over the years, it has engineered a dynamic syncretism of cultures across the generations, subtly adapting to its new pupils as each different group arrived. From its earliest days, the school employed a number of Jewish teachers, most of whom travelled from their homes outside the area to teach Jewish children in the school. Norma, one of the older participants in the study, remembers hearing the name of 'Golders Green' for the first time from her teacher. These teachers are remembered by our pre-war generation as role models whose English was excellent. Classes stopped for Jewish as well as English holidays. The school attempted to syncretise Jewish and English cultures in a number of other ways too. In respect for the Jewish religion, the school had a special timetable on Fridays; children came to school earlier in the morning, went home early at eleven o'clock for lunch and then finished at two o'clock for the Sabbath. There was also a collection box for the Jewish poor abroad, to which all tried to contribute, no matter how difficult their own circumstances might have been. At the same time, the school continued to have a daily act of Christian worship and even the Jewish children remembered the pomp and significance of the Empire Day celebrations:

I can remember, one day, being in Miss Pickard's class and singing 'God Save the King' and, each one of us, as we were able to recite the three verses, then we were allowed to go home. It was already going home time, but you weren't allowed to go home until you could recite the three verses of 'God Save the King'.

(Gloria, born in 1939)

From its opening, the school also offered a wide variety of literacy and learning activities. Abby, one of the oldest participants in our study, started at the nursery in 1920, when it was still quite new, and has vivid memories of all her subsequent classes, including the traditional housewifery classes of washing, ironing, sewing, cookery and knitting, which were provided for the girls. She also remembers learning spellings, dates and poetry by rote (which she describes in Chapter 3 of this book). However, alongside these, she recollects the regular provision of newspapers for the children to read as well as French lessons for the older children (which they paid for to help buy good-quality books for the school). One such book she remembers was Dickens' *A Tale of Two Cities* which she read at age 9. The curriculum also provided a wide range of out-of-school activities. She has memories of regular visits to Kew Gardens every year to see the bluebells when they were in bloom. Older ex-pupils remember bus trips to Epping Forest and nature walks in Victoria Park.[26] Similar memories of exceptional teaching and teachers were shared by all our pre-war group, summarised neatly by Abby:

I think the education we had at Commercial Street [Canon Barnett] School was excellent. It wasn't forced, but you learned well . . . the teachers were marvellous.

The Jews' Free School: from foreigner to English citizen

I was appointed by Dr Bernstein, Head Teacher of the Boys' School and I was given the first class of children, aged from 11 to 12. Amongst these there were children from all backgrounds. Some of them came from fairly comfortable backgrounds but there were very many very poor children. In fact, at the Jews' Free School, we used to supply some clothing for them and free school dinners were provided as well, for the very poor . . . I think the teachers and the pupils were closer together at the Jews' Free School. I don't know whether we actually recognised it as such, whether we realised that we were all strangers in a new land . . . I think it was a kind of communal feeling . . . I mean Sunday morning, for example, we had to go to school to teach Hebrew, only Hebrew. We did teach Hebrew in the first period by the way, but we also had Sunday mornings and we got paid extra for that.

(Ralph, born 1910)

By the late nineteenth century, many new Jewish immigrants were arriving in Britain. The Ashkenazim 'pale and puny, haggard, helpless creatures without funds, without skills, without contacts'[27] arrived in great numbers, destitute and desperate to settle down and earn a living. Just as the nineteenth-century promoters of English state education were motivated by religious idealism, so the settled Anglo-Jewish establishment were anxious that the newcomers should be educated as Jews and protected from the 'baneful influence' of 'non-Jewish ideologies such as Christianity and Socialism'. A further aim of the Anglo-Jewish elders however, was that the newcomers should be fully assimilated into English society.

> The perplexing problem growing out of the presence in our midst of a large number of foreign poor can only be solved by education. To train the parents in the social and intellectual scale is a task which at best only partial success can be hoped for. The children offer a much more promising field of effort. They at least can be rescued from the baneful influence which oppression and some civilised surroundings have exerted upon their elders. . . . The children . . . may be trained to become elements of the future communal well-being, instead of being a draw on the material resources of the community and a danger to its stability. The work is clearly educational; and the Jews' Free School does the bulk of it. Of the 3,000 children within its walls, the great majority enter it practically foreigners; they leave it potential Englishmen and women, prepared to take their part in the struggle of life in the spirit of English citizens.
>
> (*Jewish Chronicle*, 1888)[28]

The Jews' Free School was established in 1840 by Moses Angel who remained its headmaster for the next 51 years. By the end of the nineteenth century, it was the largest elementary school in the world with over 4,000 pupils. Providing a balance between Jewish and English education, it was considered to play a major role in the anglicisation of Jewish youth.[29] Not all members of the school were enthusiastic about its aims, however. Israel Zangwill, the novelist and schoolmaster at the school, objected to its anglicising role in his novels and short stories. Like Ralph, he remembers 'the bell of the great Ghetto school, summoning its pupils from reeking courts and alleys, from garrets and cellars, calling them to come and be anglicised', but with anger rather than affection.[30] He later resigned his position at the school after his stories, which celebrated a Yiddish-based lifestyle, were received with disapproval by the authorities.

The Jews' Free School nevertheless exerted a powerful and positive influence over thousands of Jewish children who later escaped the poverty of East London. It was a traditional and strict school with high standards for both teachers and students alike. Ralph Barnes, teacher at the school from 1931 until 1972, recalls its sway over the whole area:

> *Dr Bernstein, the headteacher, was an academic and the school produced a magazine which encouraged every boy to write a poem or short story, which would be published in time. And in fact the staff were also involved. I had one or two short stories published. I had written a story about the school bell. One day I went for a walk in the market in Petticoat Lane, and we used to have a school bell reminding us it was time to return to school after lunch. I was walking down the Lane listening to a man who was trying to sell something to a crowd of people. I'd forgotten all about school and the time and I heard the ringing of the bell in the distance and I had to go running back to school like a schoolboy. Luckily, I got there in time . . .*

High expectations and a deep empathy with the children and their families accompanied the strict regime. Teachers felt convinced that the children worked harder than their local English counterparts; both children and their parents felt that the key to success in life lay in education. In an interview, Ralph Barnes speaks of his keenness to instil accurate grammar and good spoken English in the boys he taught:

> *To what extent do you think economic deprivation affected their achieving decent linguistic and literacy skills?*
>
> **Ralph:** *I think that's a very, very important question. If they came from homes where their parents did not speak English correctly, then it was difficult for them to pick up, to speak English correctly, so when they came to school, they had to be taught, of course, and grammar was something I was very, very keen on. Still am. I'm still very conscious whether people speak correctly or incorrectly . . .*

Parental participation in teaching their children at home played no part in the school's expectations. Parents attended the school on Prize Day or went on school outings, but apart from that their task was to ensure that their children were well behaved and respected their teachers. And, as Ralph Barnes stresses, most of them did.

Mediators of literacy in East End communities

Jewish religious classes

In spite of the educational ideals of their Anglo-Jewish elders, the first Ashkenazim were reluctant to abandon their own culture and religious practices. Unused to the formality and grandeur of such places of worship as the Great Synagogue, with its anglicised rabbis, the newcomers remained resolutely in their own communities and established their own chevras or religious associations. The latter establishments 'combined the functions of a benefit club for death, sickness and solemn rites of mourning with that of public worship and the study of the Talmud'.[31] The thirty or forty chevras in the Jewish East End formed the hub of social life, providing members with the opportunity to assemble with other exiles. The associations were often named after a town or district in Russia or Poland which had once been home: the Plotzker, the Vilna, the Dzikower, for example, reflecting as Fishman notes, a 'poignant attachment to the heim (homeland) which had dealt with them so harshly'.[32] For the Jewish community, the chevra was 'their salon and their lecture hall. It supplied them not only with their religion but their arts and letters, their politics and their public amusements'.[33]

Worship took place in stieblech, small house-based synagogues where

> the accommodation usually consisted of two large rooms knocked into one with the rear partitioned off for the use of the women. The furniture was bare benches, a raised platform with a reading desk in the centre and a wooden, curtained ark at the end containing parchment scrolls of the Law, each with a silver pointer and silver bells. The back windows gave onto the yard and the contiguous cowsheds, and 'moos' mingled with the impassioned supplications of the worshippers.[34]

Beatrice Webb describes men arriving at the stieblech to pray: 'early in the morning or late at night, the devout members [would] meet to recite the morning or evening prayers or to decipher the sacred books of the Talmud [the rabbinical commentaries on the Bible], and it [was] a curious and touching sight to enter one of the poorer and more wretched of these places on a Sabbath morning'.[35] In spite of the poor surroundings, worship was enthusiastic:

> they dropped in mostly in their work-a-day garments and grime and rumbled and roared and chorused prayers with a zeal that shook the window panes and there never was a lack of minyan – the congregational quorum of ten.[36]

On the Sabbath of course, even the poorest would arrive well washed and scrubbed and in their best clothes.

It is not surprising perhaps that the distinguished leaders of the Anglo-Jewish establishment disapproved of these small, noisy stieblach, condemning them as insanitary and overcrowded. A move to build a large synagogue in the East End, to coax the poor away from their local places of worship, came to nothing however. Finally, the Federation of Synagogues was established in 1887 by Samuel Montague, MP for Whitechapel, which permitted the small synagogues to continue to worship as they wished.

An important function of the chevras was to teach Hebrew and to prepare boys for their bar mitzvah. Bermant claims that by 1891 there were some 200 of these classes in the East End with 2,000 boys on their roll. The children attended in the morning before school, during the lunch hour or after school. In 1895 a Talmud Torah opened in Brick Lane. In this school, the children received an intensive Jewish education in Yiddish and were fed and clothed. Within ten weeks of its opening, it had 500 pupils. A second Talmud Torah was opened in Commercial Road, and the third, in Redmans Road, had 1,000 pupils by the beginning of the twentieth century.

The movement of the Jewish population out of the East End following the severe bombardment in World War II, however, meant that religious education in the area declined. As the population moved out to West Hampstead, Hendon, Highgate or Golders Green, they transferred to the more anglicised synagogues of the north and west where 'most of the synagogue classes owed more in character to the Church of England Sunday School than to the old style Chadarim of Eastern Europe'.[37] One hundred years after its opening, the synagogue in Princelet Street, locked and neglected since it closed in the 1960s, is about to start a new phase as a Centre for the Study of Immigration.

Qur'anic and Bengali classes

Hasna, a Bengali community class teacher in Spitalfields, describes her classes:

> *Our lessons are planned with each other. We have books, games and pictures. I have another teacher and we work together. The whole group is 65, so we have half each. The age group is 15 to 16. First, we test them in very small groups, four or five, and teach them according to their ability. We teach them for six hours a week; three evenings for two hours, from five till seven.*

Nina: *Is there a special curriculum? Like the National Curriculum?*

Hasna: *Our community sets our curriculum. Also, as teachers, we set it.*

Nina: *What do you start with?*

Hasna: *They must know the alphabet. Then we teach reading, spelling, writing, poems, stories; also how to write letters. Also, English to Bengali translation.*

Nina: *When do they learn to do this?*

Hasna: *When they've learned the alphabet and are able to write and spell.*

As in the Jewish community, supplementary education for Bangladeshi-British children in Spitalfields began with religion: a madrassah,[38] where children were instructed in the tenets of Islam, and in the Arabic language, was started by the late Haji Taslim Ali at the East London Mosque in Whitechapel High Street in the 1960s.[39] With the arrival of more families in the 1970s, similar classes were set up elsewhere, run by volunteer teachers in a whole variety of premises, including people's homes. By the end of the twentieth century, opportunities to learn the Qur'an in Spitalfields were numerous, ranging from individual tuition for children in their own home and small classes held in the living rooms of teachers' homes to large organised classes in the surrounding mosques. Excited groups of children still spill out of these classes every evening, scuttling to their homes in the same way as their Jewish predecessors did nearly a century ago.

But Qur'anic classes are only one extra learning activity of Bangladeshi-British children in Spitalfields. In 1977, two educational pioneers, Mr Mohammed Nurul Hoque and Mrs Anwara Begum, joined a group of parents who were concerned at their children's lack of access to their own culture and language and set up the East End Community School. The school started with just thirteen children, two volunteer teachers and a management committee composed of parents and a few local activists. For some months, the school ran with no more 'official' support than a few exercise books, chalk and play items donated by Toynbee Hall. After eighteen months, by which time the school had sixty-three students, the teachers began to be paid for a few hours a week by the (then) Bethnal Green Institute of Adult Education. However, the majority of their time has continued to be given voluntarily.

The school's expansion did not continue smoothly. As its reputation grew, the scandal of its overcrowded and unhealthy conditions became known to the local authorities who attempted to close it. After a long battle and many bureaucratic delays, the school was moved in 1980 into a Portakabin on a temporary open space, which provided safe and secure premises.

At present, the school is open from 4.30 p.m. to 6.30 p.m. on weekdays and from 10.00 a.m. to 5.00 p.m. on Saturdays, with special activities on Sundays and school holidays. There are currently over seventy children between 6 and 16 on roll and over forty on the waiting list. Some children are fluent English speakers, others still at a beginner stage. Subjects taught include English and Bengali language and literature (especially poetry), maths, Arabic, general science, history, geography, singing, needlework, knitting and other crafts and art. Caroline Adams, whose interviews with older members of the Bangladeshi community have been referred to earlier in this chapter, perhaps best summarises the importance of the school in the lives of the Spitalfields community:

There is no question, for anyone who has known the children and the school for any length of time how much the children have grown as individuals, spiritually and mentally, and that their increased skills and confidence have contributed to their development within mainstream education. For children and parents alike, the school has been a focus, which has given them, as nothing else in their life in Britain has given, a sense of belonging and significance. The school is also a haven of happiness and creativity, one of the few 'nice' places in an often depressing environment.

We shall hear more about the school in Chapter 5 of this book.

Libraries: friends to the poor

The object of all labour is not so much the production of wealth, is not the extension of empire, but is to enable the English nation to grow great men whose lives are stored in books.

(Canon Barnett, opening the Whitechapel Library, 1900)

As early as the fifteenth century, there was a growing public demand in England for books and reading materials. In 1423, a bequest in the will of Lord Richard Whittington was used to establish the first lending library next to the Guildhall in the City of London, for the use of citizens as well as clergy.[40] (It was plundered and destroyed by the Protector Somerset in 1549.) The publisher John Shirley, who died in 1456, also ran a lending library comprising 'little ballads, complaints and roundels'. Large numbers of books and manuscripts were imported. In 1480, for example, customs recorded the import of 1,300 volumes. By the time Caxton introduced the printing press at Westminster in 1476, it would appear that considerable sections of the population could read. Records of male witnesses to the court in 1470 show that about 40 per cent were literate. Under Wynken de Worde, Caxton's assistant, who took over the business on Caxton's death in 1491, the press moved to Fleet Street to join other presses springing up there. By the time he died in 1535, Worde had published 800 books. Alongside the devotional and doctrinal literature, a popular culture of broadsides, ballads, fables and fairy stories was emerging. Fleet Street was to remain the national centre for printing until the 1980s.

Middle-class Londoners, therefore, had long secured access to books and reading. In the seventeenth century, circulating libraries became popular until by 1800 there were some 122 in the capital. West End clubs and professional associations had libraries, as did scholarly institutions such as the Linnaean Society, the Royal Geographical Association and the Royal College of Physicians. Mudie's on New Oxford Street and W.H. Smith had large lending libraries. Free municipal libraries, however, were slow to develop. Although, in 1850, local authorities were authorised to fund libraries from the rates, few ratepayers felt that the poor should be 'civilised' at their expense and only one London parish opened a free public library as a result. Opinion gradually changed, however, and by the 1880s there were several municipal libraries, many of them opened to commemorate Queen Victoria's golden jubilee. By 1910, only two London boroughs, Marylebone and Bethnal Green, were without a free public library.

The Whitechapel Library, which features so frequently in the memories of our participants, was officially opened in 1900. Mr Passmore Edwards provided £6,454 towards the scheme and this was matched by £5,000 provided by voluntary donations. The library was an immediate success, opening with a total of 20,734 volumes, which had increased to 50,455 by 1906. In the year 1902/3, 136,000 books were issued for home reading and 48,636 were consulted for reference. The average daily attendance in the reading room in 1905 was approximately 3,000 people. The library was used by a wide range of borrowers. An early survey found that, apart from women for whom no occupation was recorded, eighty-five different occupations were listed among the borrowers, ranging from students and scholars (the most frequent users), clerks, bookkeepers, civil servants, teachers, to tailors and cutters, actors, bakers, blacksmiths, cap-makers, dairymen, domestic servants, and so on.

By the end of the 1940s, the number of volumes had increased to 283,026. The popular story hours for children were introduced, attended in 1948 by 8,500 children. Throughout the 1950s and 1960s, the library grew and expanded and innovatory schemes introduced. In 1958/9, for example, they increased the numbers of books for parents to read to pre-school children to 14,000 volumes. All the participants in the book have used the library at some stage in their lives and it is still widely used both by local people and by schools in the vicinity.

Toynbee Hall

*And Toynbee is, well, a world in itself. To me, it was escapism, somewhere I would go and get away from my real life which was horrible. Down in the bottom was the theatre . . . Yeah, Toynbee has always been **the** place. And that's never changed. Yes, Toynbee Hall was a brilliant experience for me.*

(Tony, born in 1957)

The cholera epidemics of the mid-nineteenth century had alerted the public to the living conditions in the East End and drew social workers and clergymen to the area, but it was not until the 1880s that the conditions of slum-dwellers became a national issue. Early in 1883, George Sims published a series of articles in the *Pictorial World* called 'How the poor live'. This was followed by the publication in October of a penny pamphlet entitled *The Bitter Cry of Outcast London: an Enquiry into the Condition of the Abject Poor*. The anonymous tract, now widely acknowledged to have been the work of Andrew Mearns, secretary of the Congregational Union, warned the public:

Plates 9 and 10 Painted figures
showing Sir John Cass School
pupils in eighteenth-century dress

seething in the very centre of our great cities, concealed by the thinnest crust of civilisation and decency is a vast mass of moral corruption, of heart-breaking misery and absolute godlessness . . . Britain must face the facts and these compel the conviction that THIS TERRIBLE FLOOD OF SIN AND MISERY IS GAINING UPON US.

Mearns went on to outline, in vignettes, the desperate lives of inhabitants of the slums and to point out that 'only a merest edge of this great dark region' were practising Christians. The work was publicised in the *Pall Mall Gazette* and in the *Daily News* and caused an immediate sensation. Letters flooded in, the great and the good took up the debate. Lord Salisbury began work on plans for a Royal Commission on housing: the Prince of Wales and Queen Victoria discussed the situation with Sir Charles Dilke at Windsor. Bad housing, it was feared, could lead to civil unrest, even to socialism (Karl Marx had recently died).

The 1883 publications precipitated not only action but also a change in attitudes to the poor. Although the sentiments expressed by the authors were not new, the two works 'appeared just at the right moment'[41] coinciding as they did with the final stage of a process of change in Victorian England which Beatrice Webb described as 'A new consciousness of sin among men of intellect and men of property; a consciousness at first practical and philanthropic . . . then literary and artistic . . . and finally analytic, historical and explanatory'.[42] The poor were no longer considered depraved, but rather deprived. The site of much of the educational and philanthropic activity was Toynbee Hall in Commercial Street, Whitechapel. A month after its publication in 1883, *The Bitter Cry* was the subject of a sermon preached by the Reverend Montague Butler, headmaster of Harrow School, at St Mary's Church, Oxford. Soon after, the Reverend Samuel Barnett, Vicar of St Jude's, Whitechapel, said by the Bishop of London to be 'the worst parish in the diocese inhabited mainly by a criminal population', addressed a meeting of Oxford undergraduates and called upon them to join him in the East End. In December of the same year, at a debate in the Oxford Union, the motion 'In the opinion of this House the condition of the poor in our large towns is a national disgrace' was carried unanimously, and voluntary, municipal and state action was called for. By the end of 1883, a decision had been taken to found a university settlement in East London. The scheme had powerful supporters, MPs of all parties, academics from Oxford and Cambridge, the Duke of Clarence, the Duke of Westminster, and Arthur Balfour, the future Prime Minister, among others.

Intellectuals, wealthy philanthropists and devout Christians flocked to the East End and, although poverty was not eliminated, there followed a period of intense philanthropic, educational, intellectual and religious activity in the area, so much so that by 1896 an international survey of urban poverty

Plate 11 May Day at Sir John Cass School *c.* 1929

Plate 12 Ralph Barnes as a young teacher at the Jews' Free School in 1932

stated, 'Awakening is not needed. Every thinking man has his mind on the matter'.[43] In 1886, Charles Booth began his survey of East End life; in 1887, Queen Victoria opened the People's Palace in Mile End; in 1887, the Salvation Army included social reform as a prerequisite for the saving of souls; in 1885, Toynbee Hall was opened.

Arnold Toynbee, a young social philosopher from Oxford, who firmly believed that it was the duty of education 'not to deal with the individual man but with the citizen, with a view to showing what are his duties to his fellow-men',[44] was a friend of Samuel Barnett and had been a frequent visitor to St Jude's in the 1870s. He, like Barnett, was convinced that social problems could be solved through education. On his tragically early death in 1883 at the age of 31, Barnett and his friends decided that Toynbee should be commemorated in the new settlement. Samuel Barnett was appointed warden in 1884 and Toynbee Hall was officially opened in 1885.

Over the next half century, Toynbee Hall pioneered some of the most important advances in education to be introduced in Britain. Barnett's vision of education for all, regardless of social class, led him to criticise Oxford and Cambridge for closing their doors to poor students. The two universities were, in his view, no more than expensive schools, 'the patrimony of a particular class of society', 'The public school boy rules colleges and dons. He is the finest product of the times because he is strong and rich, looks down on the other boys and patronises his "clever smug" from the elementary school'.[45] Toynbee Hall on the other hand would be a great and democratic university where the poor students would, as in medieval times, 'crowd around the feet of the scholars'. Barnett's dream was for university education for all: 'not merely for boys and girls who had been at school full time until 18 but also for young men and women who had entered the workshop at 14'. Barnett's fervour was not confined to reform at university level. He deplored the poor training of Board school teachers and arranged for groups of teachers to attend courses in Oxford and Cambridge, and was behind the establishment of 'Day Training Colleges' at universities. He worked to improve opportunities for all children, the poorest of whom received little or no education. He strove for bigger and more scholarships, for the prohibition of paid work for children under 14, for the half-time school system to be abolished and for the introduction of compulsory schooling until the age of 16. (Although he fought for the last reform all his life, the school leaving age was not finally raised to 16 until 1972.)

From its inception, Barnett's vision for Toynbee Hall was that it should provide opportunities for the social classes to mix, a place where privileged Oxford students would live and work side by side with the people of the East End; that it would involve 'not only settlement, but shared experience, not only contact but community'.[46] Barnett regretted the flight of the middle classes from the East End. It was estimated that in 1891 only 2 per cent of the people in the East End could be said to be of the upper or middle classes:[47]

Plate 13 Toynbee Hall as it is today

Plate 14 Whitechapel Library

'It is this practice of living in pleasant places which impoverishes the poor. It authorizes as it were a lower standard of life for the neighbourhoods in which the poor are left'.[48] Barnett impressed upon the new student residents that they should not see themselves in any way superior to the East Enders: 'There must be no consciousness of superiority. They [the undergraduates] have not come as missioners, they have come to settle, that is to learn as much as to teach, to receive as much as to give'. In the same vein, he insisted that the education and facilities offered at Toynbee Hall should be of the very best, 'Nothing that can be learnt of the University is too good for East London'.[49] It was this initial concept that permitted the poorest sections of the population to come into contact with some of the greatest thinkers, writers, artists and musicians of their time.

The list of the great and good who were inspired to join the work at Toynbee Hall is impressive. Margaret Nevin, a contemporary of Barnett, wrote: 'all the most eminent in literature, art and politics came to pour their wisdom into the poor of Whitechapel . . . Henry Sidgewick, Charles Booth, Holman Hunt, Oscar Wilde . . . '. There were religious leaders such as the Dean of Westminster, politicians such as Asquith, Haldane and the socialist Tom Mann. Pierre de Coubertin stayed there as a young man and was inspired by 'the sympathetic intermingling of peoples of different backgrounds';[50] the young Marconi gave the first demonstration of the wireless there; Lenin took part in the debates on foreign policy. There were lectures on topics that ranged from morality and metaphysics to electricity. In the mid-1890s, there were 1,000 students attending lectures, the majority of whom were schoolmasters, schoolmistresses and clerks, but with an increasing number of artisans. Some went on to achieve notable success: J.M. Dent, who later became a publisher and launched the *Everyman* series, attended his first classes in 1886 and was 'literally lifted up into a heaven beyond [his] dreams'.[51] Albert Mansbridge who had attended extension classes at Toynbee launched the 'Association to Promote the Higher Education of Working Men', which in 1905 became the Workers' Educational Association', a body which still flourishes across Britain. The Barnetts were totally committed to bringing beauty to 'the paralysing and degrading sights of our streets' and organised art exhibitions that brought West Enders to the East. So popular were these shows and so successful were the Barnetts at fundraising that they were able to open the Whitechapel Library in 1900 and the Whitechapel Gallery in 1901.

Toynbee Hall was also a centre for political debate and reform. It played a significant role in the early trade union movement (see Chapter 1 of this book, p. 35) when it became the meeting place for occupational unions such as the Stick Makers, the Boot Makers, the Cigar Makers. It offered not only premises, but support and help with the workers' struggles against unfair conditions. Residents were active in their support of the Matchgirls' Strike in 1888 and during the Dockers' Strike in 1889, they provided not only food and clothing for the families, but also campaigned for the dockers' cause.

There were few reform movements in which the Toynbee residents did not play a role. In 1903, William Beveridge, a brilliant Oxford graduate, was selected as sub-warden by Barnett, who realised that solutions to the deprivation of the East End required more than goodwill and charity. 'Society needs facts and not sensational stories . . . facts as to infant mortality, as to the necessity of casual employment . . . The East End demands well thought-out schemes of relief and government'.[52] Charles Booth had paved the way for such work by undertaking the first social analysis of the East End using scientific methods, published as *Life and Labour of the People of London*, between 1892 and 1897. Beveridge, who believed that the alleviation of poverty and unemployment should no longer be left to charities and the Poor Law, but should be the responsibility of a state-run 'department of industrial intelligence', set up a committee, which included academics and politicians, to sit in the manner of a royal commission on the unemployed,[53] and in 1905 the Unemployed Workmen Act was passed and a central body was set up to manage relief schemes for the unemployed. It was from these beginnings in Toynbee Hall that Beveridge went on to become one of the most influential economists of the twentieth century, and to produce in 1942 the Beveridge Plan, the social security scheme which was to provide the basis for the UK's present Welfare State.

The pioneering artistic, academic and welfare work of Toynbee Hall went on into the twentieth century and throughout the two world wars under the leadership of the charismatic and energetic Jimmy Mallon, 'the most popular man east of the Aldgate pump'. In 1938, a new extension with a concert hall was built. The King and Queen were the first of many celebrated visitors, who included Val Gielgud, Tyrone Guthrie, Jean Renoir, Lady Diana Cooper, Mrs Israel Sieff, Constant Lambert, Frederick Ashton, Rex Harrison and others. Britain's first children's theatre was opened there; George Bernard Shaw offered all his plays without fee and Alec Guinness produced *Great Expectations*. In two years, 300,000 children saw 550 performances.

Toynbee Hall and its residents were instrumental in social reforms: the 'Poor Man's Lawyer' scheme which introduced free legal advice for the poor; boys' clubs; two scout troops; the Girls' Dinner Club, which provided cheap, nourishing lunches for the ill-paid young women working in the sweatshops. The first children's tribunal to be held in a place other than a police court was held there and the premises were subsequently used as one of the eight London Juvenile Courts. Legislation directly influenced by Toynbee Hall included the Education Act of 1936 which would eventually raise the school leaving age to 15, the Public Order Act which came into force after the Fascist marches of the 1930s, and the Hire Purchase Act which introduced fairer terms for hirers in 1939.

It is hard to overestimate the importance of Toynbee Hall. For the past hundred years it has not only enriched the lives of the inhabitants of what is still one of the poorest boroughs in the country, but the pioneering and altruistic spirit promoted by its founders has engendered some of the most important social and educational reforms of the twentieth century. Once again we turn to our theme of contrasts, for it was the alliance of the poorest and most wretched people in the capital with the 'golden youth', the privileged, intellectual élite, which led to the establishment of the Welfare State, trade unions, Legal Aid, free secondary education, the Workers' Educational Association (WEA), juvenile courts and many other reforms that have benefited the whole population. Add to that the linguistic and literacy heritage we have gained from the inhabitants of the area over the past four hundred years and we might conclude that, despite the economic poverty of its population, in cultural terms Spitalfields must be one of the richest boroughs in the country.

Part II

CHILDHOOD MEMORIES OF LITERACY AND LEARNING

INTRODUCTION

People make their own histories, but not under conditions of their own choosing.

(Karl Marx)

It was in 1888, just twenty years before Minnie, the oldest participant in this book, was born, that Annie Besant exposed the terrible conditions of the matchgirls working in the Bryant and May factory in Bow:

> A typical case is that of a girl of 16, a piece worker;[1] she earns four shillings a week, and lives with a sister, paid by the same firm, who 'earns good money – as much as eight or nine shillings a week'. Out of the earnings, two shillings a week is paid for the rent of one room. The child lives only on bread and butter and tea, alike for breakfast and dinner.

Horrified by the matchgirls' terrible working conditions and the 'phossy jaw' (phosphorus necrosis which causes intense pain from inflamed teeth and jaws and ultimately terrible disfigurement) that they suffered from, she provided the leadership and support they needed to organise the first successful strike for better working conditions in Britain.

These young workers seem a million miles away from Tahmin, growing up in Spitalfields a hundred years later, when she claims: 'my parents would never say, "Go and get a job". In fact, my dad's so old-fashioned that if you're going to work, it has to be a job that has some prestige, otherwise it's demeaning to work as a secretary, it's demeaning to work in a shop . . . '. So are Tahmin and her peers simply worlds apart from the East End matchgirls a century ago? The answer, strangely, is both yes and no. There can, of course, be no comparison between the choices open to both groups. For a nineteenth-century East End girl, there was little choice but to take whatever work she could find and, for most, the East End was a prison. In the twenty-first century, Tahmin has been to university and is thinking of studying for a doctorate in the USA. As Tahmin says in Chapter 5, the world should be her oyster. Yet we cannot just dismiss any thought of comparison across generations. We need only to probe a little beneath the surface to recognise similar faces of anger and humiliation. The anger of the matchgirls is reflected in Tahmin's description of her own '*success by default*', whereby she feels she could just as easily have ended her career stacking shelves in a supermarket. And the anger, humiliation, freedom, choice or imprisonment of both groups are centred upon *literacy* in its widest sense.

Tahmin and the matchgirls reveal the power of literacy in a number of ways. First, they show how literacy can be used as a powerful means of defiance in the lives of the oppressed. The nineteenth-century matchgirls consciously withheld their signatures, fully aware of the possible consequences of such an act for their own lives and those of their families. Similarly, Tahmin tells of her rejection of what she refers to as 'Withering Heights' and the English classics in favour of Malcolm X in school, knowing that her refusal of school-sanctioned literacy could have led to her failure. Courage paid off in both cases. The matchgirls' act of mass solidarity had historic consequences in setting off a new pattern of unionisation that would inspire the dockers in the following year and workers for the next century.[2] Tahmin went on to complete an MA at a prestigious British university and carries her anger for justice with her to the charitable organisation where she now works.

Second, we see the influence of mediators or catalysts of literacy. In the same way that Annie Besant, a highly literate woman, supported the matchgirls and enabled them to give voice to their anger in a powerful way, so Tahmin remembers a woman teacher who wrote encouraging her not to lose her aggression in a hostile world. Finally, these women remind us of the important role of literacy skills themselves in enabling such acts of defiance to take place. The matchgirls' strike and the withholding of a signature marked the beginnings of the Union of Women Matchmakers, with its own committee for which literacy skills would be crucial. Tahmin was able to reject the classics because she had the skills to read them. Literacy does indeed provide the key to open doors. Whether one chooses to use or lose the key is another matter. Without it, however, entry is impossible. None of the participants in the three following chapters take education and literacy lightly. Nor do they take it for granted.

In Part II of this book, we hear about literacy learning in homes, schools and communities from three generations growing up in the City and in Spitalfields during the twentieth century. The theme of *contrasting literacies* runs like a thread across and between the different generations as we see the impossibility of explaining success with reference to any one particular paradigm. The contrasts already begin to emerge as Minnie, born at the beginning of the twentieth century, describes her father as a role model for literacy, although he arrived in England speaking no English at all, and are epitomised much later by Tahmin's rejection of the English literature canon.

But in spite of the differences both between individuals and groups, there are a number of core themes linking all the individuals in this section. First, none of the families were able to send their children to school with the confidence that they understood what was expected and needed to ensure[3] a smooth path to success. Second, most members of the group, even the very youngest, feel that they were unable to reach their academic potential in school. Third, as each thinks back and tries to recollect early literacy learning, we are reminded that 'literacy', 'reading' and 'writing' cannot be separated from 'learning' in general and, indeed, the whole of 'getting on in life'. Fourth, the children participated in a wide variety of language and literacy practices, in different domains, using different methods and with different mediators or at different access points. None relied solely upon their parents to assist them outside school.[4] Fifth, just as literacies blend with other learning and living practices, so there is a dynamic syncretism between home, school and community literacies in children's lives. Finally, as exemplified through Tahmin and the nineteenth-century matchgirls, we see that literacy is a serious affair and one that can involve struggle, anxiety and pain. Thus, the following three chapters show how the education and literacies of each generation are framed by similar sets of interests, conflicts and struggles, but played out in different ways according to the wider social, political, economic and educational circumstances of the time.

3

LITERACY FOR SURVIVAL

At one time, you had a cinema in Brick Lane. Children lived for cinemas. You'd go regularly, Saturday morning. Now television's done away with it. We used to watch plays at Toynbee in the quadrangle. There used to be weddings. We used to have Christmas parties, club rooms, a theatre . . . But there were no cars, so we could play in the street. We had charabanc outings to the seaside. There was always something to do. Cricket, football. And sometimes, when the ice-cream seller and his barrow came round, you could get a bowl of ice-cream. It wasn't like you get it today, it was all Italian made. It was gorgeous . . .

(Abby, born in 1917)

Abby, one of the oldest participants in the book, shows how memories of learning mingle with other memories of life. For the older members of the Spitalfields study, reading is seen as an integral part of living and learning. Recalling learning to read, therefore, cannot be separated from reliving other experiences. Paradoxically, it is the oldest participants whose early memories are most vivid and vibrant, some remembering the name of every teacher who taught them and every child in the class. Some, too, have detailed recollections of learning to read at school, in the community and at home, of 'special' people in their early reading development whose influence has continued throughout their lives.

The focus in this chapter is on those born before the outbreak of the World War II in 1939.[1] The seven people whose voices we hear below have taken very different paths in life. Yet all share the common factor of being successful readers and writers, of using reading and writing frequently in both their work and their leisure activities. Our aim in this chapter is to ask: How did they manage this success, apparently against all the odds? What do they remember to be important in their early literacy lives? We unpick the scope, span and nature of learning to read and write at school, at home and in the community and examine the role played by parents and other key mediators of literacy in their lives as children in the first half of the twentieth century.

72

Throughout the chapter, we return to our theme of *contrasting literacies* as the key to early literacy success.[2] Were school practices repeated in the home? If not, in what ways did they contrast with each other and what were the implications for learning to read?

At the close of the twentieth century, Minnie was 90 and Abby and Stanley were in their eighties.[3] They started school barely half a century after huge tracts of land had been torn up for the railway lines, which were to divide east London,[4] less than thirty years after Jack the Ripper had terrorised his victims just a stone's throw from where they were to live[5] and less than twenty years after animals were driven into open slaughterhouses at Aldgate. When Abby, Minnie and Stanley began school, horse-drawn buses, bicycles and hand carts could be seen competing for room as workers streamed into the City along the Whitechapel Road.

By the time that Gloria, born in 1939, and the youngest member of this group, was leaving primary school, immense physical changes had taken place in the area. Both the City and Spitalfields were peppered with bomb-sites where children were warned not to play (but often did).[6] One bomb had partially destroyed Commercial Street School. Planes and cars had already replaced railways as symbolising progress but were still for the rich. Trolley buses had replaced the horse-drawn buses and charabancs streaming along the Whitechapel Road into the City. A row of butchers' shops and mangy dogs were all that were left of the Aldgate slaughter houses.

Significant changes had also entered the world of education. The school-leaving age had been raised from 14 to 15.[7] Class sizes had been reduced substantially,[8] permitting the introduction of less rigid teaching methods in primary schools.[9] The impact of the war and evacuation on educational standards had been considerable. The London County Council's chief inspector of education reported in 1943 that, in an average term, about one-third of London children missed a quarter or more of their classes, either through illness, work or family duties, or because parental control had weakened. Reading tests conducted with 13- to 14-year olds in the same year showed significantly lower achievement.[10] Nevertheless, as we shall see in this chapter, the reading progress of members of our group was hit more by hospitalisation through illness than by bombs and evacuation. From the war, it emerged largely unscathed.

This is a chapter of contrasts. Although, as children, our group all lived in the same streets in and around the City and Spitalfields and, to the outsider, all shared the dubious privilege of being 'East Enders',[11] the Jewish children led very different lives from the English Londoners.[12] There were different ways of 'getting on in life' open to the two groups, forced upon them by external circumstances, as we shall see below. At home, they participated in different traditions involving different networks of learning and different literacy practices. The children also saw themselves as living different lives. Significantly, our English Londoners walked or travelled by bus past Commercial Street Board School, whose pupils were predominantly Jewish, on their way to school. But there were important contrasts within as well as between the groups. The English Londoners walked out of the poverty of Spitalfields and stepped into Sir John Cass, a school steeped in the traditions of the wealthiest square mile in the country. The Jewish children also left behind family traditions and, on crossing the school threshold, entered the world of England, a massive three-storey building, just twenty years old.

Paradoxically, this is also a chapter of syncretism, of blending new cultural practices with old, familiar ones. Throughout the chapter, we see how new ways of being and seeing were grafted on to old. This syncretism is most evident in the lives of the Jewish families; children often spoke a new language, participated in unfamiliar cultural practices and learned about a new religion. But the English Londoners also learned to graft new City ways on to their repertoires in a way that was unknown to their parents. The schools were clearly mediators, enabling this fusion of old and new to take place through opening children's eyes to new worlds of opportunities and 'Englishness'.

Toynbee Hall classes, the libraries, cinemas, theatres and comics enchanted the children of both groups. This chapter, then, traces both the contrasts and the syncretism of old and new in the lives and early literacies of our group of children in and around Spitalfields during the pre-war years.

The families: 'getting on' in a land of contrasts

The English Londoners: one foot in the City and one outside

Eric's wife: *He's a freeman of the City.*
Eric: *Yes. I can drive my sheep over London Bridge.*

> *I became a freeman of the City of London by paying for it . . . I was a parish clerk then. Parish clerk at St Peter Paul's Wharf which can still have a parish clerk under a charter of Charles 1st . . . Then I went and had my parchment redone at the Guildhall, at the court of aldermen, and so it's now for my children and apprentices forever . . .*

(Stanley)

'Getting on' in the City for our English Londoners during the first decades of the twentieth century meant accepting hierarchies and knowing your place in them. As the nineteenth century drew to a close, the square mile of the City housed a concentration of personal wealth without parallel in the world.[13] Such a huge establishment of trade needed servicing and generated around it a mass of black-coated workers, the clerks. From the mid-nineteenth century, the City appeared to be 'a very city of clerks'; 'Clerks of all ages, clerks of all sizes, clerks from all quarters, walking slowly, walking fast, trotting, running, hurrying into the Bank from the very moment the clock strikes nine, till, at the latest, a quarter after'.[14] By 1911, shortly after Minnie, the oldest member of this group was born, half the City's 364,000 working population was employed by banks, finance houses and similar merchant enterprises.[15]

Becoming a City clerk at the beginning of the twentieth century symbolised success and 'getting on' for many of the poorer classes of the East End. Jobs were often obtained through family connections and recommendations or being 'spoken for'. For those staying with one employer, remaining loyal, dressing well and having neat handwriting often secured a job for life and a comfortable middle-class status. Although financially, earnings differed little from those of artisans, socially, clerks achieved a very different status, which was not just a result of 'wearing or not wearing a white shirt everyday'[16] but visiting and borrowing from the library and generally creating a good impression. Yet there was a price to be paid for this security. It was easy for employers to foster a culture of dependence whereby clerks knew their place and rarely rose to become merchants or bankers themselves. This culture, characterised by both benevolence and exclusivity, had some impact on the lives of each of our children attending the Church of England school.

Wealth and poverty

Stanley and Eric know a lot about being 'spoken for' and City hierarchies. During the first two decades of the twentieth century, they were growing up with one foot in the wealth of the City, the other in the poorer environment of the East End. Both originated from parishes adjacent to but even poorer than Spitalfields.[17] During their childhood, steady employment meant comparative wealth and unemployment meant poverty; the latter was always lurking around the corner. Stanley remembers the poverty and prostitution in 'Tiger Bay', as the area was originally known:

> *The majority worked in the docks, those that could get work, but of course, in those days, if you were unemployed, there was nothing. You used to see people scavenging in dust-bins to try to find something . . . and there used to be the Boards of Guardians who went round and they would go into people's houses and say, 'You've got that piano, sell it' . . . in the hall at St Georges-in-the-East downstairs there used to be a place where they got free cooked meals. I can remember children coming in without shoes or socks.*

Stanley and Eric's fathers both had secure jobs. Stanley's father was superintendent at the public baths and wash houses in Beck Street and the family lived on the top floor. Eric's parents both descended from Huguenot weavers but, like many others, his ancestors had been forced out of this trade long before he was born. His grandfather had been a plate layer working for the Great Eastern Railway company, who used to boost his income by 'fogging' (clipping little explosives on the line during fog to warn train-drivers in advance). Eric still remembers how he used to stave off the cold by eating a baked onion before leaving home for a night's work. His father started work as a junior clerk in a firm of paint manufacturers and rose to the position of London area manager. During his employment, he studied at evening classes, eventually gaining academic qualifications equivalent to a degree. He had earlier been head boy at Cass, which was later to serve his son well.

The two boys were accepted at Cass School because of their Church of England upbringing and, in Eric's case, his connections as son of an old Cass pupil. The memories recounted by both reveal the privilege they felt as they left the poverty of their area to enter a different and unique world:

> So at the age of 8, my father thought it was time that I should go to Cass School. He felt that I was old enough to travel because I had to go by bus . . .
>
> (Eric)

> I walked there . . . and, Christian as I was, I called for the son of the bell founder in Whitechapel . . . I used to come right up from St George's to help him across the road . . . I used to go along Cable Street, up Leman Street and past the Old Mahogany Bar . . . and all the children from Cass's, we all met on the way and joined up.
>
> (Stanley)

Upon arrival, the feeling of 'uniqueness' (a word often used by both ex-pupils) and exclusivity was even stronger:

> You had to have a new uniform every six months . . . And then, at the age of 14, you had a school leavers' uniform. It was absolutely unique.
>
> (Eric)

> Cass's was harder to get in . . . it was unique in giving you hot milk and all the classes were mixed . . . When you got into the preparation class, you went to a posh school like St Olave's Grammar School.
>
> (Stanley)

School and work

The high aims of their City school and the uncertainty of real East End life continued throughout Stanley and Eric's school careers and beyond. Both Stanley and Eric's expectations for grammar school and advanced education were awakened when Stanley passed the scholarship and Eric similarly was awarded a place at the City of London School, all fees paid. However, neither was able to go on to secondary school. Stanley remembers his father's determination that his son should find work before his own retirement. So Stanley left school in 1931, the start of the slump. Assisted by an employment secretary at Toynbee Hall, he went to work at a local clothes warehouse where he earned 12/6d. per week. He immediately started evening classes to learn bookkeeping but this was cut short by his being called up for the war. Eric also recalls his father's words when he gained a scholarship:

> *When I proudly went home to my father to tell him I'd got this opportunity, he said 'No, no, you'll learn more in six months out at work than you will at that college'. So I went out to work.*

Eric left school in 1937 after passing the London Chamber of Commerce examination, which enabled him to begin his career as a clerk with a firm of City secretaries to tea, textile and rubber companies. Unfit for military service because of poor eyesight, he continued his career by entering local government as a junior clerk, eventually rising to become Chief Committee Clerk.

Dependence and independence

Stanley and Eric retained their dual association with the City and the East End throughout their later lives. Stanley's aim had always been to go into the Church. At home, he used to play at churches:

> *Most of the rectors in those days were Oxford MAs, with the red hoods. My mum was going on an outing and she'd bought a very nice red silk blouse. I thought it would make a nice hood so I got a pair of shears and made one and put it away.*

He carried his aim with him throughout the war and, upon returning, made an attempt to be enter the ministry:

> *and the Bishop of Madras said to me, 'Don't think you're going to have an easy time because you've never been to university or anything like that'. Anyway, I came back and I had to go to a selection board. Now we came back from the Far East in the coldest winter, 1947 . . . They sent me to Litchfield and the first one who interviewed me said, 'How much money have you got?' And I said, '£75 gratuity'. He said, 'I don't know why the clergy sent you up here. The church has no money'. Well if it hadn't been for the Canon Missioner of Southwark, and the old Chapter Clerk of Durham Cathedral . . . I would have left immediately, but they kept me up there. Then I came home, . . . didn't hear anything. Then I had a letter saying they wondered why I hadn't been*

called for lay work or a monastic and my mother kept saying to me, 'Why don't you get rid of those fantasies and get yourself a job?' So I went to the labour exchange. I'd never seen so many people. I demanded to see the superintendent and he saw me and I poured out my soul to him and he said, 'You're very lucky. I'm the secretary of the Readers Board for the Diocese of Chelmsford'. He said, 'While you're deciding to be the Dean of St Paul's, I'll give you a letter to the matron of Whipps Cross Hospital. You might like to see the other side of life before you go into the Church'.

Consequently, Stanley trained as a State Registered Nurse, worked for thirty-four years in the Health Service and eventually became a clinical nurse teacher, a profession he loved, until he retired.

Meanwhile, after the war, Eric was working as chief committee clerk for a district council. His chief officer told him he should take articles:

I had to start right from the bottom because I hadn't got a degree . . . by this time, I saw an advertisement for the appointment of an administrative assistant at Sir John Cass's Foundation and a colleague saw the advert and he said 'You going to apply for it, Eric?' And I said 'What about you?' He said, 'You're more likely to be successful than I am with your school background'. So I applied and was appointed in 1960.

Eric gained promotion to deputy clerk and finally clerk to the governors, a highly responsible post, which he held for some eleven years until his retirement. This office carried responsibility for the administration of the Foundation's considerable assets including lands, residential properties, farms, shops, and schools, and the allocation of grants to educational organisations and individuals and for research projects. One such project was the funding of a radar training vessel, which was sunk by a Greek ship in the Thames:

Overnight I was not only confronted with maritime law because the Greek vessel was involved but we previously insured it for its actual value but only six months earlier I'd decided we ought to insure it for its replacement value which enabled us to go a long way towards a brand new radar training vessel . . .

Eric remained as clerk to the Foundation until his retirement.

The Jewish children: from the outside, looking in

Minnie: *I couldn't have been more than 7 years old . . . by then we had had the First World War and, of course, a lot of them got on their feet and became quite wealthy.*

78

All the men weren't able to work you know, they were rejected from work so they made money . . . buying and selling. That was the thing, if you could do that.

AW: *Did your father manage to do that?*

Minnie: *My mother did . . . I remember around the corner they used to hire out barrows for people that went to market. They used to go for miles with their greeneries and their bits of cloth . . . '*

'Getting on' for our group of Jewish East Enders during the early decades of the twentieth century was a very different task from that of our English Londoners. In some respects, it involved making the opposite choices from those made by English East End families. Largely excluded from the benevolence of the City since, as immigrants, they were unlikely to be 'spoken for', the Jewish families in our study sought independence by setting up in business or by trading. Thus we find that Abby's father had a City licence[18] and stalls in Petticoat Lane, Billingsgate and Covent Garden; Norma's parents also had stalls locally and Aumie's father was a cap-maker, while his mother used to supplement the family income by going round the neighbourhood selling butter and eggs, as well as at Passover time acting as an agent for the main wine distributor in Commercial Road.

Not everyone was fortunate enough to be self-employed: Minnie's father worked as a tailor and Gloria's as a presser, jobs which meant sudden and seasonal laying-off during slack periods. However, being an outsider, a 'foreigner' with different customs and traditions from those of the host population, fostered independence, even in the women's lives:

And some of the Yiddisher women had no gas stove where they could make proper cakes . . . So they'd make the cakes at home and take them into the Jewish baker's to bake it for them in Cable Street . . . My mother was a beautiful baker. She never bought bread. She used to make her own chollas, those plaited loaves of bread, beautifully made, and then smaller ones my mother used to make for neighbours and children.

(Minnie)

Poverty and wealth

Minnie, the eldest of all the seniors, witnessed greater poverty as a child than anyone else in the group. Her parents had escaped from Russia with her two older sisters shortly before her birth in 1908. They had lodged in Chicksand Street, just around the corner from where Abby lived, with an old uncle whom they helped by making tables and chairs for 'the odd shilling' until they found a small terraced house off Cable Street. Minnie still remembers the rat-infested rooms and the children in her school whose clothes were torn and who had no shoes to their feet. Minnie recounts the good and bad times of her father, who was a tailor:

he used to go to work at seven o'clock in the morning and come home when he was busy ten o'clock at night and then, when they were slack they had no work at all. There was no money coming in. And . . . I remember in Whitechapel . . . facing Black Iron Yard on the pavements, when the men that owned these tailors shops needed staff, they'd come along and say 'What are you?' . . . and if they took them in it was only for a time when they needed them, you know.

But it was not only individual poverty which affected children's school and home learning. The poverty of the area generally meant that children became sick with illnesses such as scarlet fever, diphtheria, rickets and TB[19] and went into hospitals which did not include education in their care. Long hospitalisation affected both Abby and Gloria's later lives:

I've never done algebra – 'cos I missed that. I was in hospital for six months just when I was 10. When I came out, I had to do exams . . . and I failed by half a mark to have higher education.

(Abby)

Gloria blames her poor spelling on having missed school:

at the age of about 6, I had a very severe bout of jaundice and I was in hospital for six months . . . and I didn't learn the building of words . . . I've never really got to grips with it, because although I must have been in hospital a very long time – with convalescence it must have been about six months, at no time did a teacher come to teach us. You know, I was just left there.

Minnie carries with her to this day the memory of the tragic death of her sister while her mother was in hospital recovering from the birth:

My aunt . . . was bathing the baby and it was wintertime – a beautiful child – the seventh one that had blue eyes . . . And the window blew out, the wind was so strong. The child caught a very bad chill and those days they didn't know what to do and the child was so bad they had to get the doctor. In those days, if you got the doctor home for babies it cost half a crown and that was a fortune. Anyhow, Dr Midgeley sent it off to Shadwell Hospital. It died within a few days. And my poor dad, he used to go to the hospital and every time she [her mother] asked about the baby he used to tell such lies . . .

The lives of the pre-war Jewish participants in our study have been transformed by economic and social success. Only Abby, one of the oldest members of this group, still lives in Spitalfields; Minnie, Aumie, Norma and Gloria have long since moved into far more affluent suburbs. Yet their efforts to remain independent have been reflected in later life: Abby went into the Land Army during the war and went on to study with the Royal Horticultural

Society. Now in her eighties, she represents the elderly on the Community Health Council as well as being in the Pensioners' Action Group and the Joint Planning Group for people with disabilities; Minnie went into business; Aumie became head of the public relations department of a large business and went on to set up an educational trust to research and publish nostalgia picture books and videos on the Jewish East End; Norma and Gloria both work for the Jewish Board of Deputies, and in addition Gloria makes 'talking books'[20] for the blind. From her large detached house overlooking a landscaped garden in Hendon, an affluent London suburb, Norma's story perhaps symbolises the transformation which has become at least conceivable for all: 'I can remember telling my teacher, "One day, we're going to live in a house in Hendon". And this was my father's house . . .'.

Jewishness and Englishness

Whereas the exclusivity of City practices meant that membership was uncertain and had to be fought for on an individual basis, our Jewish families expressed a confidence in being accepted by their religion whatever their material circumstances. In spite of the humiliation felt by Minnie's father through unemployment, the whole family went to the synagogue every Saturday where her father was sure of being accepted. He was regarded as highly knowledgeable about his religion and was a very devout Jew.

Membership of the Jewish faith was particularly powerful in Aumie's life. His family had come to England from Poland in 1910. His father had served in the Russo-Japanese war, making caps for the Russian army and he continued his cap-making business in one room in their small terraced house backing on to the railway in Bow, two miles down the Whitechapel Road east of Spitalfields. This income supported his eight children, of whom Aumie was the seventh. Unable to speak or read much English, his father's knowledge of Jewish tradition and synagogue practice was substantial and he soon became a lay reader of a small synagogue and a collector of synagogue membership fees. His family were educated to be devout and orthodox Jews. Unlike the difficulties faced by Stanley in attempting to enter the Church of England, Aumie was accepted to attend the Yeshiva[21] four evenings a week and Sunday mornings to learn the Talmud. Aumie remembers that Judaism was at the centre of life at home:

> *whatever problems might be within the families in terms of struggling to earn a living, the home on a Saturday was completely transformed, and on Friday night with the lighting of the candles and being blessed, the table-cloth being pure white, the two Sabbath loaves of plaited bread and the wine. The evening meal would begin with father saying the blessing over the wine and the blessing over the bread followed by the washing of hands before you ate, and then grace after the meal itself.*

Abby, Norma and Gloria's families had moved to England earlier and were already well established in the country when they were born. Abby's father was of Dutch descent[22] but born in a house in Copthall Close in the heart of the City where the family kept goats; he left school at 11 as Abby's grandfather was blind and needed help. Norma and Gloria's parents came as young children to England. Nevertheless, Abby went on later to attend the Jews' Free School and all went to Hebrew classes and the synagogue. They all felt that membership of the Jewish religion made them *different* from their Cockney peers. Gloria reveals this as she explains her entry into nursery at the age of 4:

> *being a very precocious child and being born to older parents, I grew up old and I went the first day to school and I said to the teacher . . . when they all stood up to say prayers in the morning, at the age of 4, I stood up and said, 'I'm not allowed to say these prayers because I'm Jewish. I'm only allowed to say the shema'. The teacher said, 'That's perfectly all right, Gloria, you're allowed to sit down'.*

Nevertheless, there was a gradual syncretism between Jewishness and Englishness in everyday life. For the parents of our pre-war generation, knowledge of English culture was very limited, as Aumie's example shows:

> *my parents weren't aware of English culture. Their whole culture was Jewish. A classic example . . . the first time my mother went inside a cinema was when the cinema was used for High Holy Days' services, when she went with the rabbi's wife . . . she was up in the gallery and she said to me 'Mir haben gekriecht in Himmel heran' [We've gone up to heaven] to listen to the prayers. Going into a cinema was the closest she got to English culture.*

This lack of awareness of English culture resulted in Aumie's parents not even knowing that his official first names were English. They thought they had named their son Abraham Mordecai but a more anglicised friend had entered the names Albert Marchant on the birth certificate. So that, at the start of the war, when his name was called out by the teacher to confirm that he was to be evacuated, his mother, who was with him in the school hall, called out in Yiddish, 'Wo gehst du hin?' (Where are you going?). When Aumie explained, 'That's my name', she said, 'Das ist nicht deine Name!' (That's not your name!). This was the first time she had heard her son's name in English. The relationship between Aumie's parents and his English school typifies that of many immigrant parents at the time. Most had little contact with their children's school except for speech days and other official occasions. Nevertheless, all parents had a vital impact on their children's language and literacy learning, as we see below.

Reading at home: the role of parents

My mother and father were both working very hard from morning till evening and all they did was feed us and clothe us and look after us. They didn't teach us anything.

(Norma)

Norma was referring here to the formal teaching she associated with the classroom. The parents of our pre-war group did not get involved with the work of the school. Nor did they talk to teachers about work they should complete with their children at home. Teaching children to read formally was viewed as the school's role, not theirs. In any case, all the families worked long hours in the home or outside and, apart from Abby, parents of the Jewish group generally could not read or write well in English. And yet although none were familiar with the practice of 'bed-time storyreading', nor did they 'teach' their children formally, all our group look back on their parents as key figures either as *role models*, as *catalysts* or as *providers of opportunity* in their language and literacy lives.

Parents as role models

but my father spoke about the world. He was fantastic . . . he read the Jewish Times, I think, and . . . he used to read the Sunday paper right through and the very exclusive daily paper, he would read it. And there was a lady in the Burdett Road and she used to teach these foreign people to read and then he got naturalised after she taught him and he loved it and he learned to read all these papers.

My mother never learned to speak or to read English. She spoke to her children in Yiddish.

(Minnie)

Parents of our pre-war group were role models of multiple literacies in different languages. Like Minnie's father, the literacy skills of Aumie's parents stood in stark contrast to their lack of formal education:

The only education they would have had would have been Jewish religious education. My father didn't go to a Polish school and nor did my mother, but my father in particular was considered quite a learned person in Jewish law, Jewish prayer and Jewish tradition. My mother was also fluent in reading Hebrew and Yiddish and what was interesting was that there would be Yiddish translations from the Hebrew text which were full of lovely fairy stories which my father would ridicule: he was more learned in Jewish law and the correct understanding of Jewish tradition, whereas the book my mother had would be a kind of Yiddish fairy-story translation from the Bible. I remember constant disagreement when my father would reject some of the fairy-tales. 'Bubemeisers', we would call them, 'grandmother's tales'.

In some families, it was the mother who was the literacy broker. Stanley's mother did all the paperwork for his father:

She was a copperplate writer and, in the end, 'cos in those days there weren't clerks for it, they took her up to the main baths and she used to write out all the statements from the committee meetings and all that.

She had two books per week from the library until she died. Stanley was encouraged by his mother to read Dickens as a child: 'The first book I ever got hold of was *Oliver Twist* and then *Pickwick Papers* and I still pick them up with relish'. These books belong to his large collection of classics and poetry books.

Parents as catalysts in language learning

Jewish parents acted as catalysts in their children's language learning without explicitly being aware of it. Minnie and Aumie's parents spoke Yiddish to each other and to their children. Significantly, however, Aumie and Minnie and their siblings spoke English to their parents. In other words, the children listened to and understood the Yiddish but responded in English; their parents listened to and understood the English but responded in Yiddish. The maintenance of the mother tongue was not seen as important in England and both sets of parents were so keen that their children should learn English that conversations in different languages were seen as no problem. In spite of working sometimes until 10 p.m., Minnie's father made time to try to learn to read English with a private teacher; Aumie's father used the local Yiddish daily newspaper which carried many English adverts as well as having English words written out in Yiddish characters to improve knowledge of his English.

Dual language conversations heightened the children's linguistic awareness. Aumie remembers clearly the way his mother 'massacred' the English language.

She would talk about things like 'I went to Matzos' (for Marks & Spencers) and for Selfridges she would say 'suffragettes' but what was interesting was that the balance of sound stayed the same. The classic example was when she would say 'I need an ambulance' but what she meant was that she wanted an envelope. So it was the same number of syllables 'amb-ul-ance'; 'en-vel-ope'. And also, she would take English expressions and automatically assume they were Yiddish. For instance, she would say 'Ich glacht eim nicht. Er ist ein grosser nosey-parker', which means 'I don't like him. He's a nosey-parker'. I explained to her, 'Why do you say "nosey-parker" when it's English?' No, no, she was adamant. 'Nosey-parker' was the 'hoech Yiddish' [top Yiddish]. These were the confusions.

Parents as providers of opportunity

Stanley recounts: 'My mother used to buy me books to read. She was an avid lover of Dickens'. However short of money, the parents of all the pre-war group made sure that their children's language and/or literacy was fostered in whatever way possible. Stanley was unusual in the group in that his mother managed to buy classics and poetry books for him to read as a child. They still line the walls of his flat today. Abby's mother also bought her daughter annuals. Like Stanley, Abby has a large collection of books on every topic – all of which she has read – in her small flat. Some parents provided their children with a whole variety of comics at home; Aumie had boys' magazines such as *The Magnet*, *The Wizard*, *The Adventurer* and *The Rover* and Norma could add *The Beano* and *The Dandy* to these. Gloria, Norma and Eric also refer to comics bought by parents.

However, the main role of the parents of this generation was to provide access for their children to both mediators and access points of culture and literacy outside the home. This took place both formally and informally, as we shall see below.

Funds of knowledge in the community

My mother had ideas above her station. She liked to take me to Lyons Corner House[23] and she taught me how to use a serviette and general table manners like not talking with food in your mouth and not eating with your mouth open . . . She would take me to matinées at the theatre and show me how to behave when you go out with other people . . . This is all education . . . This was an education from my mother that few children of my age got, you know.

Gloria's mother took her daughter out to wealthier areas of London to give her access to the sort of cultural and literary activities she hoped she would need in later life. All the parents of this generation realised the importance of sending or taking their children into the community to learn literacy-related skills, but, generally, relied on other mediators of literacy to teach their children. Four major funds of knowledge[24] were significant in the young lives of our senior participants: Toynbee Hall (the Universities Settlement); English literacy classes; the library; and Hebrew classes (for the Jewish children). Each of these had a special meaning for different children, as we see below.

Table 2 Literacy-related activities at home and in the community: the pre-war generation

Type of practice	Context	Participants	Purpose	Scope	Materials	Role of child	Language
Hebrew class	formal; in small groups	group of single sex	to study the Bible and Jewish prayers	approx. 10 hrs for boys; 4 for girls	Bible and prayer books	listen and repeat pattern	explanation in English; reading in classical Hebrew
Yeshiva	formal class	boys	to learn Jewish law (Talmud)	10 hrs plus per week	Talmud	listen to lectures by teachers	Hebrew, Aramaic
Synagogue	group	adults and children	prayers, hymn singing	daily	Prayerbook and Scrolls of the Torah	listen and observe	Hebrew
choir	formal; in synagogue	mainly boys	practising hymns for synagogue	Sabbath and festivals	Prayerbooks	practise	Hebrew
Jewish club	informal	group: boys and girls	acting, games, sport	weekly	various	play	English
Toynbee Hall (music, drama, guides, scouts, dancing, English classes, etc.)	usually formal, some informal	group or one-to-one, e.g. music lessons	learning about English culture: a skill; or for pleasure	usually once a week or whenever learning place	various: books, newspapers, music scores, lectures took	learner or apprentice etc.	English
English literacy or numeracy work	formal; at someone's home	group	to learn English literacy/ numeracy	weekly	books, primers	repeating, practising	English

Table 2 continued

Type of practice	Context	Participants	Purpose	Scope	Materials	Role of child	Language
elocution	formal	one-to-one	to learn to speak well	weekly		repeating, practising	English
library	informal	alone or with siblings	to gain access to good books, newspapers and English culture	as often as possible	library books	active reader, meaning maker	English
comics	informal	alone or with siblings	pleasure	weekly	comics	active reader, meaning maker	English
play with sibling/friend	informal	group	fun	daily	songs, rhymes, etc.	mimicking, copying	English
theatre, cinema	formal	group	pleasure	weekly	various	listening, watching	English
reading with mother	informal	one-to-one	pleasure	frequently	classics, poetry	listening	English

The magic of Toynbee Hall

Canon Barnett said the working man would never have a voice in his government unless he was educated so he used to have the Workers' Educational Association there . . . and Lenin attended some of them . . . I went there for evening classes, then I tried to learn the violin – you paid half a crown and you had some strings on a piece of hardboard and a bow, but the neighbours complained, so I never became a violinist . . .

(Stanley)

All our group spoke of the 'magic' of Toynbee Hall as an oasis of excitement and of cultural and literary activity in their lives. Norma had piano lessons there; Gloria learned ballet; most attended plays and a whole variety of talks. There were even sports and other English cultural activities; Abby remembers Christmas parties and maypole dances. Toynbee Hall's literary and cultural activities were attended by Jewish and non-Jewish families alike. Toynbee Hall and its influence has been discussed more fully in Chapter 2 and will recur again in Chapter 4.

English literacy classes

Minnie: *At Henriques.²⁵ I was about 13 . . . and I continued that English literacy class until we moved to Forest Gate. My mother didn't like me going there on the bus because even those days, the cost was fourpence for me.*

AW: *And what did you do there?*

Minnie: *We did all sorts of things. Mrs Henriques used to read to us and teach us . . . she read English, all English. Some were very poor. They used to run there from school because their mothers went to work and they'd come about 7 o'clock and some of my friends got to the top . . . very able . . . they couldn't even afford fourpence for a gas mantle . . . A lot of the boys learned to read. And Mrs Henriques used to say, 'It is a very important thing'.*

Minnie was not the only child to attend formal English literacy classes outside school. Norma's mother sent her to elocution lessons so that she could erase any trace of Cockney accent from her speech. Both Minnie and Norma's parents paid for this extra tuition.

The library: escaping everyday life

I remember going to the library, and in those days you could go by yourself. I went on my own. I remember, it used to be dark. I suppose it was the middle of the winter. Pitch black . . .

(Norma)

All our group were regular users of the public libraries. In the main, this was the Whitechapel Library which had opened in 1900 with 20,734 books and a reading room.[26] Canon Barnett's opening speech had stressed the library's function in being 'a friend to the people of Whitechapel' and most of the group remember the first books they borrowed with great emotion:

> *I found a release in books . . . I still remember the books I read because they were so different from my everyday life . . . There was one particular girl who went right through all this series of books and I couldn't wait to get the next book . . .*

> (Norma)

For the Jewish children, library books provided an access to learning about England and English culture, typified for Aumie by public schools:

> *the most interesting books that engaged us were those about public schools . . . this wonderful place where boys would go where they would sleep in dormitories and play cricket and rugby . . . books about public schools . . . as if that was what we seemed to aspire to and want to become involved in . . .*

Norma and Gloria also mentioned adventures from across the world[27] and added a variety of Enid Blyton stories to their list.

Hebrew classes: 'the be-all and end-all' for our Jewish families

> *We would go five times a week. So you'd come home from school . . . and then by five o'clock, we would be in Hebrew classes until 7, and, as far as I was concerned, by 8 o'clock I was back in the Synagogue choir for rehearsals twice a week . . .*

> (Aumie)

Many boys followed the same routine, while the girls like Minnie, Gloria, Norma and Abby attended only once or twice a week. Although Aumie has difficulty in remembering how reading was taught in his English school, the method of teaching classical Hebrew remains clear in his mind:

> *You would learn phonetically, the twenty-four letters of the Hebrew alphabet . . . We would learn letter by letter and then build up the words . . . Learning Hebrew phonetically like this we were soon able to read quite quickly. We would read mechanically without understanding the words . . .*

At the age of 8, Aumie also became a student at the Yeshiva at Aldgate, where he studied the Talmud, or Jewish law. At this age, therefore, he would be expected to read and have legalistic discussions on both the Talmud, written in Aramaic or classical Hebrew, and the rabbinical commentaries. The Torah (the Five Books of Moses) would be practised and sung for bar mitzvahs. Aumie was also a member of the synagogue choir and spent considerable time practising hymns and melodies. Minnie attended Hebrew classes until she was 14 and maintained it was 'the one thing my brain has always remembered'; only Abby, who attended for just one year from the Jews' Free School, maintained 'we never really picked it up'.

The school as mediator of literacy, literature and life in the world of the Empire

EG: *On thinking back, what would you say you learned most from Commercial Street School?*

Abby: *Reading. 'Cos I'm a great reader. I read a lot. And how to live with other people – with different religions and that. We learned to live and mix. I was brought up to mix with people whatever colour and see them as you would yourself.*

In what ways did school literacy learning build upon the home and community experiences of our group as outlined above? A simple reply is that it did not – at least, not intentionally. It aimed to present a world of 'Englishness' which included a detailed knowledge of history, geography, respect for the British Empire, as well as literature and poetry, which were to be learned by heart. But we see below that children did manage to draw upon home learning as they made sense of what happened in the classroom. We also see that, looking back, the older generation in this study have a broad view of the literacy-learning process, which included poetry, literature, hymns and prayers as well as visits outside the school (see Table 2, pp. 86–7). Literacy learning, then, is interpreted by all to be more than just *methods* used by the teacher to teach reading – although these are seen as important too. Below, we examine the way our group remembers learning about literacy, about literature and about English society in general.

Early days at school: learning to read by rote and memorisation

Abby: *We used to do everything by rote. It would be put up on the board and we would repeat what the teacher said. 'Cat', 'Dog', that kind of thing . . .*

EG: *Can you remember if you learned it by the sounds, like 'k' 'a' 't' [sounds it out] or did you learn the whole word 'cat'?*

Minnie: *'Cat' [the whole word]. You might have learned the letter sounds as well, like 't' and that kind of thing, but it was the whole word and you repeated it by rote. Mostly you said the letter names 'c', 'a', 't' and then 'cat'. You didn't pronounce* it 'k' 'a' 't' [sounding it out] *the way the schools do now. And we used to have chalk slates . . .*

The older members of the group remember learning to read in the same way and are convinced that this method of rote learning is beneficial because, in Abby's words, 'you repeated things, you looked at things on the board. It stuck in your mind'. Exercise books for handwriting practice were distributed at the beginning of a lesson and collected at the end. Reading books were not given out until children were about 7 or 8; children then stood up to read them out loud around the class. During the 1920s, children at Commercial Street School had reading and oral spelling tests every six months.

> *We always had tests and exams and we had school inspectors who came round to see how you were doing. You had to stand up and repeat some of the things you knew . . . We always had spelling tests when the inspectors came round. For writing, you used to learn a script . . . italics and that. First you practised on the blackboard, then you had to do it into your book . . .*
>
> (Abby)

Minnie is the only member of our Jewish group who remembers that her class had many children whose English was limited and that this was recognised in the teaching of reading:

> *Yes, well, learning to read, it was articles on the board or on your table. So you should be able to pronounce them first and know your 'cup', your 'saucer', your 'knife', your 'fork'. And when you got to know a number of those objects they started to teach you to write but what could you spell? You were glad after a couple of months to learn the ABC . . .*

Nevertheless, the importance of grammar and spelling (mentioned by most) during the early stages rather than reading whole stories and texts may have inadvertently given Jewish children an advantage over their monolingual peers:

> *at the age of 7, we were learning Hebrew grammar, which is far more complicated in many ways than English grammar, so when we were in the English school, adjectives, nouns and verbs, things which our non-Jewish friends would just be beginning to grapple with, were all very natural to us. Maybe, in some ways, it gave us an advantage in that we were aware that language had a structure. In Hebrew, you see, you have the 'root' of a word . . . you could have one word in Hebrew which when translated would be five words in English. So even as 7-year-olds those of us who were competent in Hebrew already had a sound grammatical basis when we looked at English grammar.*
>
> (Aumie)

By the time Gloria started school towards the end of the war, new methods of teaching reading were being tried out:

> *I remember coming home with this book, this* Phonoscript First Primer *and sitting down, not very often, but I do remember sitting down, I can't remember how old I was – this is when it was printed, 1929, and somebody helping me with it. But I know I had a lot of difficulty with it . . .*

(Gloria)

This unusual book followed two phonoscript reading charts but introduced capital letters which, 'on the principle of presenting to the child only one difficulty at a time, are omitted from the charts and introductory primer'. Gloria could not quite remember the code to interpret the different diacritics but it appears that, in vowel sounds, they showed how a letter was pronounced. For example,

Ơ   Ơ   Ꝋ   Ꝋ   O   Ꝋ

Λ   əʊ   aʊ   u: ɒ   ɔ

Instructions at the front of the book stress, however, that 'It is unnecessary to teach a child to "transfer" from Phonoscript to ordinary print. In the earlier stages it is inadvisable to encourage it, as it leads to "guessing." It is, however, impossible to prevent children from reading, or trying to read, ordinary print outside the classroom, and it will be found in actual practice that "transfer" proceeds parallel with the progress made in Phonoscript'. In spite of forgetting the precise rules of Phonoscript, Gloria has kept this book carefully alongside all her other treasured first books.

Reading as an introduction to literature and culture

> *I remember, when we were very good, Mrs Stokes used to tell us a story. It was written on a scroll, which she held lengthwise across the desk and on the side facing the class were the pictures. As she told us the story, she unrolled the scroll and the pictures moved along. I wonder what happened to that scroll . . . I wonder if they've still got it in the school . . .*

(Gloria)

Reading was by no means just about learning to say 'c – a – t'. Like Gloria, our other members of this group stress the importance of literature from the beginning of their schooling. Most remember the regular recital of poetry. Abby recalls learning Wordsworth's 'Daffodils'. Later on in school, Aumie describes how children learned and acted out Shakespeare – an important influence on him, since he considered taking up an acting career later in

1. We could put bread,
2. butter and cakes in a
3. bag, take a tin kettle
4. and make some tea.

LESSON 13.

5. F, f; O, o; O, o.
6. Out Owl Fowl-house
7. Mouse Shout Spout
8. To Food Roof Shoe
9. Do School Foolish

10. As soon as ever
11. Ada was told about
12. the plan she ran into
13. the house to get the

22.

1. food ready and find
2. a kettle. In an out-
3. house Sam found an
4. old leather bag that
5. would hold all we had
6. to carry. So away we
7. went in high spirits.

23.

Plate 15 Excerpts from Gloria's first reading book, *Phonoscript First Primer*

1. We two, Sam and 1,
2. proudly led the way.
3. over the lawn. It was
4. a lovely day. The sun
5. was bright; the sky was
6. blue. No day could
7. be finer.

LESSON 14.

8.   O, o; Ꝺ, ꝺ; ꞃ,(-e).
9. On Not Shock Knock
10. Or Nor Door Shore
11. Corn Tore Bought

12.   We went for a
13. mile or more along

24.

1. the river bank until we
2. came to the lock-gates.
3. Then we got into a
4. very narrow, shady
5. lane. On the banks and
6. in the hedge-rows we
7. saw all, or nearly all,

25.

Plate 16 Excerpt from Gloria's first reading book, *Phonoscript First Primer*

Plate 17 Aumie's family in the 1920s

Plate 18 Stanley's class in 1923. Stanley is fourth from right, second row

Plate 19 Abby's class at Canon Barnett in 1924. Abby is on the extreme left, front row

life. But a special storytime is etched into Stanley's memories as he thinks back over seventy years:

> *but the great thing there was on Friday afternoons after play at 3 o'clock, till we went in for the last hymn at quarter to 4, they were allowed to pick a book and read to us, the teachers, so we had* King Solomon's Mines *and all these good ones and we always used to look forward to those.*

Stanley still has a large library of poetry and the classics at home. Hymns, prayers, songs, newspapers and atlases were the most commonly mentioned reading material in school. Abby described how the children in her class also enjoyed the visits to Kew Gardens every daffodil time. She went on later to become a horticulturalist.

It is Aumie, perhaps, who remembers the most original and innovatory reading practice set up by his school.[28]

> *in our school, the headmaster was . . . particularly keen on good speech. And so we had a speech choir as distinct from a singing choir. Bearing in mind we were 12- to 13-year-olds, for us it seemed so odd that we would have to recite* 'Hickory, Dickory, Dock, the mouse ran up the clock. The clock struck one, the

96

Class __2A__   Term ending October __1934__

SUBJECT.	Max. Marks.	Marks Gained.	SUBJECT.	Max Marks.	Marks Gained.
Reading	40	23	Science	20	13
Recitation	10	10	Drawing	20	4
Composition ...	50	35	French	50	34
Grammar	20	15	Shorthand	20	NT
Spelling	20	9	Needlework or Practical Mathematics	30	30
Penmanship ...	10	7	Woodwork or Cookery	30	26
Arithmetic... ...	100	81	Typewriting ...	20	N.T
Geography... ...	40	35	Homework ...	100	57
History	40	21	Conduct		V.G

Number in Class __43__   Position in Class __10__

Remarks:

It is a steady, industrious boy and has improved his position considerably.

N. Dunstone   Class Teacher.

Class __2A__   Term ending March __1935__

SUBJECT.	Max. Marks.	Marks Gained.	SUBJECT.	Max Marks.	Marks Gained.
Reading	40	25	Science	20	17
Recitation	10	10	Drawing	20	11
Composition ...	50	40	French	50	40
Grammar	20	13	Shorthand	20	N.T
Spelling	20	13	Needlework or Practical Mathematics	30	19
Penmanship ...	10	7	Woodwork or Cookery	30	26
Arithmetic... ...	100	87	Typewriting ...	20	N.T
Geography... ...	40	22	Homework ...	100	65
History	40	28	Conduct		Ex.

Number in Class __34__   Position in Class __5__

Remarks:

I am pleased with his work and behaviour. I hope he will do very well next year.

N. Dunstone.   Class Teacher.

Plate 20 Sir John Cass school report from 1934/5

mouse ran down, Hickory, Dickory, Dock'. We would go to other schools and recite various poems as examples of good speech ... It was an oddity ... Looking back, it could have been a political gesture on his [the headmaster's] part to establish his contribution in a so-called Cockney area ... to improve the quality of speech.

Now none of our Jewish group has a Cockney accent, due perhaps as much to elocution lessons and the choral speaking as to the fact that it was not the dialect of their parents, nor of their Jewish friends. As Gloria comments:

> *The prize I got in my senior school was for nothing academic. I won the oratory competition prize. And it was presented to me by Dame Sybil Thorndike. And it's funny, because I was a child of the East End.*

Teachers as guiding lights

> *And this was a book given to me by my very special teacher, my favourite, favourite teacher, when I was so ill in the hospital . . . and I corresponded with her up until the day she died.*
>
> (Gloria)

Gloria's admiration and love for her teacher was reflected in the words and reading worlds of many of this generation. In general, it was the teachers rather than the parents who transmitted a love of literature to their pupils. As we have just heard, Gloria still has the present of a small book given to her by her teacher. Stanley speaks of his love for poetry, which he learned from both his teacher and his mother. His mother, in turn, learned her love for poetry from her own teacher: 'they had a teacher who was an ardent follower of Alfred Lord Tennyson, well, through all her life she could declaim the *Lady of Shalott* and *Enoch Arden* and a few more of those poems'. Aumie refers to the 'humanity' of the excellent teachers he respected so much. 'Respect' is a word used over and over again as the seniors recall so many of the names of their teachers alongside their special skills at teaching or initiating learning for them. Abby, who was a school governor until recently, has perhaps the most interesting way of expressing herself. She refers to all her teachers as 'university educated'. When it was pointed out that all today's teachers are university educated, she replied confidently, 'Well, ours just *seemed* to be university educated, that's all'.

Entering the British Empire: syncretising new and old worlds

> *And they [the teachers] taught us about England. Most of us came from a foreign background and I think they taught us about the British Commonwealth, which I didn't know anything about . . .*
>
> (Norma)

> *They taught us the meaning of life as well, didn't they?*
>
> (Gloria)

I can remember, one day, being in Miss Pickard's class and singing 'God Save the King' and, each one of us, as we were able to recite the three verses, then we were allowed to go home. It was already going home time, but you weren't allowed to go home until you could recite the three verses of 'God Save the King'.

(Gloria)

The school saw its aim as teaching all pupils to become respectful citizens of the Empire. In this, it saw no difference between bilingual Jewish or monolingual English children. Teachers did not expect children to enter school knowledgeable of schoolbooks, stories or learning practices. Nor did they expect parents to 'teach' these to their children at home. It was up to all children in their own way to blend new school-learning practices with those they knew from home. All members of this generation in the study highlight the intricate blending of traditions, languages, literacies and whole ways of thinking from their families with the 'high culture' of England introduced by the school. These old and new beliefs then permeated their later lives.

The stories recounted by the group show how their parents' lives had also been in flux. Aumie, Gloria and Minnie's parents were coping with new languages and cultural traditions and beginning to blend these into their own lives. Stanley and Eric's parents were also shifting from different jobs and ways of life from those of their own parents. Stanley and Eric's fathers recognised the huge disadvantage of a lack of formal education in their lives.

At first glance, the syncretism of old and new ways of life seems of a very different nature for our Jewish and English Londoners. Through the school as mediator, the Jewish children grafted a whole new language, new customs and traditions on to the well-established traditions of their families. As Aumie stresses, they had the benefit of syncretising two cultures, both of which were very explicitly promoted. Elocution lessons, visits to Lyons Corner House and the theatre, speaking English, even to non-English-speaking parents, and choosing books about public schools – all seem to indicate a conscious decision to find the key to 'getting on' in English society.

In contrast, our English Londoners already spoke English and were familiar with many of the cultural practices they met in school. But were the two groups in fact so very different? Our English Londoners were also faced with grafting new accents and ways of speech on to old as they practised reciting poems to teachers who were not from East London. They, too, were learning about the history and learning practices of wealthier English families through literature. In some ways, the odds may have been more stacked against them, since they were not as *conscious* of difference as their Jewish peers. Whereas our group of Jewish seniors appeared to accept their disadvantages in not continuing to grammar school, Stanley and Eric were clearly both surprised and disappointed at their fathers' decisions to end their schooling at 14 and 15 respectively. Likewise, Stanley was later disappointed and surprised at his rejection by the Church he wished to serve.

We see from our pre-war group that successful reading was not just a product of the method of reading tuition used in school. Nor, indeed, was it the result of parental storyreading at home. Most of the group remember being taught to read using explicit and structured approaches. But even those who have forgotten the method used remember early books or comics they read. All recall excellent teachers, not for the method they used but for the encouragement they gave or simply for the sort of person they were. In this chapter, we have examined the home, community and school learning of a group of seven people aged between 60 and 90, who have learned to read successfully against many odds. Interestingly, almost all the group later entered charitable work or the caring professions. It is, indeed, as if all have passed into different worlds but all have kept the first world of their childhood deep within them.

4

LITERACY FOR EQUALITY

> And school – school for me was fine – knowledge, books,
> reading, devoted teachers. The world was beginning to open
> up, at least in print.
>
> (Bertha Sokoloff)[1]

The people we meet in this chapter, Eileen, Robert, Christine, Joy, Tony, Linda and Chris, were the first post-war generation. They were born in a London that was scarred with bomb-sites and beset by shortages and were to lead lives very different from those of their parents. Rani was born in Kenya of Muslim Asian parents.

World War II brought unprecedented changes in all aspects of people's lives. Many urban families had led a nomadic existence during the war years, flitting between the dangers of the Blitz and the unaccustomed quiet of the countryside. Robert, who was a child during the war, moved with his mother into Somerset 'and came back when it looked as though things were improving, and then went back again when it seemed as though it wasn't letting up'. Some estimates suggest that there were sixty million changes of address during the war period and that two out of seven houses were affected by bomb damage. In 1939, 750,000 children were evacuated from the cities.[2] In London, the East End boroughs of Shoreditch, Poplar, Stepney and the City lost between 45 and 50 per cent of their population.[3] Such shared hardships, it has been argued, united the nation and brought about a collapse of class barriers: throughout the country all social classes shared canteens and cooperated in the rescue effort (even the royal family stayed in London throughout the Blitz); rationing and shortages meant that people dressed in the same utility style. On the radio, the medium of rich and poor alike, listeners heard the voice of Churchill and the music of Vera Lynn; and everyone, from aristocrats to ammunitions workers, sang and danced to 'The White Cliffs of Dover' and 'We'll Meet Again'.

Some of the greatest changes came in the field of education. It was precisely this wartime spirit, it has been suggested, that paved the way for the 1944

Education Act. The atmosphere of cooperation, nurtured by the collective war effort, generated an impatience with the rigid social hierarchies and class divisions of pre-war society. In addition, the mobility brought by the war broadened horizons. Evacuees encountered new experiences and new ways of life outside the cities. Recruits to the armed forces, whose poor educational standards shocked the government, discovered new areas of interest and new skills in the adult education classes, lectures and discussions which were instituted for servicemen and women. They subsequently emerged from the war with a new awareness of social and political issues. It seemed that finally, the passionate belief in 'education for all' that had been one of the strongest tenets of the founding fathers of Toynbee Hall in the nineteenth century (see Chapter 2) was beginning to gain wider acceptance. 'Access to education' was one of the four main planks of Beveridge's 1942 social welfare plan for the construction of a fairer Britain. A principal objective of R.A. Butler when he introduced the 1944 Education Act was that 'the education system should be accessible to all'.

As we saw in earlier chapters, pre-war educational opportunities had correlated closely with social class. The education system had merely 'succeeded in bestowing and confirming advantages on males, on the upper and middle classes and through the medium of the British Empire, on Anglo-Saxons'.[4] Hitherto, education had not even been considered a major concern of the state. As we noted in Chapter 2, schools were run by church authorities or private organisations, and regulated by the school boards. They were divided into elementary schools, which educated children to 14, and fee-paying secondary schools. The majority of children in Britain, as we saw in the case of Eric, Minnie and Stanley, attended the free elementary schools and, even if they succeeded in passing the scholarship for secondary school, most were unable to take up their free places since poor families could not cope with the expense of uniform, sportswear and other costs. (In 1895, of every 1,000 children who attended elementary school, only four or five went on to grammar school.) In 1926, the national figure for scholarship places in grammar schools was 9.5 per cent, while in London the figure was 6.5 per cent.[5] Bertha Sokoloff, growing up in Spitalfields, recalls the inequity and prejudice inherent in the pre-war system.

> My sister having just missed winning a scholarship, reached free place level. When she went for interview at the grammar school concerned, the headmistress was frank. She would not be given a place because it was clear that my mother (on relief) could neither afford the uniform, nor could she keep her at school until the age of 16. She spent years in the same class at the elementary school, doing odd jobs for the teachers, making the staff tea, yet both her children went to university with ease.[6]

The 1944 Act brought substantial and significant changes, making 'as important and substantial advance in public education as this country has ever known'.[7] It created a Ministry of Education with Central Advisory Councils for England and Wales; it aimed to phase out the one-school elementary education which most children had followed hitherto, and to reorganise schooling into three successive stages for all children: primary, secondary and further education. Most importantly, it introduced free secondary education for all, an innovation which meant that most of the participants in this chapter would be able to benefit from an education to which their parents could never have hoped to aspire.

Families

Eileen, Robert, Christine, Joy, Tony and Linda grew up in the City and the Spitalfields area in families that were typical of Londoners of that period. Like many other migrants in earlier centuries (see Chapter 1), their parents or grandparents had moved to the capital early in the century either to find work during the Depression or to escape from the poverty and hardships of agricultural life. Eileen and Robert's parents came from large families living near the docks: one grandfather was a carpenter, then a milkman and then unemployed during the Depression; the other, the son of a lighterman on the Thames, worked for the Gas, Light and Coke Company on the docks but died young. Joy and Christine's great-grandfather was a drover by trade, bringing sheep from Gloucestershire to the capital, but he found work in the cloth industry in Soho where he settled and raised a family. Their father married a Gloucestershire woman who had nursed him during the war and moved to London to work in 1950. Tony, Linda and Raymond's father grew up in Wales and, after being invalided out of the mines, had come to London to work on the railways, marrying a London Irish woman who had been born in the workhouse.

For this parental generation, secondary and higher education had been unattainable goals. Some, like Eileen and Robert's mother and Christine and Joy's father, had gained scholarships to secondary school, but poor family circumstances had prevented them from taking up their places. Others like Tony and Linda's father had been forced to go out to work at an early age to contribute to the family income. It was in their children, born in the 1940s of Beveridge and Butler, that the parents were finally able to realise their own educational ambitions.

Home learning

Living in the City, the families of Eileen, Robert, Joy and Christine were closely involved with the traditions and practices of the Square Mile: their fathers were housekeepers (caretakers) in the large City office blocks, cleaning out boilers, shovelling coal and carrying out maintenance jobs; their mothers cleaned offices or cooked in the canteens of the same firms. Like many of their generation to whom a fulfilling education had been denied, these parents were natural autodidacts. In Tony's words, they were 'naturally intelligent without being taught'. His father, who had left school early to go down the pit, nevertheless insisted his children join the library and was himself an avid reader and crossword addict. Joy and Christine's father who was 'artistic and scientific' and who 'would have achieved more if he had had a better education . . . was always reading: newspapers, adventure stories, westerns . . . '. Their mother (like many women in pre-war days) was trained as a dressmaker and in Joy's words 'didn't achieve anything academically'. She did not share her husband's passion for reading, having inherited from her own mother the Victorian rule which stipulates that women should not sit and read when they could be sewing, cleaning, ironing or polishing. In many cases, mothers passed this guilt on to their daughters: Joy, although now in her fifties, still feels guilty if she finds herself 'sitting and reading during the day'.

Having 'missed out on' education themselves, however, all the parents were eager for their children to succeed in the new post-war climate of 'education for all' and made every effort to ensure their children received a good education. Eileen recalls her mother's fierce determination that her daughter should have the luxury of choosing a career rather than being obliged to do the kind of unskilled work she herself had been obliged to do. Christine, who was good at maths, remembers her dad bringing used envelopes from the offices he maintained on which he wrote long division sums for her to do. Eileen's father, one of a family of keen and talented musicians who regularly played and sang together, played the piano and sang nursery rhymes with her in the evenings, teaching her the musical notes and the words at the same time. Tony's father took his children to the Whitechapel Library. Tony recalls, 'If you said, "I don't know how to do something", he would say, "Go and get a book out of the library" . . . the library was the big thing in our lives'.

Their neighbours in those days were almost uniformly white and many were Jewish. Tony remembers his street:

> *Brick Lane where we lived was all Jewish. It was lovely, really lovely. Without the Jews, I don't think I would have survived. Cos they used to give me pennies. Well, I looked a bit desperate. They used to say 'Weh, give him a penny,' and I used to buy a bit of bread or a roll.*

Christine remembers a Hungarian refugee child arriving in her class in 1956 and her surprise at seeing the little girl's drawings full of explosions and fires: 'I thought that it was amazing to have her in the class and to know that all was not safe in the world'. Although the children were growing up surrounded by bomb-sites, with V-2s and V-1s – or doodlebugs – still very much alive in everyone's memory, they felt secure and at home in their city environment. Robert was a keen footballer and played for the Oxford and Bermondsey Boys Club. Eileen attended Brownies in the grand premises of the Guildhall, where she recalls the little elves and pixies, singing songs round their improvised camp fires beneath the august portraits of long-deceased lord mayors and aldermen. In spite of the post-war shortages, the children were resourceful and active. Joy and Eileen remember the ballet classes, the roller skating, skipping and ice-skating, and of course the exciting days of the first children's TV programmes when they all crowded into a long-suffering neighbour's front room to watch *Rin Tin Tin* or *Heidi*. There were comics too. Robert recalls 'graduating' from favourites such as *The Beano* and *The Dandy* at age 8, to *The Wizard, The Champion* and *The Hotspur,* later still going on to more grown-up publications such as *Film Fun* and *Radio Fun*. Eileen and Joy took *Girl* and *Schoolfriend* every week. In these homes there was no stigma attached to reading comics, 'everybody bought them', and *The Beano, Girl* and *Schoolfriend* annuals were perennial favourites in the Christmas stocking. The children's classics were read just as voraciously as the comics, however, and Eileen remembers saving up her pocket money and the excitement of going to Woolworth's with her 2/6 to choose one of the red hard-back classics published by Dean and Co. *Little Women* and *Good Wives* were favourites and were read tearfully over and over again.

Pioneers: the schoolchildren

Janet and John *across the world*

In their primary schools, methods of teaching seemed not to have changed much since Minnie and Eric's schooldays. Christine recalls her first teacher in 1949, 'a short lady in a flowery overall with plaits around her head', who administered whacks across the knuckles with a ruler for infant misdemeanours.

> We used to write on slates and they would be scratchy and we used to do our letters, lines of 'a's and lines of 'b's all joined up. And we learned by rote: the alphabet we learned and learned and learned.

Learning to read in school in the 1950s meant becoming acquainted with *Janet and John.* Chris, learning to read in a primary school in Romford, comments: 'It was all by rote. There were never any creative approaches, certainly no contemporary literature: just this ideal world of *Janet and John*'. Even in the mining village in East Africa where Rani grew up, Janet and John were familiar figures: 'I don't really remember anyone teaching me to read. I know we used to have *Janet and John* as our first reading scheme'.

105

Table 3 Literacy-related activities at home and in the community: the post-war generation

Type of practice	Context	Participants	Purpose	Scope	Materials	Role of child	Language
church	formal	group	worship	weekly	Bible, prayer books, hymn books	active participant	English
youth club	informal	group	pleasure	weekly	games, sports, discussion groups	active participant	English
library	informal	alone or with friends	work and pleasure	regularly	homework, reference books, novels and poetry	active reader	English
reading books	informal	alone	pleasure	regularly	Enid Blyton, *Biggles*, school stories, classics	active reader	English
reading comics	informal	alone or with friends and/or siblings	pleasure	regularly	*The Beano, The Dandy, Girl, Schoolfriend, The Eagle, Film Fun, Radio Fun,* etc.	active reader	English
Guides, Brownies, Scouts	formal/informal	group	learning skills and to work in a group	weekly	written instructions, manuals, etc.	active participant	English
Toynbee Hall: music, drama lessons, poetry readings, etc.	formal/informal	alone or group	learning a skill or craft	weekly	music scores, play scripts, poems	learner, apprentice	English
cinema, radio, television	informal	alone or group	pleasure	weekly, daily	various	listening, watching	English

Geographical distance seemed immaterial too when it came to teaching methods. Chris Searle in Romford recalls his own primary school, where 'we had class reading: teacher reads, individual child reads, going round the class' and Rani in her small African village recalls:

> We also had reading where everyone had to stand up and read a certain passage from a book and we used to do that in rotation around the whole class. So rather than concentrating on what the others were reading, I would try to work out which bit I had to read so that I could practise beforehand so that by the time it came to my turn I would be able to stand up and read fluently.

Some children became so proficient in listening and memorising that it was never clear whether they could read or not. Christine, who proved to be dyslexic, listened intently to the other pupils reading *Janet and John* around the class so that she could reproduce the text from memory when asked to read, thus persuading the teacher that she was a fully competent reader when in fact the opposite was true.

The happy, ordered existence of *Janet and John* so familiar to children around the world contrasted sharply with the lives of some of the readers however. Tony lived in Brick Lane and went to a nearby Catholic primary school. One of seven children, his family was desperately poor and there was rarely enough food or clothing to go round.

> one of the reasons I got expelled from that school was because I didn't have any shoes and Sister S decided to have me up in front of the whole school and she stood me on the stage and my face was always filthy and I always had scabs and cold sores. I remember her standing there and holding me like this [gesture of disgust] and she said, 'Get out', and I ran. I just ran out. Going through that at 8 years old, I should have been put off education. I should have said, 'Sod you, sod school, sod learning'. Luckily, I didn't. It made me go the other way and I wanted to learn as much as I could about everything and then I was lucky enough to get into Sir John Cass.

Tony's experience, although possibly unusual for the 1950s, was quite commonplace in the nineteenth century when children were frequently sent home for being dirty. Sir John Cass's logbooks for 1846 record children being sent home for being 'slovenly', or 'to have his shoes mended' or 'to clean her clothes'.

Thus the primary schools of the 1950s still had much in common with pre-war schools. In spite of the egalitarian rhetoric of the new education act, some have argued that post-war secondary schooling merely perpetuated pre-war patterns.

Secondary school

There is a substantial minority of angry (middle class) parents who see their children of moderate ability (having failed the eleven-plus) deprived of the opportunity of grammar school education. There is good reason for believing that many such children would achieve more in grammar schools than the theoretically more able children from poor homes.

(Geoffrey Howe)[8]

Although revolutionary in some ways, the 1944 Act nevertheless relied heavily on pre-war thinking in its provision for secondary schooling. In the immediate post-war period, views on education were still influenced by the 1930s psychometricians whose work on cognition and types of mind led them to divide children into those who were capable of abstract thought and those who were 'better at practical activities'. Their views, influential in the production of the 1938 Spens Report, also influenced Sir Cyril Norwood's 1943 White Paper on Educational Reconstruction.[9] This document distinguished three types of pupils: first, those who were 'interested in learning for its own sake, [could] grasp an argument or follow a piece of connected reasoning' and were 'sensitive to language as an expression of thought'; second, those who 'had an uncanny insight into the intricacies of mechanism, whereas the subtleties of language construction were too delicate for [them]' and finally those who 'dealt more easily with concrete things than with facts' and whose 'horizons were limited'. This division of pre-adolescent children into three groups fitted the tripartite division of secondary education into grammar, technical and modern schools, introduced by the 1944 Act. Selection was by means of the eleven-plus examination, a written IQ test backed up by arithmetic and English attainment tests. Even Labour politicians believed in the tripartite system and that 'a differentiated social system offered the best hope to disadvantaged social groups'.[10] R.H. Tawney, ex-Toynbee resident and tireless promoter of working-class education, wrote as early as 1922, 'Selection is necessary but it should be selection between alternate paths, not as in the past between educational opportunity and the absence of it'.[11] Labour politicians such as Ellen Wilkinson, also a close associate of Toynbee Hall, strongly supported a selective system and claimed that, as Education Minister in the new Attlee government, she would ensure that 'no boy or girl [was] debarred by lack of means from the education *for which he/she is qualified*' and that she would 'remove from education those class distinctions which [were] the negation of democracy'.[12] The older participants in this chapter sat the selection test at age 11 and went on to secondary school on the basis of the results.

The 1950s and 1960s were the heyday of the grammar schools and the secondary modern schools. In those two decades, the number of grammar school pupils rose from 500,000 to 750,000 and the number of pupils in secondary modern schools from 1,270,000 to 1,641,000. Many of the new grammar school pupils, including the participants in this chapter, were first-generation secondary schoolers.

The grammar school: 'an indispensable kind of citizen'

On one single day in the January of our last year in primary school we were marshalled into the gymnasium of our local secondary school and asked (not told) to take three papers: in Mathematics, English Language and something called General Intelligence ... All these papers lasted about half an hour so after one and a half hours the die was cast, our educational fate was sealed.[13]

The successful ones would go on to the grammar school. Eileen, Robert and Joy passed the eleven-plus and went on to Greycoats, St Olave's and St Saviour's respectively. Christine, who did not pass the examination, was awarded a governor's place at St Saviour's and Chris went first to a secondary modern school before passing the thirteen-plus and going on to grammar school. Ten years later, Tony went to Sir John Cass School when it was a new comprehensive and Linda to the grammar stream of Bishop Challoner Comprehensive School. Rani, as a new immigrant to the country, was given no choice but placed in a secondary modern school on her arrival in London.

Sir John Cass Primary School did not send many children to grammar school. Christine remembers 'there were two people in our year who passed the eleven-plus. One went to Greycoats and the other to the City of London. They were clever little girls and they were pushed'. Joy and Eileen, two of only five in their year of approximately seventy children to pass the scholar-ship, were unrepresentative of their social class. In spite of the public image of grammar schools as the 'agency whereby children from all social classes might mix together in the pursuit of truth and excellence', the reality was that even in the booming post-war years they remained largely the preserve of the middle classes. In 1956, the year Christine left Sir John Cass for St Saviour's, only 9 per cent of children from unskilled workers' homes went to grammar schools as opposed to 60 per cent of children from professional backgrounds. Mary Evans (1991) recalls her first day at a grammar school in a London suburb: 'Arriving at ... School on the first day of the first term, the most striking characteristic of the other new pupils was that they too arrived in cars, from detached homes and with standard English voices'.[14]

Not surprisingly, perhaps, when they arrived at grammar school, Eileen and Joy recall feeling somewhat set apart from their wealthy, confident middle-class schoolmates. Eileen found few girls from working-class families and tended to make friends with those who were from similar backgrounds to her own. Joy recalls: 'I enjoyed being there but there was a feeling of being

Plate 21 The London Blitz in 1940. Robert was reading comics in an underground shelter on the right when this bomb fell in front of the Monument

Plate 22 Christine, aged 6, on her way to Sir John Cass School feeding Silver, a fishmonger's horse, from Billingsgate Market

110

quite lonely'. For working-class children there were many shameful reminders of their origins and few grammar schools appeared to acknowledge the social and economic differences among their pupils. Evans describes the annual shoe inspection in her school, 'when "good" [expensive] shoes made by Clarks and Start-Rite, shoes of the middle class, were immediately passed as acceptable, whereas 'bad' [cheap] shoes sold in shops such as Freeman Hardy and Willis were held up for condemnation'. In *The Uses of Literacy*, Richard Hoggart writes memorably of working-class boys embarrassed by 'the stigma of cheaper clothes, of not being able to go on school trips, of parents who turn up for the grammar-school play looking shamefully working class'.[15] Language too was a clear marker of social class. The desirable accent was RP (Received Pronunciation) or near RP, and standard English, the only acceptable grammar. In Christ's Hospital, the working-class accents of scholarship boys were soon ironed out.

> Many boys used to become bilingual . . . but to the influence of master and other boys has now been added the all-pervading voice of the BBC and the problem has greatly diminished. When it occurs it is deliberately faced and tackled.[16]

Eileen, a prize-winning pupil at Sir John Cass, recalls putting her hand up enthusiastically to answer questions when she arrived at her smart West End

Plate 23 Sir John Cass children on an outing to Brighton in 1953. Joy and Christine are in the centre wearing kilts

grammar school only to be 'corrected on every word [she] spoke'. She 'never spoke out in English for the next seven years, only in French and Latin'. Even the reading habits of the working-class children were subject to stigmatisation. At her preliminary interview for grammar school, Joy was asked by the headmistress. 'What do you read?', to which she replied, 'Enid Blyton'. 'Well, we'll stop you doing that before long' came the response.

It seems inevitable therefore that, in spite of their proven academic ability, many working-class children failed to stay the course. In 1949, out of 105,000 leavers, 25,000 left before the age of 16. The trend continued through the 1950s and 1960s with working-class children shown to be the most likely to drop out early.[17] Some able working-class children stayed on, however. Eileen, Robert, Christine, Joy and Chris were all successful pupils, completing A-levels and going on to further education. Two are now professors, one a senior lecturer, one a senior health visitor and one a chiropodist. The one field in which they could compete on equal terms with the middle-class children was in academic work, and they soon realised that, if children were able, teachers appeared to make no distinction between the rich and the poorer pupils. Eileen remembers working so conscientiously that her mother regularly had to persuade her to break off and go to bed. Hoggart captures the experience of being a working-class child in a selective school:

> Brains are the currency by which he [sic] has bought his way and increasingly brains seem to be the currency that tells . . . his school-masters are the cashiers in the new world of brain-currency. Consequently, even though his family may push him very little, he will push himself.[18]

The benefits of being treated as an intellectual equal were exhilarating, however. Chris recalls his English teacher at Hornchurch Grammar School who 'sent me and my mate to some *Critical Quarterly* conference when I was 18 and we met Ted Hughes and Sylvia Plath'. The same teacher 'used to take us to the West End to the Old Vic and the Royal Shakespeare Company. The first play I ever saw was Judi Dench as Juliet at the Old Vic. All the boys fell in love with her'.

The modern school: a 'practical and craftsmanlike tradition'

Although the grammar schools had been presented as the model for secondary schooling, educationists were at pains to stress the role and the importance of the secondary moderns. Such schools, suggested the *Times Educational Supplement* (TES), had 'the noble task of restoring to the ordinary people the intellectual and emotional freedoms they had lost over the years', and to this end they should not offer merely a 'watered down version of the

Pussy can sit by the fire and sing,
   Pussy can climb a tree,
Or play with a silly old cork and string
   To 'muse herself, not me.
But I like *Binkie* my dog, because
   He knows how to behave;
So, *Binkie's* the same as the First Friend was,
   And I am the Man in the Cave!

Pussy will play Man Friday till
   It's time to wet her paw
And make her walk on the window-sill
   (For the footprint Crusoe saw);
Then she fluffles her tail and mews,
   And scratches and won't attend.
But *Binkie* will play whatever I choose,
   And he is my true First Friend!

Pussy will rub my knees with her head
   Pretending she loves me hard;
But the very minute I go to my bed
   Pussy runs out in the yard,
And there she stays till the morning-light;
   So I know it is only pretend;
But *Binkie*, he snores at my feet all night,
   And he is my Firstest Friend!

Plate 24 Eileen's favourite poem as a young child, taken from *The Jungle Book* by Rudyard Kipling, a prize at Sir John Cass

grammar school curriculum, but should 'develop their own more practical and craftsmanlike tradition' which could be achieved by using the new 'activity methods'.[19] Rani and Chris attended secondary modern schools with very different experiences. Chris, who went to Hylands in Romford, recalls wonderful teachers: 'Some of the best teaching I had was in that secondary modern school and the commitment of those teachers was phenomenal. I count myself lucky to have been there, even though I hated the idea of the eleven-plus'. Among the 'wonderful group of teachers' was an extraordinary music teacher, a woman who ran a fifty-piece orchestra in which 'almost every second boy in the school took part'. Chris attributes the success of the school mostly to the committed and enthusiastic staff but also to plentiful resources: 'the 1950s and 1960s were a golden age to be at school in terms of resources. Everything was there for you. You didn't have to pay for anything'. (If the secondary moderns appeared to be so well provided for, how much better equipped were the grammar schools which received 50 per cent of the funds allocated to the secondary sector while educating only 30 per cent of the school population.) Tony and Linda, who attended comprehensive schools, also felt they had had 'a very good all-round education. There was nothing lacking in our education at all'. Rani, on the other hand, newly arrived in Britain from Uganda, was taken by her father to the nearest school in East Ham. 'They gave me a place and never even asked us what subjects we'd been doing or anything.'

> They put me in a class and said, 'Because you're behind, do typing. They totally disregarded the fact that I had been doing physics, chemistry and biology and that these were the subjects that I wanted to do. Nobody asked me about these. Here, I had to take on new subjects like typing, commerce, office practice, things that were totally alien to me. It wasn't until about two years after this that I discovered that, had I known about it, I could have gone to a grammar school.

Guiding lights

Notable in all the accounts of schooling are figures who helped to shape the lives of the young people they encountered. Eileen, Joy, Tony, Linda and Chris all have vivid memories of adults who inspired them to learn. Some motivated their pupils through discipline. Tony recalls: 'Mr Owens who taught us English was particularly good because he was so strict. He was about 60 and everyone was terrified of him. So I was a bit of a swot. I loved reading'. Others provided adult role models for their pupils to aspire to in a London where teenage culture was still to be defined. The French teacher, Mrs Rouve, whose example inspired Eileen to read French at university, was what many young girls hoped to be: 'a professional woman who was beautiful, well dressed, cultured and married to a French film director'. Chris's secondary modern school in the early post-war years was full of real-life heroes, the emergency-trained ex-servicemen who had fought and defeated Fascism' and who 'laced their teaching with narratives from the war'. His form teacher was particularly memorable: an ex-submarine lieutenant who taught geography 'so when he taught us about places, he'd been to them', and 'telling us about oceans, he'd been down into them'. These teachers were 'charismatic and full of narrative'. Others inspired by their example. At grammar school, Chris had 'a wonderful English teacher who became a published poet and chairman of the Poetry Society' who was adventurous in his approach to English teaching and was 'possibly the first schoolteacher in Britain to put on a Brecht play'. For some pupils it was the extra kindness of teachers that remained in the memory. Joy remembers a maths teacher giving her additional coaching after school because she needed a good pass at GCE in order to train as a nurse. Christine recalls the dedication of the women teachers at St Saviour's and St Olave's, many of whom had been young at the time of World War I and had never married and who 'gave their all' to the school.

Institutions were also able to inspire and provide contexts for successful learning and literacy. The libraries and adult education centres that were established as a result of Canon Barnett's drive to improve the lives of ordinary people were, for many, quite literally the means of escape from the poverty of the East End. For it was in centres such as the Whitechapel Library that children who lived in small crowded flats were able to find a warm and peaceful setting in which to do their homework and thus move on to careers that would lead them away from east London. Bertha Sokoloff's memories echo those of many teenagers of the 1960s:

> Like the rest I made the regular pilgrimage to the 'Ref' above the Whitechapel Public Library near Aldgate, where rather incongruously there was an attendance of two kinds of people. First there were the boys and girls from the grammar and central schools, all beavering away at maths, science and languages. Then there were the down and outs of whom Stepney has always had more than its goodly share who came in to read the newspapers or just to have a warm, quiet sit or snooze.[20]

For other children, it was Toynbee Hall that provided inspiration and escape. Robert learned music there and still sings and plays today. For Tony, it was the first stage in a career that would take him to the West End.

Toynbee Hall was a world in itself. To me it was escapism, a place where I could go and get away from my real life which was horrible. I was 10 when I did my first play, The Italian Straw Hat. *Toynbee Hall has always been*

the place and that's never changed – Asian, Jewish, Catholics . . . Toynbee
Hall has never changed.

(Tony)

True to its original ideals, Toynbee Hall employed the best teachers. Tony's coach for English at the age of 10 became a famous producer. Tony himself went on to become an actor.

Pioneers: the teachers

Just as Eileen, Robert, Christine, Joy and the others broke the mould as first-generation secondary schoolers, so Chris and Rani themselves became pioneering teachers. From boyhood, Chris was passionate about literature and poetry. He studied English at Leeds University, then emigrated to Canada where he wrote his MA thesis on Isaac Rosenberg, the East End Jewish poet and artist killed in World War I. After a spell teaching in the Caribbean at the time of emerging black power, he returned to work for an MEd at Exeter University where he came under the influence of Marjorie Hourd, 'an inspiring woman already in her mid-seventies', author of *The Education of the Poetic Spirit* and *Coming into their Own*. It was Hourd who inspired Chris to encourage his own pupils to write. From Exeter, Chris went straight to Sir John Cass, by now a comprehensive school. The pupils were 'mostly white East End children, whose dads worked in the City, on the docks, in the markets, in local industry, as street porters, brewery workers and in the rag trade'. These were working-class Cockney children from families with no tradition of writing for publication. 'The first thing I did was to get them to write poetry. They were terrifically motivated. They would write in rhyme, in short and long lines, in ballad stanzas or in Whitmanesque lines. They loved it.' So enthusiastic were the students that Chris arranged for a photographer to take photographs of the area to accompany the poems. 'They would see their poems superimposed on Ron McCormick's photos of the actual district and that caused them to write with more realism and social insight.'

The children wrote about their environment. Tony, who was in Chris's English class, wrote about Brick Lane:

> a horrible place where everyone has a gloomy face
> There isn't one little space to play football
> Everyone plays in the dirt
> Filling their hair with dirt
> I always try to be happy and cheerful
> Now I begin to get doubtful.

(Tony Hussey)

They wrote about poverty:

I come from Stepney, lived there all me life
Loads of cheap markets
Bargains at half price
Jumpers and skirts, trousers cheap
All muddled up in any old heap.
                              (Diane Colman)

They wrote about tower blocks where 'when it rains there's nothing to do, only sit and watch it pour'.
    They wrote about the characters who lived in Spitalfields:

The old man's hair is grey and bald
His clothes are shabby and torn
But he still walks in the park
Until his feet are worn.
                              (Jean Webb)

They wrote about being an immigrant in a poor white community:

I am just a Pakistani boy
No one likes me
When I think of all the boys playing
I wish they would let me play
But no they put their fingers over their noses
And say Go away.
                              (Charley Mason)

The poems are vibrant and expressive and, to anyone who knew the area, a true reflection of the children's lives and environment, and Chris made plans for publication, much to the delight of both children and parents. Although the school itself was happy with the work, the governors refused to allow publication because 'they were uncomfortable with the realism of the subject-matter'. Undaunted, and with help from local dignitaries such as Jack Dash, the dockers' leader, and Trevor Huddleston, Bishop of Stepney, Chris collected enough money to publish *Stepney Words* himself. He was subsequently dismissed.

It was only then that the true impact of Chris's teaching made itself felt. On hearing of his dismissal, the 800 pupils of Sir John Cass promptly went on strike. One of the strike leaders, Zeinaida MacWilton, recalls: 'it just didn't seem fair that a teacher everyone enjoyed and liked was being thrown out'. The following day, joined by pupils from neighbouring schools, they marched with banners to Trafalgar Square. It was one of the first pupils' strikes in London. Chris was eventually reinstated, but did not remain long before leaving to work in the newly independent Mozambique. He has continued to encourage and to publish children's writing throughout his teaching career.

Rani too was a pioneering teacher. Having grown up in a small mining village in Uganda, she fled to England with her family when she was 12. Although she'd been at a grammar school in Africa where she had studied academic subjects, in London she was put in a secondary modern school where, in spite of her protests, she was made to learn typing and business studies. On reaching the fourth year, she told the careers advisors of her ambition to become a teacher:

> *They must have looked at me and thought 'Ha ha, little Indian girl, what does she think she's up to!' And they told me the best thing for me was nursery nursing. And then before I knew it, I was at college studying to be a nursery nurse. Half-way through the course, I realised it wasn't about teaching at all, it was just like child-minding. So I investigated teaching and was told 'Oh you have to have A-levels if you want to do teacher training'.*

So determined was she to become a teacher that, while attending the nursery nurse course in the daytime, she studied for her A-levels at night and finally got a place in a teacher-training college. Since then she has worked in east London and, as the current head of Canon Barnett School, is one of the few Asian headteachers in an area where most of the children are from Bangladesh. Her own multilingual background, growing up in Uganda speaking Punjabi, English and Swahili, and her childhood experiences as an immigrant in Britain, give her special insights into the lives of her pupils and their families.

Over the years, she has developed an approach to reading that suits her bilingual pupils:

> *I'm very much of the old school. I'm not in favour of the real books method . . . particularly with the children we have here. I think you've got to teach them through a very structured process, and if you are going to expose them to language, which is meaningful and that they can relate to, then it's got to be taught. For us, the approach has to be a mixture – a good balance of approaches. When we expose them to books and materials, it's not only got to be culturally appropriate but it's got to be in a language they will understand.*

Pioneers: the mature students

Not all children were as fortunate as Eileen, Robert, Christine, Joy, Chris and Rani in having parents who could support them both emotionally and financially through higher education. Tony and Linda, living in a three-bedroomed flat in Brick Lane with their parents and five siblings, left school at 15 and 16 respectively, and went out to work. Tony says: 'I had had enough of school. When I got to about 15 I thought "This place can't teach me any more. Let me out."' So difficult were conditions in the family home that, as soon as Linda got a flat of her own, 14-year-old Tony left home and moved in with her. Tony continued acting and doing shows, while training as a hairdresser. It was only after working for some years that they both decided to return to studying. Just as in their early childhood they had supported each other through difficult and stressful times, now in early middle age they chose to do a degree together, 'to study together'. 'We both did the same thing, BA (Hons) in Education, Training and Management.' Having reawakened the 'craving for knowledge' and rediscovered how much they 'adore learning', Linda is now embarking upon an MA at the Institute of Education, London.

Christine, who, as a dyslexic child, was convinced that in spite of her considerable scientific ability she would never succeed in arts subjects, has, at the age of 50, developed a passionate interest in history and, family and work commitments notwithstanding, has passed history A-level. The inhibitions about her writing and spelling that she experienced as a young person have disappeared thanks to the computer and she now publishes articles and reviews.

The brief life histories recounted in this chapter have demonstrated the power of learning and literacy to change lives. For Eileen and Robert, whose parents could not even aspire to secondary education, success in schooled literacy brought academic careers and international recognition. For Joy and Christine, whose mother had practised as an amateur nurse, literacy brought professional qualifications: Joy is now a senior health visitor, and Christine a chiropodist with her own practice. The stories have demonstrated that literacy can be a source of empowerment: that a passionate belief in the power of poetry to educate and transform lives can give even the poorest children the confidence and strength to challenge authority. They have shown how, through reading and learning, children and adults can regain the self-esteem so easily shattered by a childhood spent in abject poverty. They have shown how the experience of acquiring literacy in another continent can be used to enable young learners in the East End to adapt to their new environment. All these 'first-generation secondary schoolers' seized the opportunities offered to them, and, taking advantage of the 'education for all' policies of the post-war politicians, showed that high standards in literacy and learning are no longer the preserve of a privileged élite.

5

LITERACY FOR CHOICE

Literacy is about giving someone confidence within themselves, to learn how to develop their own skills, to give them confidence to feel they can achieve whatever they want. Education is about feeling you can do whatever you want. It's about encouraging someone. It's about feeling on top of the world . . . It's about giving children choices, to make them feel they have abundant opportunities in life. 'Cos I think . . . that has to come from an early point in your life, because it affects your development in so many ways.

(Tahmin, born in 1975)

Like many other participants in this book, Tahmin finds it impossible to separate 'literacy' from 'education' and 'getting on' in life. In this chapter, we return to Canon Barnett School half a century after Abby had left and we listen to five young women whose parents came from Bangladesh to live in Britain. Nina, Noshi, Sima, Tahmin and Ros were born between 1969 and 1977 and were between 20 and 30 years old at the start of the twenty-first century. All either attended Canon Barnett as children or went to nearby schools and now have young children at Canon Barnett or Sir John Cass School.

Nina, Noshi and Sima are married with young children at one of the two schools. Nina and Sima were both born in Spitalfields. Noshi, their neighbour, was born in Sylhet in 1971 but came to Britain and lived in St George's Ward, adjacent to Spitalfields, as an infant in 1973. Nina and Noshi live just opposite Abby, whom we met in Chapter 3, on a small estate of new houses and flats built in the shadow of Canon Barnett School. Tahmin and Ros, born in 1975 and 1977, are the youngest of the group, and single. Tahmin was born in Sylhet but came to Britain as an infant; Ros was born in Spitalfields. Both have university degrees from prestigious institutions; Tahmin has a degree in History and Politics and a masters in International Relations, Ros has just completed a degree in Politics, Philosophy and Economics at Oxford. Apart from Tahmin, who returned to Bangladesh for fourteen months during her primary school years, members of the group have spent all their lives in Britain, returning to Bangladesh only for holidays.

When Sima, Ros and Nina's fathers first came to Britain during the 1950s and 1960s, life in Spitalfields was very different from that which their daughters later experienced. During the early years of immigration, living conditions were harsh. Most of the more affluent Jewish Londoners, including Norma, Gloria and Aumie, had moved out to the suburbs, leaving the older and dilapidated Victorian tenements in the west of Spitalfields empty (Asghar 1996: 66). It was to these flats that the new immigrants came. David Widgery, a local doctor, reported his shock at making home visits in the area:

> I still remember the shock of visiting the shared home of six Bangladeshi clothing workers in Hanbury Street in the early 1970s . . . The flat was dark and bare . . . In this bleak room they had lived a sealed-off life, self-sufficient in the extremity of its poverty, grateful to be exploited by co-religionists, hope for the future as barred as the windows . . . '
>
> (Asghar 1996: 71)

By the time our group of young women were in school, housing conditions had improved considerably. Unlike the early decades of the twentieth century, when property remained in the hands of exploitative private landlords, housing associations during the 1970s took over a considerable amount of accommodation and helped renovate, refurbish and redevelop flats as well as replacing some of the worst tenements with attractive low-rise blocks and larger houses with gardens.[1] It is in these houses and flats that our group of women lived with their families.[2]

Spitalfields children of the 1970s and early 1980s did not grow up in extreme poverty, nor were they forced out of school at the earliest possible moment in order to get a job and support younger members of the family as Minnie and others had done fifty years earlier. Likewise, they escaped the hurdle of the eleven-plus,[3] which was a turning point in the education of Robert and our group of children in Chapter 4. Yet in the eyes of society and particularly in the eyes of the education world, they had all the odds against them. They were growing up at a time when influential education reports such as the Bullock Report (DES 1975) and the Cox Report (DES 1988)[4] were telling teachers that young children who came from homes which were not classed as 'advantaged' or 'educative'[5] or who did not participate in listening regularly to written narrative (the bedtime-story routine)[6] were likely to find learning to read in school difficult. Born to immigrant parents, many of whom were unable to speak, read or write English, and living in one of the poorest areas of Britain, our group would certainly not have been classed as 'fortunate'. Yet all are successful insofar as they have gained first or higher university degrees or entry to the professions.

This chapter presents a different set of contrasts and different types of syncretism from those described in the last two chapters. Instead of survival and equality, the contrasts in the lives of this generation are framed by choice: choices of identity, future profession, whether to leave the area or whether to stay. But choices are not always simple, especially when growing up in a family where girls, in particular, are unaccustomed to such privilege. In this chapter, we continue to explore our theme of *contrasting literacies* as a paradigm for early reading success. We ask the same questions as in Chapters 3 and 4. How have these young women managed to succeed in school, apparently against all the odds? What do they remember to be important in their early literacy lives? How are they passing this knowledge on to their own young children? What is the nature of syncretism as they blend traditional practices from their home learning as children with that which they have experienced in school? We find contrasts on different levels: between their own and their mothers' literacies, between home literacies of the group (both when they were children and now as mothers) and the officially recognised literacies of school, and between literacy practices in the home and those of the community when they were young. Paradoxes appear and reappear throughout the chapter: definitions of 'good teaching and learning' and the way that 'competitiveness', 'enjoyment', 'fun' and being 'pushed' by teachers fit within them or clash with the commonly accepted paradigm of what counts as desirable learning in homes and classrooms today.

The family as provider of love, language and literacy

The role of love, pride and tradition

Oh, a job was always out of the question, 'cos my parents aren't materialistic. They would never say, 'Go and get a job'. In fact, my dad's so old-fashioned that if you're going to work, it has to be a job that has some prestige, otherwise it's demeaning to work as a secretary, it's demeaning to work in a shop. So money was not a question. He almost felt embarrassed for us.

(Tahmin)

Tahmin's words are echoed by other women in this group. All speak of the help they were given as children in terms of love, moral support in Tahmin and Nina's words, and financial assistance; this support could not, however, extend to 'teaching' children through officially recognised home-literacy practices such as English storyreading. The women speak of the great contrast between their own educational opportunities and those of their mothers. Noshi, who worked as a senior administration officer at Thames Water Utilities before the birth of her second daughter, contrasts her career with the life chances of her mother:

*being a girl and living in a village at that time, a long time ago, they didn't
allow girls to continue past primary school, whereas my dad and my uncles
were able to go to mosque school or even to college.*

Ros, whose grown-up sisters have benefited from university education, finds
it difficult to imagine her mother's youth:

*I don't think my mum had any formal education. She did go to school but
stopped very early, she got married relatively young. It's amazing how different
my mum's and my own experiences are, but we are very similar people in so
many ways. I mean, I always think it's amazing. I don't know how my mum
gave up her life in Bangladesh and came to a completely different country and
culture. Something I don't think I'll ever do.*

But such differences do not necessarily give rise to difficulties in communication. All the group emphasise the close family links between generations.
Partly, this link is fostered by strong cultural traditions within the family.
Nina, Noshi and Sima left formal education for marriage before university
level because of parental expectations that they would marry or in order to
give their families support at home. Nina's father died when she was 13,
leaving her mother with five children, of whom Nina was the eldest. She felt
responsible for looking after her younger siblings as well as contributing
to the household budget. Nina, Noshi and Sima all married young, and are
trying to combine a career with having young children. Tahmin and Ros have
not yet married and tell of how their parents have 'grown with them' as they
have continued into higher education. When asked by Nina, 'So your parents
must be proud?', Tahmin replies, 'My parents would be proud of me whether
I do well at school or not'. Ros's father mirrored his daughter's studies by
completing his MA in Government and Politics just two years ago. He has
been a local councillor for twelve years. Nevertheless, like Nina, Sima and
Noshi, Tahmin, Ros and their siblings also grew up in families described by
Tahmin as 'culturally strict', which meant a strong frame of religious and
moral expectations, conducted, as we see later in this chapter, through
community religious and language classes.

Families as teachers of language and literacy

Tahmin: *I didn't read* Winnie-the-Pooh *or* The Jungle Book *or anything like
that. You know, if I speak to a lot of my white friends, they were really into* Winnie-
the-Pooh *and it was an integral part of their bedtime stories. You know, the
concept of 'bedtime story' didn't exist in my family.*

Nina: *Would you have Bengali stories read to you?*

Tahmin: *No. It depends on the dynamics of your family unit. Some families do, some
families don't and it's got nothing to do with the nationality of the family. It*

123

depends on the dynamics of that family. And I didn't have any Winnie-the-Pooh bedtime stories or their Bengali equivalent.

Nina recalls slightly different memories:

> *I didn't have much support at home with reading because my parents couldn't . . . well, they could read the basics but they wouldn't have been able to read us long stories. But they did know the basics of the alphabet and simple words but they couldn't read us English stories . . . they weren't so confident in reading English and they wouldn't have been able to express their feelings in English. But they would tell us Bengali stories instead. Not when we were going to sleep, but just before we did – in a group, not every night if we were doing other things – we were quite a large family, there were five of us there. But they did a good job on bringing us up.*
>
> (Nina)

It was not just love, financial and moral support that was offered to their children; Bangladeshi-British[7] parents played a vital role in fostering both language and literacy development. Parents did not participate in the English storyreading practice. But, like our previous two generations, they found other mediators of literacy to support their children, both inside and outside the home. Most of the group had comics regularly and all attended libraries to read newspapers, do homework or, more often, to borrow books. Like some of our post-war generation in Chapter 4, books were also purchased by parents. These were generally the hard-back Ladybird books which are widely available in newsagents, but sometimes included beautiful storybooks, as Ros describes below. For all, however, learning to read was a *serious* matter, which needed to be tackled formally and in a structured fashion.[8] Ros shows below the seriousness with which her father took his role as a 'reading teacher' to his children:

Ros: *I remember before I joined nursery my dad trying to teach us to read and he'd bought me my first book which was a* Peter and Jane *book.[9] I remember that, which was great fun . . . I remember Dad going through the* Peter and Jane *book and then I was repeating and then Dad would check up and, as time progressed, we'd be reading harder books and stories and Dad would be listening to us.*
Nina: *Do you think that helped you?*
Ros: *Absolutely, simply because Dad had pushed us at home. He always had and that gave us, I mean, we were so many steps ahead of everyone else in the classroom and those traditional methods complemented what we were doing in school . . . it always revolves around my father, it's amazing. I remember my dad buying a huge book called* The Treasury of Literature for Children *and it had all things like* Aesop's Fables *and* Hamelin *stories – traditional fairytales.*

124

Paradoxically, this structured teaching, viewed as anathema by many early years teachers in Britain during the 1980s, when Ros and her siblings were learning to read,[10] was remembered by them to be 'great fun'. We hear more about being 'pushed', 'traditional methods', 'hard learning' and being 'checked' later in this chapter.

Traditional, structured storybooks have a special significance in all the women's memories of learning to read. Noshi recalls the Ladybird fairytale series: 'The Ladybird books I read were *Cinderella, Beauty and the Beast* . . . You remember them because you still believe in them kind of thing. Sounds like it's going to happen and it's true'. From our group, we begin to see that interpretations of 'fun' and 'seriousness', 'work' and 'play', as well as what makes an 'interesting' text, are a cultural matter. Ros shows us that a serious and formal approach to teaching, even at a very young age, may also be 'fun' and enjoyable if undertaken by a person who is trusted and loved. Noshi is entranced by *the story itself* in her Ladybird book, not the quality of English in which it is written. It is unimportant to her whether the book has been written expressly to teach reading or not.

The refrain of 'being pushed' through challenging and 'serious' teaching is one which recurs as a positive feature as the women refer to their own education and as they now educate their own children. Noshi speaks of the serious way in which she 'taught' her younger brothers:

> *I used to teach my younger brothers different things, like how to spell certain words and teach them how to use the dictionary and tell them to read their books. I thought I was teaching them, but there was no one to teach me.*

Others in the group all speak about their feeling of responsibility in 'teaching' younger siblings – even if, like Tahmin , they have difficulty in finding time:

> *My younger sister who's 11 now, has expressed an interest in going to the library and sometimes she'll ask if I can go with her and I'm so busy I don't have the time . . . I actually have to make an appointment with my sister to go to the library and that's sad . . . And she doesn't want to go with my mum because my mother doesn't know all the titles and she wants to go with me or my other sister . . . My parents were so busy with other things and also the culture isn't there to support your children's educational activities. Many Bengali parents don't have that . . .*

Tahmin's view of literacy teaching is serious enough that she believes it requires special skill:

> *It's the literacy side, you know, reading and writing, that I'm not particularly good at and I think parents in general . . . I think teaching literacy requires*

Table 4 Literacy-related activities at home and in the community: Bangladeshi-British women born 1969–77

Type of practice	Context	Participants	Purpose	Scope	Materials	Role of child	Language
Bengali class	formal: in class or small group	group of mixed ages	to become literate in standard Bengali	usually 6 hrs or more per week	primers from Bangladesh	listen and repeat pattern; also questions, spelling tests, numeracy	standard Bengali for reading; Sylheti for discussion
Qur'anic class	formal: in class or small group	group of mixed ages	to learn to recite the Qur'an	usually 6 hrs or more per week	preparatory primers and Qur'an	listen and repeat pattern	recitation in classical Arabic; some discussion in Sylheti
library	informal	alone or with siblings	pleasure and to practise reading in English	frequently	books	active reader, meaning maker	English
reading-scheme books	formal/ informal	one-to-one with parent or sibling	to learn to read in English	frequently	reading-scheme books	listen and repeat pattern	English
traditional stories	informal	one-to-one (with parent) or family	pleasure, to practise reading and to learn English	frequently	Ladybird books: traditional tales; 'beautiful storybooks'	listener and active meaning maker	English and discussion in Sylheti
storytelling	informal	family	pleasure	approx. once a week	parent	listener	Sylheti
TV	informal	family	pleasure	after community classes and at weekends	TV: TV listings in newspapers, etc.	active meaning maker	English and some discussion in Sylheti

Table 4 continued

Type of practice	Context	Participants	Purpose	Scope	Materials	Role of child	Language
videos	informal	family	pleasure; to watch Indian films	approx. once a week	Hindi film videos	active meaning maker	film in Hindi; discussion in Sylheti
songs, rhymes, games	informal	friends, siblings	pleasure	frequently	songs from school; Hindi videos; playground skipping rhymes	active meaning maker	English; Sylheti; Bengali
homework	formal/ informal	alone and with siblings	to learn English literacy, numeracy	varied	schoolbooks	sometimes teacher, sometimes learner (with siblings)	English and Sylheti
translating and interpreting	formal	with parents and officials	to assist parents	varied	official letters, documents, etc.	child as mediator of language and literacy	English; Sylheti; standard Bengali

*a special training. It's really difficult to get under a child's skin and approach
it as they would.*

All the group share a devotion and dedication to pass on the 'new' cultural,
linguistic and literacy knowledge of the host community, which they are the
first generation to have.

But sometimes there are resources that the family simply does not have.
Like Nina, the eldest child in the family, Tahmin also remembers in detail
how she had to teach or 'push' herself with her English-literacy skills:

> *I always used to feel limited with my English language, 'cos I never felt I had
> enough words to play with. In the third year, we went back to Bangladesh for
> fourteen months and we came back and I became even more obsessed by my
> lack of vocabulary because every year you develop in so many ways and I was
> aware that I'd missed out on that learning process and then, I think I worked
> out that if you read a lot of books, it improves your learning anyway, and it
> did . . . I think I spent one summer trying to get my reading . . . you do it
> unconsciously. At that age, I hadn't really worked out that by reading you
> develop in so many ways – your critical abilities, your faculties, your spelling,
> your learning. You know, I didn't consciously work it out in my head, but
> subconsciously, I worked it out. Oh, it's getting easier, what you have to do.
> But if you'd had parents, if you'd come from a more literate family, they would
> have been drilling you, that kind of stuff . . .*

It is precisely this purposeful and serious approach which has been
adopted by Nina, Noshi and Sima as they bring up and 'teach' their own
children to become literate. Nina's words symbolise the seriousness with
which all three tackle home literacy: 'As I've gone through the education
system, I know it's my duty to teach them and to make sure they're getting
the extra support they need'. All have taken teaching into their own hands,
providing methods and materials that have not been suggested or provided
by the school. Nina, whose boys are 6 and 8 years old, has, perhaps, the most
rigorous programme of homework. She explains the comprehensive nature
of this work:

> *I do give them moral support and always ensure that they're learning, reading,
> doing their maths, doing their homework and giving them additional tasks,
> doing my own worksheets, giving them different books, buying them books to
> do this task and that task from W.H. Smiths and giving them some space also
> for themselves. You know, when I'm out in the street with them and we see car
> registration numbers, I ask them if they can add up the numbers on the number
> plates. You know, if a number is 712, I say, 'Add up the numbers and what
> would it be?'.*

Nina's repertoire extends to writing comprehension questions on the books she has bought for them as well as spelling and reading tests. Her expectations are high:

> *Sometimes I type up my own worksheets and give them comprehension to do at times, although Wasif [the 6-year-old] doesn't do it as much as Wasak [the 8-year-old] does. Wasak tends to concentrate much better, but Wasif tends to twiddle around and get distracted quite quickly. But he's still quite young at the moment.*

Nina's serious approach to getting her children off to a good start in literacy is shared by both Noshi and Sima. As a primary assistant, Sima has access to school materials, approaches and to the 'language of literacy' used by teachers. She works regularly with her 6-year-old son who attends Sir John Cass: 'I help him with his homework. I set up my own tasks as well. We do a lot of practical stuff. Like at school, he might do water games and I do those – certain things I know will help him'. Noshi's expectations for her eldest daughter's home and school learning are equally high (she is three and a half and has recently started the nursery at Canon Barnett):

> *My daughter already knew nursery rhymes, the alphabet and counting rhymes [before starting school]. I taught her those about a year ago. But, as yet, she doesn't seem to have learned much at school . . . I would have expected her to have learned more . . .*

This group of young women are taking responsibility for their children's early literacy learning in a way undreamt of by our parents in Chapters 3 and 4. Their approach is also very different from that promoted as necessary for early reading success in both research studies[11] and official education reports.[12] But teaching literacy at home is only one part of the duty felt by these women towards the language and literacy development of their children. A very separate part is the transmission of a cultural and religious inheritance through community-organised classes. Like Minnie, Abby, Aumie, Gloria and Norma in Chapter 3, all these women had attended community classes as children. Unlike our Jewish group who learned classical Hebrew, these women all learned simultaneously about Islam at Qur'anic classes and standard Bengali at language and literacy classes. Following the tradition of their parents, all send or intend to send their own children to the classes when they are old enough to attend. Nina's boys already attend Bengali classes and will start Qur'anic classes soon; Sima's son attends Qur'anic classes and will start Bengali when his English literacy is established. Noshi's three-and-a-half-year-old daughter began Qur'anic classes about a year ago, then stopped, but will return later:

I sent my daughter to the mosque class. That was last year. But she's too young, I think, to understand that you go there to sit quietly and to read, not to talk. But I'll send her back when she's a little older . . .

Noshi perhaps sums up the feelings of all three mothers towards their children's cultural and religious inheritance, the third strand in their literacy lives:

Yes. I want her to learn Arabic and Bengali. Bengali she should know because it's her mother tongue, just to read and write. She doesn't have to have a degree in it, just to get by with reading and writing. She'll go to classes after school or at the weekend, hopefully.

So what do these women remember of their 'third literacy' in terms of the skills and benefits it has endowed?

A treasure trove: literacy in the community

Qur'anic classes

Arabic, actually, when I say Arabic, it was basically to learn how to recite the Qur'an and so any understanding you have of what you are reading has to come from the teacher, not necessarily from your own understanding of what you've just read. So it was really just to learn how to recite the Qur'an. They hadn't really thought through the Arabic language as such. The teachers probably couldn't speak Arabic either. They could speak and understand Arabic in relation to the liturgy or the prayers that they were teaching, not separate to it. When you say Arabic classes, I think it's a total misconcept. They're Qur'anic classes. 'Cos if you look at Qur'anic Arabic at the moment, no one speaks it in the Middle East, it's something you have to go to special classes to learn.

(Tahmin)

All the group had attended Qur'anic classes from an early age. In many ways, these classes were similar to the Hebrew classes attended by our pre-war Jewish group described in detail by Aumie in Chapter 3. Like the Hebrew classes, learning took place in a language the children could not understand, and in a classical form of the language which is no longer spoken. Like the Hebrew classes, teaching was highly structured, involving phonic recognition and memory, learned through recitation. Jewish girls attended these classes only twice a week; Bangladeshi-British girls, however, were treated equally with their brothers, attending about five or six hours per week at classes, which took place after school or at the weekend. Nina spoke for the whole group when she described many of her evenings:

130

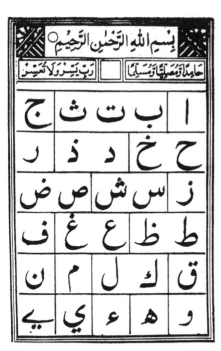

Plate 25 During their first year at mosque school, Ros and her friends would prepare to read the Qur'an in classical Arabic. Learning began by the decoding of individual symbols and proceeded to the deciphering of joined-up script (as shown at the top of this plate)

Plate 26 Page from a Bengali reading book used by Sima and the group at their community class

After school we would go to the mosque and read Arabic and there we would really not understand what we were reading. We would do it for religious purposes. We would need to read the Qur'an and make sure we could practise it at other times. So every day we used to come home from school, get changed, have something to eat and start Arabic classes around 5 until 7 o'clock. Then we would come back, have our dinner and then we wouldn't really have much time – and we'd go to bed after that.

Apart from this, little was said by the women about Qur'anic classes. There was a common understanding of their necessity and importance, especially since all were being interviewed by Nina, herself a member of the Islamic faith. We investigate further the nature and significance of Qur'anic classes in Part III of this book.

Bengali classes

Yes, I remember them, yes, from an early age. We were very lucky – although we didn't think so at the time. We had the East End Community School organised by Nurul Hoque and Anwara Hussein. They are very well known in the community and I think they've done wonders for people of my generation. I have fluent Bengali with GCSE grade A and I owe it to them . . . it was incredibly tiring because it was straight after school and we had to go and then we'd miss things like Neighbours *. . . It was Monday to Friday, like 4 till half-past 6. We'd have Arabic Friday and Saturday. It was more Bengali-based, which is why our Bengali is so much better than our Arabic.*

(Ros)

All the group retain very clear memories of the methods and materials used by their Bengali teachers. Key features, common to all classes, were their competitiveness, their structured approach, starting with the alphabet and phonics and using a lot of repetition, and the way in which children were 'pushed' to get ahead. What counted as successful learning were perseverance, motivation and a sense of 'belonging' to the group. In Sima's words: 'You all learned it in the end. From what I remember, you memorised everything. No matter how long it took, you just memorised it'. When asked by Nina: 'Did you find that interesting?', Sima replies: 'It was very competitive. That was the good thing about it. Because the group I was working with, we would always be in competition. And that made us learn. Sort of kept us motivated . . . '.

Ros and Nina both reflect upon the way in which their Bengali classes complemented the very different type of learning taking place in the mainstream English school:

132

The Bengali class was a lot more strict than the English school. It was a lot more rigid. I mean, our primary school education at the time, the curriculum was challenging traditional methods of teaching the 3 Rs. This [the Bengali school] was very strict. It was like proper learning, reciting, memorising and you'd be punished if you didn't do well or if you hadn't done the homework. You had to do homework as well for these lessons. It was handwriting lessons then, and if you got it wrong you had to write it out 100 times.[13] But there were very good aspects to it. There are things I've learned there which I've remembered and I know I'll take them for the rest of my life. I'll never forget them simply because they were drummed into us . . .

(Ros)

Nina reiterates this through a more direct comparison:

Learning to read in English and Bengali was quite different. Bengali was more structured and you had to learn the alphabet and do strict spellings and do your homework, whereas in the English school you would learn through play and activities and have different topics and different areas. It was all enjoyment. I'm not saying that I didn't enjoy learning Bengali. I did. And now I can read and write Bengali . . .

Like Ros earlier in this chapter who challenged accepted notions of 'fun' when she referred to repeating a structured reading-scheme text after her father as 'great fun', Nina explains that there are different types of 'enjoyment', depending on whether we are considering short- or long-term rewards.

Nevertheless, Bengali classes were not unanimously appreciated. On looking back, Tahmin does not feel comfortable with the principle of 'competitiveness':

There [the Bengali school], it was very hierarchical. It was based on merit. It was based on how good you are, your abilities. Very competitive. You only progress through the system by results. If you don't have the results, you're seen to be lacking and you're esteemed if you have high results. I came at quite a late stage and I performed quite respectably. But, looking back, I don't think I'm comfortable with this results-based outlook and judgement. I don't like the idea of people being valued for the results they achieve. I think it's wrong.

However, she does not question the value of these classes as such, but views improvement in terms of better organisation and resources:

the children's Bengali is not as good as it should be because they've not thought through their criteria, their curriculum, 'cos they're very badly equipped in terms of resources. Basically, they just have one teacher to thirty or forty students, talking at a class, and I don't think it's individualised. And also, there's no differentiation between levels of ability. Everyone's there in one go and all the students are competing for the one teacher's attention . . . supplementary teaching is not formalised in any sense because of funding . . . it's not really been thought through . . . I think when parents get concerned that their kids aren't learning Bengali they don't realise that part of the reason isn't that they're spending too much time learning English, it's because the Bengali classes aren't as effectively organised around those pupils' needs, as they should be. But parents won't know that because they have to be extra-involved and concerned. That's how you get to know about the shortcomings. Otherwise you just take it for granted that they're teaching you Bengali and that's it!

Nevertheless, all the group, including Tahmin, have successfully mastered Bengali literacy, though to varying degrees. Ros has the most advanced skills and is most positive about her classes; Nina, Sima and Noshi feel more comfortable reading and writing in English but are confident in tackling simple books as well as newspapers in Bengali. Even Tahmin, who says she can now write but no longer read Bengali, says,

My Bengali was actually really good at some point but then I stopped practising and I lost it . . . It's a matter of reading a newspaper fairly regularly and then it would all come back to me, 'cos I have the basics. It just means brushing up on it.

The women's confidence in their literacy skills in a second language and script, plus their determination to ensure that these are transmitted to their children, must point to the success, even if qualified, of their Bengali classes.

There are some ways, however, in which both the Qur'anic and Bengali classes resemble the Hebrew classes of Aumie, Minnie, Norma, Gloria and Abby. In both cases, our participants remind us of the enormous investment they made in terms of long hours spent reading texts in different scripts, and using languages with different and complex grammars, from those used in the English school. Both Ros and Aumie refer to their community classes as an extra literacy resource, a treasure trove upon which to draw in the English school. Interestingly, it is both Aumie and Ros who are also most fluent and confident in their third, or community, literacy.[14] There are also links between Ros's interpretation of the benefits of her Bengali class and Abby's memory of school and the advantages of rote learning. When Ros says she will never forget some learning from her Bengali class because it was 'drummed into her', she is echoing Abby's memories from over half a century earlier: 'You repeated things, you looked at things on the board. It stuck in your mind'. The words of both women suggest that our equation of 'enjoyment' with immediate 'fun' in Britain may, indeed, be a cultural matter.

Why didn't they say 'the world is your oyster'? Literacy, language and learning in the English state school

I don't ever remember being taught to speak or read English simply because of our curriculum – or the teachers at the time – it was more of a natural approach, that language comes through interaction and, I don't know . . . We had reading that was good and we had certain stages that we had to meet . . . I don't have memories of being conscious of learning . . .

(Ros)

In 1974, when Nina started school close to Canon Barnett, she was the only Bangladeshi-British child in her class. At about the same time, Noshi's class in a neighbouring school also had only a few Bangladeshi-British children. Less than a decade later, when Ros began school in 1982, all her classmates were of Bangladeshi-British origin. Yet there had been little official recognition of the arrival of these children in school in terms of policy for English language teaching or teacher training. Innovations in methods and materials used to teach literacy[15] during the 1970s and 1980s assumed a common culture in a nation of fluent English speakers for whom a single teaching approach was most suited. At the time when our group of women were in primary school, methods of literacy teaching were influenced strongly by linguistics and psycholinguistics, which equated learning to read with learning to talk: children learned to read by listening to good stories and by being 'apprenticed' to a capable reader with whom they wanted to learn, in the same way that they learned to talk through wanting to communicate with the world around them.[16] This 'natural' approach to teaching literacy may explain why Ros and the other women have fewer memories of learning than either Abby and our pre-war generation, or Christine and the post-war children, when methods were much more explicit.

However, the English state school was only one site where formal learning took place in the lives of this group. As we have seen, all had access to a different type of literacy teaching and learning in their community schools. These parallel classes may well have been one influence on their inter-pretation of what counted as 'good' teaching and 'learning', as we see below. In contrast with the clear images of methods and materials carried with them from the Bengali classes, their memories of learning to read in mainstream school were confined to certain books such as *Charlie and the Chocolate Factory*, fairytales or authors such as Enid Blyton. They had difficulty recalling *how* they learned to read them. They remembered the relaxed atmosphere, the enjoyment of pantomimes, school plays, swimming competitions, etc., but most of the group emphasised the lack of impact those early school years appear to have had in their lives. Ros, Tahmin and Sima feel they learned English 'naturally' – or even from siblings before school. Nina and Noshi have the clearest memories of having to learn a new language when they started school.

135

I thought, being a Bengali girl, my mother tongue was Bengali at home and I used to think, 'How am I going to speak English? What if I say something wrong?' It's not something you're sort of born with, speaking English . . . That sort of worried me. I learned by watching television, listening to the teacher telling stories and speaking with friends in my class. But not with my parents. The thing is that my parents didn't speak English at home, so at home you were just speaking Bengali, and English at school. I did used to get muddled up. Like, what I knew in Bengali I probably didn't know in English, and what I knew in English, I probably didn't know how to explain in Bengali. At that time, the only Bengali teacher in my school was my form teacher . . .

(Noshi)

I sort of remember learning to speak English, though I used to speak Bengali with my parents at home. My father could speak English, although he never used to practise it with us. My mother . . . well, now she's managed to learn English and she can do the shopping but, at the same time, she didn't feel confident. There was a total contrast because we used to speak in Bengali at home and then, when I used to go to school, it was totally English. I don't remember having any other Bengali kids in my class, and when you're in school eight hours a day with just English children you just learn the language . . .

(Nina)

Nevertheless, all have misgivings about the 'natural' approach and believe that their own children need more explicit English and literacy teaching:

At school, it's 99 per cent Bengali children going there. They're not using their English as well as I did. They're always speaking Bengali – well, they're speaking English too and I don't want them not to learn Bengali, but I think that they should practise English at school and that can't be helped when there's such a large percentage speaking Bengali, whereas when I went to school it was quite different. I had to speak English and I developed good speaking skills.

(Nina)

Noshi and Tahmin express this urgent need for better English skills more strongly. In spite of her admiration for her own Bengali teacher in her English primary school, Noshi believes that the Bengali teachers are generally using their mother tongue too much, hindering the children's learning of English. Tahmin is even more critical. She asks passionately: 'Why aren't our children leaving school speaking good English?', and criticises jointly the Bengali teachers who, she argues are non-Sylheti speakers, are from a higher social class than the families and generally care little for the advancement of their

136

pupils; the Local Education Authority for their policy of inviting these teachers from Bangladesh; and the children's families who insist on their children's use of Sylheti at home because they are still frightened that the children may become too anglicised. She argues that a 'natural', 'implicit' approach to teaching English is simply not enough:

> *Why is it that kids born and brought up in Britain are growing up and speaking 'broken' English? I'm really worried about that. It's not because English has precedence over any other language and therefore we should all learn it 100 per cent and communicate in it. It's not that. I'm just concerned that because of this lack of ability to speak fluently you're hampering our development in the future. Language is so important to the way we interact in our environment. You know, to learn English is not to become English. It's different. Parents have this siege mentality that the more English you learn, the more anglicised you'll become and I don't think that's the case. I think in some ways we have to reassure parents that, just because you're giving children the tools with which to express themselves in their environment, doesn't mean that you're diluting their identity . . .*

So what might the 'good' teaching envisaged by these women look like in practice?

The teachers: 'the good ones made it hard'

Ros: *Mr Cook was West Indian and he was brilliant 'cos he was a really good teacher. He was very traditional and he pushed you and was very sharp, very strict and, compared with our other teachers who were very liberal, very easy-going, trying out these new methods of teaching, which is fair enough, but this guy was brilliant, simply because he pushed you, especially the bright kids. I mean, one thing, I always remember teachers who pushed us simply because there were teachers you could tell, who . . .*

Nina: *. . . that wanted you to go further.*

Ros: *Absolutely. Who identified different abilities and – I remember being bored a lot of the time in school and there were teachers who recognised that and who encouraged us.*

A strong awareness of an unequal start in life in comparison with their monolingual and middle-class peers meant that all the women saw being 'pushed' or 'pushing yourself' as the only way to compete in the British education system. Paradoxically, it was precisely this type of ambition or competition which was considered detrimental by many mainstream teachers during the 1970s and 1980s when these women were in primary school.[17] Ros was 'pushed' by Mr C and went on to 'push' herself: 'I was always driven to be top of the class. I was probably in the top group and probably came top . . . '. Tahmin's favourite teacher was a woman who understood the necessity for her to become 'arrogant':

> *One teacher who I really liked wrote something unusual in her 'Good luck' comments before she left. She wrote: 'People have been saying that Tahmin is becoming arrogant, but you need to become arrogant, to have some of that quality to survive in life' and she said that women are particularly good at doubting themselves and their own abilities and if I'm arrogant, then it's a good thing . . .*

Asking children to read aloud to the class was also discouraged on initial and in-service teacher education courses during the 1970s and 1980s when proponents of the child-centred approach regarded it as an unnecessarily competitive activity. Most of the group, however, saw reading out loud as something enjoyable:

> *There was one teacher . . . I got very fond of him. I remember, he always involved us in lots of activities. He used to take us, especially at lunchtimes, and then he made us read in front of the whole class. He really made you feel valued . . . gave you encouragement . . .*

(Sima)

Noshi had the same junior schoolteacher from her first until her fourth year (ages 7–11), the only Bengali teacher in the school. Interestingly, she is the only member of the group to have clear memories of her literacy and numeracy lessons. When asked what her teacher did to encourage her, she replies:

> *Like giving you a spelling test every day, making things hard; like calling you out in front of the class to do a sum on the blackboard, which made you embarrassed so you had to learn it the night before. So you had to do your homework at the right time, so you did it. And my teacher, she was a Bengali from Dhaka, she was very strict and used to tell you what to do. I had her from my first to my fourth year.*

(Noshi)

Recalling her reading tuition may not have been difficult, since her Bengali teacher used approaches Noshi would have recognised from her Bengali class:

Nina: *How was reading taught?*
Noshi: *Well, the whole class used to read a book and then we'd take turns in reading. No one could escape from reading and you'd have to read in front of the class, loudly and clearly, and it made you . . . Well, there were two girls who never wanted*

138

to read. They were so shy. They could read but never wanted to read in front of the class, so that made them overcome their shyness. They were confident then.

The urgency in everyone's voice as each speaks of 'pushing' or 'being pushed' may well stem from the women's awareness that, in spite of their academic potential, they could not hope to compete with monolingual peers where 'pushing' takes place within the family and the school. Ros, who went on to gain a place at Oxford University, is particularly conscious of this:

> *a lot of my teachers thought, 'Why Oxford? You're wasting a UCAS space' or 'You're not going to fit in, you're not going to join in . . . or you're not going to get the grades', blah, blah, blah . . . They're not in touch with Oxbridge and they don't have high aspirations for us and that's why the kids don't have high aspirations for themselves . . .*
>
> (Ros)

She goes on to say how she was totally unprepared for the interview, in contrast with pupils from schools in more privileged areas with whom she was competing. Tahmin's view is very similar:

> *The teachers didn't encourage you to achieve as much as you could have done. They never said, 'The world is your oyster' . . . I really wish that when I was younger people had given me the full range of opportunities that are there. I don't think working-class children are given the opportunities they deserve. They're not alerted to them. I just wish someone had sat me down when I was 16 and said: 'Look, Tahmin, there's architecture. There's medicine. There's a whole range of things you could be. You could be an engineer. You could be this, you could be that. That's how it's all structured'. I didn't have my family there to tell me because my family didn't have a clue any more than I did and I was 16 so I couldn't really be given that responsibility to think for myself at my age about something I wouldn't know of. Someone should have had that hindsight . . . but I don't feel anyone had. It's by default that I haven't done so badly . . .*

The lack of encouragement or ambition for their pupils, shown by both teachers and schools, results in precisely the 'success by default' so frequently mentioned by Tahmin:

> *I feel if I'd grown up somewhere different, my intelligence would have been nurtured so that I could have done a lot more with it. I'm not saying I can't do much with it now, but then it wouldn't have been by default, it would've just happened . . . I just feel that with the kind of ability and skills I have, I could have gone a lot further than I have . . .*

All the women realise that they have achieved against the odds: Nina, Sima and Noshi still have to fight for the university education they want. It is for this reason that education is a serious business. 'Fun' and 'enjoyment' may well be important when the 'pushing' comes from home. For these women, they are an extra bonus – fine once good teaching, high expectations and opening doors to choices are in place, but not before.

Syncretising literacies, languages and identities

When Ros explains how her Bengali classes enriched her knowledge about literacy in the English school, she highlights the syncretism of different literacies and different ways of becoming literate in all the women's lives. Reading fairytales, comics and reading schemes in English opens new worlds which blend with and transform the traditional worlds of the Bengali and Qur'anic classes and vice versa. But literacy only symbolises a wider syncretism between languages and identities taking place in the women's lives. Nina asks Ros and Tahmin about the role of different languages in their lives:

In writing, when I'm writing a letter or an essay, it would be English . . . but I think in Bengali as well, particularly when I'm angry. It's quite funny, particularly when I'm in a non-English environment . . . even in Oxford, I was thinking in Bengali. I caught myself having a go at someone in Bengali. You know, there are certain expressions in Bengali that can't be translated into English. But I think predominantly in English, I think English has to be my first language.

(Ros)

Tahmin's response is remarkably similar:

Well, for administrative and official purposes, I feel most comfortable in English. Also in my personal life, I feel confident communicating in English. Also, I move between languages and this happens in conversation with totally non-Bengali speaking friends. I switch between languages because it's so comfortable for me to do so. Often they don't notice that I'm using a word that they don't understand because I'm speaking so quickly. I think it gives you more vocabulary and different ways of expressing yourself. 'Cos you know how you think differently in languages. And this is how I know I feel comfortable in Bengali, because, you know, if I want to swear or if I want to express disgust, I do it in Bengali, because my Bengali is so culturally specific to that feeling of disgust at that particular moment. It's so eloquent when I do it in Bengali, so I feel comfortable.

(Tahmin)

As Tahmin describes above, language lends itself perhaps most easily to syncretism. Noshi feels just as confident as Tahmin and Ros with mixing both languages:

> *I feel comfortable speaking Bengali at home. With my children, I speak mainly Bengali because I can't speak to them in complicated English because they find it too difficult to cope or understand. With my husband I speak both, and with my mum, Bengali. When I know people know English, I speak English with them. Otherwise, with seniors or elderly people, I speak Bengali.*

(Noshi)

In general the group do not differentiate between Sylheti and Bengali, but Nina lacks confidence when she feels standard Bengali is called for:

> *I feel much more comfortable speaking English . . . I speak Sylheti fine but the standard Bengali, which originated from Dhaka, I don't think I can speak that perfectly, although I can understand it, but when it comes to speaking it I'll always have an accent. It's not 100 per cent there.*

Although many of the young women feel far more confident in reading and writing in English, they are nevertheless quite competent in using both written and spoken Bengali.

The way the women feel about their own language is reflected in the way they speak with their own or their relatives' children. Tahmin is happy speaking both languages with her nephews and nieces. She simply replies in whatever language they begin the conversation. True to her own convictions about improving their English, however, she tries to improve their language skills by choosing to speak English with them whenever she can. Noshi accepts her daughter's 'muddles' while she is learning:

> *When my daughter speaks English, she can say, 'Can I go to the toilet? Can I have a glass of water?' She can't say much. We speak mostly Bengali and a little English . . . She speaks Sylheti and standard Bengali and English. She's muddled up still. She doesn't know which one is which. 'Cos when she speaks Sylheti, she has one word of Sylheti, one word of proper Bengali and one word of English. She has it all muddled up. It makes sense to her though!*

Sima uses both English and Bengali when speaking to her son.

Language use also mirrors the way different women view their identities. Nina and Noshi both feel themselves to be 'Bangladeshi-British' in that they identify with both British and Bengali cultures.

Noshi maintains:

I think I'm Bangladeshi-British. I think I'm Bangladeshi but I was brought up in Britain. I've only been to Bangladesh once or twice. So I don't really know much about Bangladesh.

Nina is more specific:

I feel that part of me is also English as well as being Bangladeshi. I would call myself Bangladeshi-British as I have both races actually – probably I wouldn't have said I was British if I hadn't been born here. In all, I suppose I've only spent about nine or ten months of my life in Bangladesh, otherwise I've spent it all in England and in Tower Hamlets and Spitalfields. And I'm nearly 29 now . . . but I still say half of me is Bangladeshi and half English, because I follow the traditional laws and the culture and I go to festivals and cultural parties. But I also participate in Western activities. I have Western friends and I have Bangladeshi friends.

However, the issue of identity is a complex one. Some see themselves as not fitting neatly into one specific category. Sima says:

When I look in the mirror I see an individual. My origins are in Bangladesh but my upbringing was in London and then my contacts with the Jewish community during my childhood mean that I have something of all three cultures in my background.

Tahmin and Ros, the only two of the women with a university education, vigorously reject the equation of identity with nationality:

I don't really care about this nationality rubbish. I don't see myself as any of those things. I only fill those in when I'm doing job applications with these equal opportunities policies . . . I mean, you only feel something when you're in an environment where you're not that. You only react against it, so your identity and spelling something out is when you react against something . . . so I'm only a Muslim really, I only really think of myself as a Muslim when I'm in a Christian environment or when I'm in a chapel. That's when I think of myself as a Muslim. I think of myself as Bangladeshi when everyone's going on about being British . . . but I'm not any of those things. Having gone to Oxford and Kingsland in Hackney, you know, it's so irrelevant, all of this rubbish, it's overstated.

(Ros)

Her words are almost identical to those of Tahmin who says that she hates the notion of nationality. When Nina asks her how she would describe herself, she says: 'Some of it's Bengali, some of it's Islamic, some of it's British. None of it's English. Some of it's being a woman. But most of it is about being Tahmin – and that changes over time as well . . . '.

142

Coming to terms with choice

We've got to have this drive to succeed to do what the immigrant community before us, the Jewish community and the Russians did – get out of here and move on – push your kids to do well in school or work and go on to do well and assimilate. I think that's one of the greatest challenges, assimilation. I don't agree with isolation, being isolated. It's one thing being independent and not giving in to the status quo or the consensus but I think moving forward is one of the greatest challenges. Younger people of my generation and the future generations have to do something for themselves and have their own identity. I don't think it's accurate just to label ourselves as Bangladeshis or the Bangladeshi community. There are so many differences within the Bangladeshi community. I'm a different type of Bangladeshi to my mum or dad – or even to you [i.e. Nina].

(Ros)

Tahmin believes that 'assimilation' is the wrong word to use and sees 'diversification' of skills in the community as the key to being able to compete in a wider market. All the women view successful education, symbolised by high literacy skills, as enabling choices in life. Lack of choice means a loss of opportunities and freedom to move on. The group all express anxiety for boys exposed to drugs and crime on the streets of Spitalfields, dangers their parents are unable to understand or come to terms with:

I don't know how they can do it. I see how they can slip through the system and be on the streets dossing around. I personally would go mad if I were doing that, but I mean there should be options for them. I sound so conservative saying that they should get up off their backsides, which they should, but at the same time, there should be choices for them, and I don't think there are at the moment. I don't think there are alternatives. Youth groups, I don't know what state they're in, but these kids, they have so much going for them, or they had and they should be taking those opportunities . . .

(Ros)

The way in which choice increases with education is very apparent in the women's own lives. The single women, Ros and Tahmin, who have the choice of where to live, have a positive, almost romantic view of Spitalfields. Noshi, Sima and Nina, however, want to move away, preferably out of London – to Surrey, or somewhere that has good schools for their children. These three women are striving for university education themselves or, at the very least, for their children.

All the women appear overwhelmed with the amount of choice they have in life. Symbolically, all except Noshi (who wants to take up management), have chosen to work with charitable trusts or in the caring professions, rather

143

than simply professions that are financially more lucrative. We are reminded of Christine, Joy, Linda, Norma, Aumie – indeed, almost all the participants in our previous two chapters. Choice has not been part of the family background of these women: their mothers and grandmothers were locked into the expectations and traditions of their own parents and, later, their husbands. Choice of where to live and what to do in life is not always easy, especially when the world *is* your oyster. Ros has just finished her degree at Oxford and suddenly feels plunged into choices:

Ros: *I don't know what my future is at the moment. It's weird having gone to uni and been so independent and free and doing all these wonderful things and suddenly coming back here and I feel I'm back where I started. I'm confused about making career choices. I don't know about my future. A lot of my friends have gone on to do CPEs, you know, law and things . . . I don't want to close any doors . . .*

Nina: *But there are lots of options open to you.*

Ros: *Maybe. Maybe I've closed lots of doors as well. I don't think I've got an easy ride, just because I've got a degree from Oxford . . .*

Three years older, and with an MA already behind her, Tahmin is beginning to make decisions for her future:

> *I've always thought about doing a Ph.D. I didn't want to do it straight away, because I think too many people complete Ph.Ds without taking into account the environment they're in . . . also because I've never really had a specific interest in anything, so that's why I can't just do a Ph.D straight away, because it has to be something that really impassions me, that makes me enthusiastic. I haven't got that yet. I think if I do a Ph.D, I'll do it in the States . . . I'm going to apply for a Fulbright Commission scholarship, which I should get . . . I don't want to go to Oxbridge because I think they're stuffy as institutions, but I feel I would be happy at a good institution in the States.*

Such a statement would have been impossible for the women, or the men, in our past two chapters. The scope and nature of choices available for Tahmin's generation was undreamt of when Abby and Aumie, or even Linda and Tony, were young. So has a greater equality of opportunity between the economically poor and their wealthier peers been achieved for this generation of young people?

Tahmin and Ros would suggest not. Tahmin constantly stresses that she could have done better and that her academic success came 'by default': 'It could easily have gone another way and I could have been sitting at the checkout at Sainsbury's or something'. Ros feels equally angry:

I'm angry at the education I've had . . . I may have done well, but for my own personal best I don't think I have, and I think it has a lot to do with the training you receive in school . . .

(Ros)

There is little doubt that the choices available to all the group would have been as limited as for Abby and Minnie in Chapter 3, had they been young fifty years earlier. Sheer poverty would have meant leaving school early to find work. But what if they had been born at the same time as Joy, Eileen and Christine from Chapter 4? If they had passed the eleven-plus, their academic future would probably have been assured. Noshi, Nina and Sima would most probably have gained at least A-levels,[18] facilitating entrance to university. Whether the group would have managed to pass the eleven-plus as speakers of English as a second language is, of course, another matter. Even the monolinguals in Chapter 4 spoke of 'luck' in their having passed the eleven-plus from an East End school.

When Nina and Tahmin refer to their families' inability to participate in school-recognised literacy practices (for example, the storyreading practice), they highlight a crucial difference between their own and the older gener-ations in Chapters 3 and 4. Unlike Aumie and his group and Joy and the post-war generation, Nina and her peers know that their parents are supposed to prepare their children for school literacy. Thus we see embodied the edicts of the major education reports of the 1970s and 1980s discussed in the Introduction to this book (see pp. 4–5). The movement towards parental responsibility for their children's reading is a serious matter for Nina, Noshi and Sima as their children first set foot in the classroom.

LOOKING BACK

We conclude Part II of the book just as Ros, Tahmin and the other young women in their group prepare to embark on further study or on their chosen profession. Some also have young children whom they are preparing for school learning. The time and energy they devote to this task would have astonished earlier generations. When Minnie, Aumie, Joy and Christine and the others in both our pre- and post-war generations were at school, no one expected parental participation in teaching academic knowledge. The only teaching assumed was to ensure that children came to school able to behave well and, in Rani's words, 'have the right attitude to learning'. In any case, for our pre-war Jewish children, school-teaching styles and materials for early literacy scarcely privileged fluent English speakers over those learning English as a second language; if anything, Jewish children were conscious that mastery of the Hebrew language and grammar from their religious classes gave them an extra learning resource upon which to draw.

By the time that Nina and others of her generation were at school, a very different situation prevailed. Schools expected parents to work in English with their children at home – and this was not supposed to be just any kind of work. Schools were sending home storybooks containing colloquial or difficult literary language for parents to read and talk about with their children, such as the following extract from a popular children's book by the Ahlbergs:

> Each Peach Pear Plum, I spy Tom Thumb.
> Tom Thumb in the cupboard, I spy Mother Hubbard.
> Mother Hubbard down the cellar, I spy Cinderella.
> Cinderella on the stairs, I spy the three bears . . .

This type of work demanded not only a knowledge of the English language but of English literature and traditions (termed 'cultural capital' by Bourdieu (1977)), which few first-generation immigrants to a country could possibly possess. And yet, owing to a lack of understanding and recognition that some families may have *different* strengths to offer, these books were often sent

146

home with little explanation to parents of what they were expected to do.

One might, therefore, begin to wonder what progress has been made in terms of equality of opportunity throughout the century? Have Tahmin and her group's chances of success really been increased by legislation or has it come 'by default', as Tahmin herself suggests? It is true that, in certain ways, schools and teachers throughout the twentieth century have acted as 'gatekeepers', excluding children from economically disadvantaged families from vital knowledge that would enable them to increase their choices later in life. For our pre-war group, selection by the school came late. The scholarship marked out those who were privileged enough to continue to the higher elementary or secondary school rather than go straight out to work. For our post-war group, it was the eleven-plus that demarcated those chosen for academic success from those destined for the secondary school and more manual tasks later in life. But for Tahmin and her friends, selection came rather earlier: it was on entry to primary school when families were in danger of being categorised as 'deficient' if parents were unable to prepare children appropriately for school learning.

So what has changed and what has remained the same across the century? In spite of Tahmin and Ros's criticisms, the changes in opportunities available to their group should not be underestimated. Minnie and her generation could never have contemplated studying at Oxford. Thirty years on, the grammar schools opened doors to this kind of opportunity for Robert and his group. But further study in the USA, as envisaged by Tahmin, would still have been out of the question. One wonders, too, whether Tahmin and her peers, as learners of English as a second language in east London, could ever have passed the eleven-plus? There can be no doubt, therefore, that progress has taken place. However, despite the huge differences across groups, a number of common features hold members of different generations together. All recognise the pain involved in discarding old cultural practices, grafting new practices on to old and crossing boundaries between different social classes. All have great empathy for the underprivileged and many have chosen to work in the caring professions. They work in education, the health system or devote their retirement or spare time to charities. Finally, none takes education for granted. School learning and literacy are serious matters and no one can afford to take them lightly.

Part III

LOOKING AHEAD: YOUNG LITERACIES, LIVES AND LEARNING

INTRODUCTION

One hears the claim, 'All children should be treated alike.
There should be no discrimination'. It must be conceded that
to overlook individual differences and cultural differences and
to treat everyone as if they were the same, does, indeed, involve
a lack of discrimination. Think about it, it certainly is not in the
child's interest.

(Duquette 1992)

Nina and her group were leaving school at the advent of the most important changes in education since the 1944 Butler Act. In 1988, the Education Reform Act was to introduce a common curriculum, to be followed by all children in England and Wales. Prior to this, teachers and schools had enjoyed considerable autonomy in curriculum decision-making, resulting in significant differences between areas, schools and classrooms. The Act proposed to change all that, aiming to give every child the entitlement to a common curriculum. The idea of a 'national' curriculum was not new. As early as 1976, James Callaghan, then Secretary of State for Education in the Labour Party, had spoken passionately about the inequalities still existing in the English education system. His speech at Ruskin College, Oxford, mooted the future that was to be introduced only much later and by a Conservative government. In 1987, a consultative document claimed that 'a national curriculum backed by clear assessment arrangements will help to raise standards of attainment' (DES 1987: 3) and in 1988 the Education Reform Act was passed. Shortly afterwards, the first 'orders' for the curriculum were published.

In line with other policies of the Conservative government of the 1980s, education was now to enter the market place. A new discourse of education appeared, reflecting changes in structures.[1] The curriculum was now to be 'delivered', 'targets' were to be set by 'senior and middle management teams'; during the 1990s, university departments of education were to become 'providers' and student teachers referred to as trainees (Ofsted 1998). Funding was devolved to school level and the budget placed in the hands of the school governing body where parents were to be strongly represented. This body was also expected to take responsibility for the enforcement of the curriculum, the monitoring of standards and the hiring and, hypothetically,[2] the firing of the head and the teachers. In theory, then, each governing body took charge of its school.

In exchange for these responsibilities, parents were given certain rights. Most importantly, they gained the right to send their children to the school of their choice. The question, however, was how people outside the world of education should know which school to choose. The answer to this was simple. Schools were now to compete with each other through the yearly publication of test scores achieved by children at ages 7, 11, 14 and 16.[3] Successful schools would be rewarded by a funding formula for the number of children they could attract.[4] In contrast, schools deemed to be 'failing' under the new inspection system would, under the 1992 Education (Schools) Act, be put under 'special measures', including the suspension of a delegated budget and the intervention of the local education authority. Without immediate improvement, the Secretary of State would be empowered to send an education association into the school to take it over and either recommend closure or turn it into a centrally funded grant-maintained school.[5] The duty of parents from now on would be to follow the league tables and inspection and national test results to make sure their children attended successful schools.

The introduction of the National Curriculum placed 'equality of opportunity' at the core of its aims. Indeed, the term itself had been central in the various documents emerging from the Education Reform Act. It was used by Kenneth Baker (1987: 8) when he claimed the Act would 'open the doors of opportunity' for all children and reiterated in various documents emphasising that both the curriculum and the national tests must make every effort to avoid race, culture or gender bias. It was also enshrined in many of the National Curriculum Council's documents during the 1990s. The promise offered to all children in 1992 (NCC 1992: 15) was as follows:

Providing equal opportunities for *all* pupils means:
1 Treating pupils as individuals with their own abilities, difficulties, attitudes and experiences.
2 Challenging myths, stereotypes and misconceptions.
3 Ensuring that equal access to the curriculum means more opportunity to benefit.

How far were the new orders to achieve these goals?

The first few years of the National Curriculum served only to highlight existing inequalities in achievement. National publication of test results revealed to everyone the extreme differences between schools in wealthier and poorer areas as well as differences between schools in the same area.

These differences had no doubt always existed and were certainly part of the folk knowledge of older generations in our study. Nevertheless, the fact that they were now officially published resulted in some parents withdrawing their children from schools where results were particularly poor in order to place them in academically more successful schools. Changing the content of the curriculum, then, did not appear to have any immediate effect on children's performance. Politicians turned to look elsewhere.

During the first years of the National Curriculum and the SATs (Standardised Attainment Tasks) in the early 1990s, there had been no attempt to influence the *methods* of teaching used in classrooms. Indeed, individualised and small-group teaching and learning in primary school classrooms had generally been held to be sacrosanct ever since the publication in 1967 of the Plowden Report (DES 1967) advocating child-centred education. However, it was becoming increasingly clear that setting down the contents of the curriculum and testing these regularly was ultimately bound to influence methods of tuition. Coupled with this, the aim of both the outgoing Conservative and the new Labour government to raise standards led to further centralisation and control. Where better to begin than with controlling the methods used for initial literacy and numeracy teaching?

On its election in 1997, the Labour government pledged to raise significantly standards of literacy by promising that 80 per cent of 11-year-olds would be reading and writing fluently by the year 2002. In order to ensure this, a National Literacy Strategy (NLS) became mandatory for one hour a day in all primary schools in England and Wales from September 1998. This new directive gives precise instructions as to exactly what must be taught, using which materials, and in what way, throughout the entire primary curriculum. The new NLS emphasises the importance of structure and includes regular whole-class practice of phonics and letter recognition alongside word and comprehension skills. At the start of the twenty-first century, it seems likely that 83-year-old Abby might share more with today's 5-year-olds than 23-year-old Ros as they reflect upon learning to read in school. Whether this means escape from the inequalities that have dogged the lives of all our participants in Part II will be known only as the century unfolds.

The children in Part III of this book step into the midst of all these changes. Born between 1989 and 1990, they are young enough to be the first generation to have experienced the National Curriculum, but are too old to have learned to read with the NLS. When they entered Sir John Cass and Canon Barnett in the mid-1990s, the composition of the two schools had changed radically from the days of Abby and others in her group. With the occasional exception of one or two pupils, all the pupils attending Canon Barnett are now of Bangladeshi-British origin. Sir John Cass receives approximately 75 per cent of its children from Bangladeshi-British families; the remaining children are of English, African, African-Caribbean or Asian origin. The teachers, too, have come from across the world: New Zealand, South Africa,

Holland, Australia, Bangladesh and Ireland. They are joining their English colleagues in learning to live with the new ways of the English curriculum.

The theme of *contrasts* that is promoted in this book is also present in the demography of Tower Hamlets, the London borough in which Spitalfields is sited (see Table 5). Figure 2 shows clearly how the distribution of bilingual pupils in Tower Hamlets is concentrated in schools in certain parts of the borough, leaving other more eastern areas almost exclusively monolingual and white.[6] By the end of the twentieth century, Tower Hamlets had approximately 20,000 pupils with a home language other than, or in addition to, English, representing 59 per cent of the school population (see Figure 1). Although Bengali/Sylheti is the most common language with 17,231 speakers (86 per cent of all bilingual pupils), 74 languages other than English are spoken, with one secondary school recording 29 different languages. Over half (52 per cent) of the school population is not fluent in English and over a quarter are classified as beginners. After Bengali/Sylheti, the languages with the most speakers are Cantonese, Somali, Turkish, Vietnamese, French, Urdu, Arabic, Yoruba and Panjabi.

The square mile of Spitalfields is quite unique in Britain in that 95 per cent (approximately 36,000) of its population are of Bangladeshi origin from Sylhet.[7] Yet, even in Spitalfields itself, this apparent homogeneity conceals stark contrasts. During the last two decades of the twentieth century and continuing today, Spitalfields has undergone rapid and dramatic changes that polarise yet further the contrasts of poverty and wealth. Money from the City is spilling over to the East. The earnings of a growing number

Table 5 School population in Tower Hamlets by ethnic group

Ethnic group	Number of pupils	% of total population
Bangladeshi	17,151	50.7
Caribbean	1,572	4.6
Chinese	363	1.1
English/Scots/Welsh	10,720	31.7
Greek	60	0.2
Indian	276	0.8
Irish	428	1.3
Pakistani	286	0.8
Somali	318	0.9
Turkish	263	0.8
Vietnamese	248	0.7
other African	826	2.4
other black	348	1.0
other white	384	1.1
any other	216	0.6
unclassified	358	1.1
Total	33,817	100.0

Source: Policy and Performance Monitoring Unit, London Borough of Tower Hamlets (1994a)

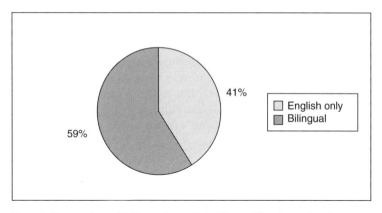

Figure 1 Proportion of bilingual pupils in Tower Hamlets schools

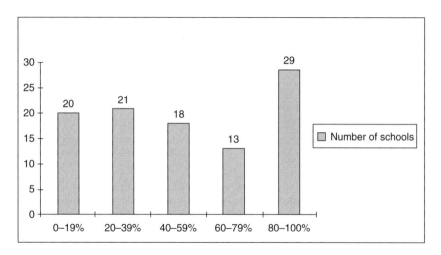

Figure 2 Number of schools with proportions of bilingual pupils

of City workers have exploded, resulting in a mushrooming of wine bars and restaurants, which overflow with City workers during lunch breaks and after-work gatherings. Alongside these, previously neglected Victorian warehouses, schools, and even the former Jewish Soup Kitchen are suddenly being renovated, their exterior façades restored to their original beauty, and their interiors converted into luxury *pied-à-terre* apartments for the business world. Significantly, the new population appears to have little real commitment to the area. At weekends, the area empties and appears abandoned. The City workers return to their country homes; the restaurants, wine bars and pubs remain closed, leaving champagne bottles alongside other rubbish piled up in the narrow Victorian alleys.

At these times, Spitalfields' 'invisible' community comes to light – a community worlds apart from the City and its wealth. This community lives largely tucked away in the side streets, in local authority accommodation. Some families survive in conditions reminiscent of those described by our pre-war generation, with seven or more children in a small Victorian apartment, and only an internal courtyard in which the children can play. The centre of the community is the new housing development of Flower and Dean Walk, built on the site of Jack the Ripper's first murder. Families living in houses here are the luckier ones; spacious flats are built around a paved, tree-lined courtyard, with a community centre where Qur'anic and Bengali classes are held. Adjacent to Canon Barnett School and the courtyard is Brick Lane, housing a building that started out as a Huguenot chapel, became a Methodist chapel, was converted into a Jewish synagogue and is now a mosque; shops and restaurants in this street are almost entirely Bangladeshi owned. Only occasional names like 'Adler Street', two twenty-four-hour bagel shops and Jewish monumental masons reveal the area's earlier history.

The thirteen families whose literacy lives are the subject of Part III all live in or around Spitalfields and all have Year 1 or Year 2 (5- to 7-year-old) children at Sir John Cass or Canon Barnett schools. The demographic data from the study highlights important factors contributing to differences in the children's home literacy practices. The family background of the children is shown in Tables 6 and 7.

As these tables indicate, the differing patterns of employment of the two groups reveal the relative isolation of many of the Bangladeshi-British families living in the area in comparison with the monolingual families, whose jobs bring them into contact with a number of different people. Although Nina, Noshi and Sima from Chapter 5 herald a new generation of British-born women whose children are now entering school, many women still enter Britain from Bangladesh upon marrying and have no experience of the British education system. They are also new to the English language and culture, which isolates them from the mothers of their children's monolingual peers. In our study, no mother in the Bangladeshi-British group was in employment outside the home, in contrast with all but one of the monolingual mothers whose work or studies demanded English literacy skills. Three out of the seven Bangladeshi-British fathers were unemployed and the employment of the remaining fathers was in the immediate vicinity with colleagues from the same country of origin. Second, six out of the seven Bangladeshi-British mothers had received their education in Bangladesh and were literate only in Bengali. The seventh mother had attended school in Britain. This contrasted with the monolingual mothers, three of whom had GCSE passes.[8] Third, the cramped accommodation of many of the Bangladeshi-British families meant that they were not able to house the arrays of toys visible in some of the monolingual families. Finally, in contrast with the monolingual children, those of Bangladeshi-British origin had a number

Table 6 Family background: Bangladeshi-British children and their families

	Position in family	Father's occupation	Mother's education	Mother's occupation	Accommodation
Uzma	4/5	restaurant owner	Grade 5*	housewife	flat
Maruf	5/5	shop worker	Grade 5	"	double flat
Shima	5/5	unemployed	Grade 5	"	house
Shuma	2/4	waiter	to age 15	"	flat
Akhlak	9/11	unemployed	Grade 7	"	flat
Henna	3/4	unemployed	Grade 4	"	flat
Shanaz	2/3	factory owner	Grade 5	"	flat

* Grade 5 indicates the final level of primary school and is generally reached by age 11.

Table 7 Family background: English monolingual children and their families

	Position in family	Father's occupation	Mother's education	Mother's occupation	Accommodation
Sophie	1/1	policeman	age 16	childminder	flat
Sarah	3/3	publican	age 16	works in family pub	week – flat weekend – house
Amy	1/1	builder	age 16	insurance clerk	house
Nadia	2/2		age 16	unemployed	flat
Ricky	3/3	engineer	age 16	access course	flat
Stewart	2/2	plumber	age 16	playleader in children's playground	flat

of older siblings living at home. These siblings constructed a distinctive home-literacy practice that is outlined in Chapter 6.

In Part III of the book, readers are invited to participate in the literacy learning of thirteen children and their parents presently living in the heart of London; children who may well carry these experiences with them until the latter part of the twenty-first century. Just how different will such experiences be from those of the generations of children who sat in the same classrooms in the early years of the twentieth century?

6

LIVING LITERACIES IN HOMES
AND COMMUNITIES

> The differences that children bring to classrooms, therefore,
> are not simply individual differences or idiosyncrasies . . .
> They are the products and constructions of the complex and
> diverse social learning from the cultures where children grow,
> live and interact . . . These, too, are dynamic and hybrid:
> mixing, matching and blending traditional values and beliefs,
> child-rearing practices and literacy events with those of new,
> post-modern, popular cultures.
>
> (Luke and Kale 1997)[1]

This chapter is concerned with the new generation of Spitalfields residents,
the children who, with their families and teachers, took part in the Family
Literacy History project in the mid-1990s. The study was carried out at a time
of grave concern over standards in education and in particular over reading
standards. Three Inner London boroughs had recently been the focus of
a special investigation (Ofsted 1996),[2] which demonstrated that children in
these inner-city areas performed less well in literacy tests than their counterparts elsewhere. Although many factors, including poverty, poorly resourced
schools and large numbers of children for whom English is an additional
language, must account to some extent for the disappointing results, parents'
own skills were also considered to play a crucial role in their children's
performance.

Home literacy practices have long been seen as a contributory factor in
a child's success or failure in school. Research by ALBSU[3] suggested that
parents' level of education was the strongest predictor of a child's success.
Large-scale studies by scholars such as Wells[4] found correlations between
home storyreading and early proficiency in school reading. Snow and Ninio
went further, stating that home storyreading was essential to provide children
with the 'skills which they have to learn if they are to participate successfully
in book reading interactions'.[5] Government reports also encouraged parental
involvement. The Bullock Report (DES 1975) stated that a major priority was

to 'help parents recognise the value of sharing the experience of books with their children'; the Cox Report (DES 1988) exhorted parents to 'share books with their children from their earliest days and read aloud to them and talk about stories they (had) enjoyed together'. More recently, the School Curriculum and Assessment Authority Report on Desirable Outcomes for Children's Learning in Nurseries (SCAA 1996) urged parents to 'support learning opportunities at home through reading and sharing books'. This was followed up by a government green paper proposing that parents should be obliged to read with their children on a daily basis.

> Parents will be asked to sign an undertaking to read with their children at home for at least 20 minutes per day under government proposals for improving literacy published yesterday . . . Stephen Byers, the schools minister, said he was fighting back against the dumbing down of British culture as exemplified by the Teletubbies and declining standards on Radio 4.[6]

It is clear then, that home storyreading both to and with children is considered to be a pivotal factor in the successful acquisition of literacy, and there would appear to exist in both education and government circles a set of beliefs concerning good practice. It is assumed:

- that story reading, as it is practised in Western homes is the most valuable preparation for literacy development;
- that the same home-reading practices are suitable for all children whether their home language is English or another language;
- that parents need to perform activities approved by the school and that successful practices are transferred from school to home;
- that it is parents rather than other family members who should carry out the literacy activities with the children;
- that very little literacy besides that taken from the school goes on in the homes.

While the government initiatives are admirable and clearly reflect a political will to improve standards for all children, they nevertheless focus on a very narrow definition of literacy; that is, that which is variously described as 'mainstream' by Heath,[7] 'schooled' by Street and Street[8] or 'official' by Dyson.[9] Little account appears to be taken of what happens in non-Western homes nor of the unofficial literacy practices in which people engage. Yet as we have seen in earlier chapters, the people of Spitalfields have a long tradition of 'alternative' literacies, ranging from studying the Talmud to publishing working-class poetry. One aim of our project was to uncover the 'unofficial literacies' in which people engage and to examine the part they can play in supporting children's school learning. We begin by looking at the reading experiences of the mothers who took part in the project and who were aged between 23 and 40 when the project was carried out.

Reading at home

The monolingual mothers

My dad was a reader. He read anything and everything from the newspapers. That's why Simon could read the newspaper; he could pick all the horses out. He was four and a half when he came here [to school] and he was reading the newspaper. He still does, the back page. At the time he could see what horses were running, what the prizes were, what colours they had, who the jockey was . . . he lot, he still does . . .

(Mrs Radford)

As we can see from the above quotation, the route to becoming literate for some of our participants did not necessarily depend on reading from approved texts, nor was it school based. The six monolingual mothers who took part in the project provided surprisingly homogeneous accounts of their formal literacy experiences in Inner London primary and comprehensive schools of the 1970s and 1980s. For the most part, their 'schooled' or 'official' reading experiences had been painful and disappointing. All felt dissatisfied with their own schooling and wanted their children to have the educational opportunities they felt they themselves had missed. Four of the women had truanted regularly from both their primary and secondary schools, afraid to go to school because of bullying or encouraged to stay at home by parents. One was dyslexic, one fell behind in her work because of her frequent absences and another left before taking any examinations because of the bullying she suffered. The feeling expressed by some of the mothers was that the 'significant adults' in the process, the teachers, had been uninterested in them and had not encouraged them to work hard nor to strive for success in school. Memories of learning to read in the formal context of school therefore were painful:

I was never really that good in school. I was partially dyslexic as well and still am with writing. They used to leave me in a corner with a picture book.

(Mrs Turner)

I was slow at reading. I was behind for a long time. My mum used to let me have a lot of time off and then once you fall behind in your work you don't want to go back any more, do you?

(Mrs White)

In contrast, true learning and reading with real enjoyment took place at home. Thus, Mrs Radford who left school with no qualifications, when asked about how she learned to read, responded, 'I've always been able to read. My dad was a reader'.

Mrs Turner, who was dyslexic, stated,

> *Whatever I learned was down to my mum and dad. They were good in that department because my mum's dyslexic. On Saturday morning, we used to get comics through the door. I used to sit there for hours. I used to get all of them – Buster, Beano, Dandy . . . my mum used to read them as well.*

Mrs Taylor who had been an indifferent student in school, and who 'just used to walk out of school a lot of the time', nevertheless 'used to love going to the library "cos [she] used to go behind the counter and sort the tickets out' and had some 'beautiful books' at home, which she bought with her dad at W.H. Smith at Elephant and Castle. All the mothers spoke with evident pleasure of the books and comics they had read at home as children. Enid Blyton was cited by all as a favourite author, along with classics such as *Black Beauty* and *Treasure Island*.

For these women, then, it was the home rather than the school literacy practices that had shaped their learning, and in almost every case there was an interested and caring adult in the home, a literacy broker or a 'guiding light'[10] who encouraged them and provided books and materials. In the case of Mrs Radford it was her father who 'was a reader'; Mrs Turner's parents coped with her dyslexia by providing comics; and Mrs Taylor's father took her shopping for books.

Interestingly, the love of reading, which they remembered so vividly from their childhoods, has remained with them and five mothers now read regularly for pleasure. Mrs White, who missed about two years of schooling, reads 'a lot now, mainly biography and horror'. Mrs Radford, who left school with no formal qualifications, is now a parent governor, chair of her local residents' association and still an avid reader, sharing and discussing books with a circle of friends. Mrs Turner, once dyslexic, now reads mainly 'on a night' and on Sundays when she 'sits on the settee all day with a book' and 'doesn't move'. Mrs Anderson, the youngest mother at 23, who left school before completing her education, says of her husband, 'He's not really a reader. I'm the reader'. Interestingly, there was no suggestion in the interviews that their reading should be educational or 'improving' in any sense. Nor was there any mention of 'good books'. For these women, reading is a purely pleasurable occupation and the authors such as Catherine Cookson, Harry Bowling, Virginia Andrew, Ruth Rendell, and Agatha Christie, whose works they read so avidly, would be considered writers of 'popular fiction'.

In this way, the monolingual mothers differed from both the Bangladeshi-British mothers (see p. 178) and from the two mainstream schoolteachers. For the latter group, there had been no 'pain–pleasure' dichotomy attached to learning to read as children and they had happy memories of both school and home reading, remembering authors such as Enid Blyton, Noel Streatfeild and Eleanor Brent-Dyer. Unlike the children's mothers, however, they felt that they now had no time to read, except in school holidays, and even then, it was suggested by one teacher, it was preferable to try to read 'good' books. The 'reading for pleasure' dimension that had been such an enjoyable part of their childhood reading patterns has now disappeared from their lives.

The children

As might be expected, the monolingual mothers viewed the reading, writing and other literacy practices in which the children engaged at home largely as activities to be enjoyed, and there was a wide variety, ranging from playing schools to attending drama classes, with the boys enjoying computer games and drawing, and the girls preferring reading, writing and playing schools, along with the usual television and video viewing. Playing schools, which involved writing registers, 'correcting' work and writing on the blackboard, was the preferred pastime of all the girls, even if they had to play alone.

AW: *What do you like doing at home?*
Nadia: *At home I like playing teachers because I've got a board and I can write on it. It's not a board, it's like . . . you know a folder, it's a folder with all paper in and I've got pens to write with and I say a few names that's in my class but some I don't know.*
AW: *And do you play by yourself?*
Nadia: *Yes.*
AW: *When do you read all these books?*
Sarah: *Sometimes when I'm playing teachers. Sometimes I play it with Amy, sometimes with Nadia and sometimes on my own.*

Writing can also be an absorbing occupation for a solitary child. Nadia and Sophie both enjoyed writing:

> *she'll sit in her room and she'll fold her legs and she'll write.*
>
> (Mrs Taylor)

> *I do stories sometimes. I've got a little diary with Minnie Mouse on it and I write in there. Not every day . . . sometimes.*
>
> (Nadia)

> *I like to write stories and I like to do my handwriting and I like to do pictures and cards and give them to everybody. I made a Valentine's card. It had hearts and Sellotape over and then I stuck them with glue.*
>
> (Sophie)

162

Unlike the girls, the boys did not enjoy solitary occupations but actively sought out other children to play with. As well as playing imaginative games with toys such as Batman, the Power Rangers and Ninja Turtles, they played computer games, which require two players:

AW: *What do you do when your mum says he's not allowed in?*
Ricky: *I just let him in and then we look to see if anyone is sitting in the chair near the door and then we creep into the bedroom.*
AW: *And what do you do in there?*
Ricky: *Play. We play on the computer and sometimes we play Sonic, Sonic 2 and Street Fighter.*

Although such games involve reading instructions and typing in names, they are not literacy-based activities in the same way as playing schools, writing or reading books, the preferred occupations of the girls.

All the children talked about books they read at home, however. The girls in particular enjoyed both reading and collecting books:

AW: *What do you think would be your best book?*
Sophie: *I think it would be my Mr Men books.*
AW: *Have you got all of them?*
Sophie: *Nearly. I've got twenty-one more to collect.*
AW: *What about the Little Miss books?*
Sophie: *I'm not collecting them yet.*

> *I've got thousands of books. I've got loads . . . I have to have two shelfs [sic] for them. I've got a collection of dinosaur books. My grandad buys all the dinosaur books and I've got ninety-nine so when I go today [to visit him] I'll have a hundred.*
>
> (Sarah)

Family size, position in the family and family circumstances also had an effect on the children's play. Two girls were 'only children' and the two others were the youngest child in the family by several years and therefore obliged to entertain themselves much of the time. All were used to playing alone, and reading, of course, is an ideal activity for a solitary child:

> *There are times when we want to relax and be quiet, and she'll be gone for an hour and she'll be down here reading on her own.*
> (Mrs Anderson, mother of Sophie)

> *I just read some books to myself in my bedroom . . . but I've read them so many times, I'm fed up with them.*
> (Sarah)

Although only 6 years old, the children already possessed many books:

AW: *If somebody gave you a present what would you choose?*
Sophie: *I'd choose a bookcase 'cos I've got so many books I have to have a toybox to put them all in and I have them on a shelf and all the rest on the landing. I can't fit them anywhere.*

Their tastes in books were wide ranging and diverse but much of their reading matter would not necessarily meet with approval from teachers, nor would it be found in school bookshelves. Luke[11] identifies two main strands in children's literature: the 'residual' tradition, exemplified in fairytales and works by approved authors; and the 'emergent', alternate tradition, which is closely associated with popular culture. Materials which fall into the latter category are rarely approved in schools as 'official' literature. At home, however, these 'unofficial' texts formed a substantial part of the children's reading, creating 'a pattern of mutually reinforcing intertextual references', with characters who appeared on television, in films, in comics, in books, and as toys.[12] Thus 6-year-old Sophie, who read the classics such as *Little Women* and *What Katy Did* with her mother, claimed nevertheless that her favourite books were based on the Walt Disney films:

AW: *Do you get books for presents?*
Sophie: *Sometimes I ask for them.*
AW: *Do you remember any that you have asked for?*
Sophie: *I asked for* Dumbo *and* One Hundred and One Dalmatians.
AW: *Have you seen the film* Dumbo *?*
Sophie: *Yes.*

Ricky, whose passion was the *Ninja Turtles* (a US television series), was firmly situated in the 'emergent' culture tradition:

AW: *What else do you do after school? Do you ever read books or anything?*
Ricky: *I only read Ghostbusters and Turtle books.*

In spite of their popularity with children however, such texts are rarely found in schools. Thus, while they fulfil the criterion of providing pleasure and fun, they are not considered suitable for school reading. Just as we found with the mothers, there still exists a clear distinction between the reading matter that is enjoyed in the home and that which is sanctioned in school.

Literacy brokers and guiding lights

Although the English mothers saw reading at home primarily as an enjoyable occupation, they were nevertheless very concerned about their children's education and in most cases were taking steps to ensure that their children did not experience difficulties in school: Sophie's mother had begun teaching her daughter to read with flash cards at the age of eighteen months so that by age 3 she could recognise simple words like 'cat' and 'dog' and 'was reading books by the time she came out of reception class'. Mrs Taylor bought Nadia maths and language-activity books in order to help with school work. Amy's parents enrolled her for speech and drama classes, which they felt would 'help her with exams later'. Ricky's mother attended special classes organised by the school to demonstrate how reading was taught in school. Without exception, the monolingual parents involved in the project were anxious that their children should succeed where they felt that they themselves had failed:

> *I wish I'd stayed on [at school]. That's my big regret. I wouldn't like her to make the same mistakes as I did.*

> (Mrs Clark)

Involvement in the children's learning was not restricted to parents however. In each of the monolingual families the grandparents played a major part in fostering the children's interest in books and reading. Sometimes, the grandparents acted as role models, as in the case of Nadia.

AW: *Do you ever read any other books at home beside your PACT (Parents And Children Together) books?*

Nadia: *Sometimes I read these, erm . . . interesting books like bird . . . about birds and . . .*

AW: *And where do you get them from?*

Nadia: *From my grandpa.*

AW: *So there are books about birds?*

Nadia: *And books about plants and some about ants . . .*

AW: *Are they interesting? Have they got pictures?*

Nadia: *Yes but they aren't really like pictures like in a book what you read . . . like . . . just interesting.*

AW: *Are they books for children, do you think, or are they books for adults?*

Nadia: *I think they're books for like 7- to 11-year-olds . . . But my grandpa's got lots of books . . . He's got all sorts of books about snakes, about birds, about insects . . .*

AW: *Does he read them?*

Nadia: *Yes.*

AW: *And where does he keep them?*

Nadia: *He keeps them in his wardrobe.*

AW: *And what's your favourite one that he's got?*

Nadia: *The one I read sometimes is this white book called* The Reindeer Book.

Table 8 Literacy-related activities at home and in the community: English monolingual children

Type of practice	Context	Participants	Purpose	Scope	Materials	Role of child	Language
playing school	informal: at home	group or individual	play	frequently (girls)	blackboard, books, writing materials	child imitates teacher and/or pupils	English
PACT (Parents and Children Together: home-reading scheme)	informal: at home	parent–child dyad	homework: to improve child's reading	daily	school reading book	child reads and is corrected by parent using 'scaffolding' or 'modelling' strategies	English
comics, fiction, non-fiction	informal: at home	individual or dyad (parent or grandparent/ child)	pleasure	frequently	variety of comics, fiction, non-fiction books	child as 'expert' with comics or books; as interested learner reading adult non-fiction, magazines, etc.	English
drama class	formal	group	pleasure and to learn skill	2 hrs a week	books: poetry and plays	child performs in group; recites as individual	English
computers	informal	individual or in dyad with friend or sibling	pleasure	frequently	computer games	active participant	English
video/TV	informal	family group or individual	leisure/ entertainment	daily	TV/videos	child listens and watches; discusses with others	English

Nadia's grandfather, like two of his brothers, had been a London taxi-driver, who, in order to qualify, had had to pass the written examination based on what is often referred to as 'the knowledge'. His early interest in general knowledge has stayed with him all his life and even now at the age of 80, he still reads widely and maintains his interest in subjects as diverse as stamps and medicine. Nadia appeared to have adopted her grandfather's taste in books and her preferred reading matter at the time of the project was her children's encyclopaedia.

Sarah and Sophie's grandparents bought books for their grandchildren. As we saw earlier, Sarah's grandad bought her dinosaur books and Sophie's grandparents bought collections of the classics as well as reference books: 'She'd brought the atlas home from school and he [grandfather] went out the next day and bought her this [an atlas]'.

Some grandparents actually taught their grandchildren to read, as we saw in the case of Simon who learned to read with his grandfather, using the racing tips in a tabloid newspaper.

> When he was 3 or 4 he was always with him . . . watched the horse-racing, read the papers, taught him to read when he was in nursery.

Clearly, the transmission of literacy skills in the monolingual English families is not seen solely as the responsibility of parents. In a society where mothers have to work outside the home, it is often the retired grandparents who have the time to take on the role of literacy brokers. The situation in the Bangladeshi-British families was quite different as we shall discuss in the next section.

Formal learning in informal contexts

The Bangladeshi-British children

The out-of-school lives of the Bangladeshi children seem far removed from those of their monolingual schoolmates. Although they too rush happily out of school with their brothers and sisters at 3.30 p.m., they do not go home to an evening of playing schools or computer games. For most of them, formal learning continues long after mainstream school has finished, as the following conversation with 6-year-old Maruf demonstrates:

Maruf: *There are eighty three children.*
AW: *Eighty three children in your Arabic class! And when do you go to that?*
Maruf: *7 o'clock to 9 o'clock.*
AW: *On?*
Maruf: *A night.*
AW: *Every night?*

Table 9 Literacy-related activities at home and in the community: Bangladeshi-British children

Type of practice	Context	Participants	Purpose	Scope	Materials	Role of child	Language
Qur'anic class	formal: in classrooms or in someone's living room	group of 0–30 mixed age range	religious: to read and learn the Qur'an	approx. 7 hrs a week	Raiel (wooden bookstand), preparatory primers or Qur'an	child listens and repeats (individually or as group); practises and is tested	Arabic
Bengali class	formal: in classrooms or in someone's living room	group of mixed age range. Can be children of one family up to group of 30	cultural: to learn to read, understand and write standard Bengali	approx. 6 hrs a week	primers, exercise books, pens	child listens and repeats (individually or as group); practises and is tested	Standard Bengali
reading with older siblings	informal: at home	dyad: child and older sibling	homework: to learn to speak and read English	approx. 3 hrs a week	English schoolbooks	child repeats, echoes, predicts and finally answers comprehension questions	English
video/TV	informal: at home	Family group	pleasure/entertainment		TV in English; videos (often in Hindi)	child watches and listens; often listens to and joins in discussions; sings songs from films	Hindi and English

Maruf: *Monday to Friday.*
AW: *Monday to Friday! You go for two hours every night! Aren't you tired?*
Maruf: *I don't feel tired.*
AW: *No? And who goes with you? Anybody from your class?*
Maruf: *I go by myself . . . And some people go from upstairs . . . juniors.*
AW: *And are you the youngest then?*
Maruf: *Yes and I'm on the Qur'an.*
AW: *You're on the Qur'an now.*
Maruf: *There's Quaida and Ampara and Qur'an.*
AW: *And you're on the Qur'an now?*
Maruf: *I'm on the last one.*
AW: *Are you . . . How many teachers are there for eighty three children?*
Maruf: *There's two.*
AW: *Only two. Who are they?*
Maruf: *One is the Qur'an . . . you know, all the Qur'an he can say it without looking.*
AW: *He can . . . What's his name?*
Maruf: *I don't know. And one is . . . he can . . . he knows all the meanings.*
AW: *Does he? Does he tell you the meanings?*
Maruf: *Yes, he does.*
AW: *So do you just read the Qur'an for two hours? Is that what you do?*
Maruf: *Yes but I don't sometimes, I talk sometimes.*
AW: *You don't!*
Maruf: *I do.*

This conversation gives some idea of the demands made upon children who participate in two very different cultures. For these children, acquiring literacy is a complex business involving several languages. The home dialect of the London Bangladeshis is Sylheti, an unwritten variety of Bengali, and so parents feel that it is important that their children learn to read and write standard Bengali if they are to maintain their own culture. Second, in their mainstream school they have to learn to read and write in English in order to function successfully in Britain. Finally, as practising Muslims, the children must read the Qur'an and therefore attend Qur'anic school and learn to read in Arabic. Already at age 6, Maruf realises that literacy is a serious business and that punishments lie in store for those who do not apply themselves.

The class which Maruf attended every day after school is typical of Qur'anic classes everywhere. The sessions are usually two hours long: few concessions are made to the young age of some of the children and even the smallest are expected to concentrate for long periods:

> In this particular class there are two male teachers, one of whom is working with the more advanced children who are tackling the complicated word structures of the Qur'an. The other group

169

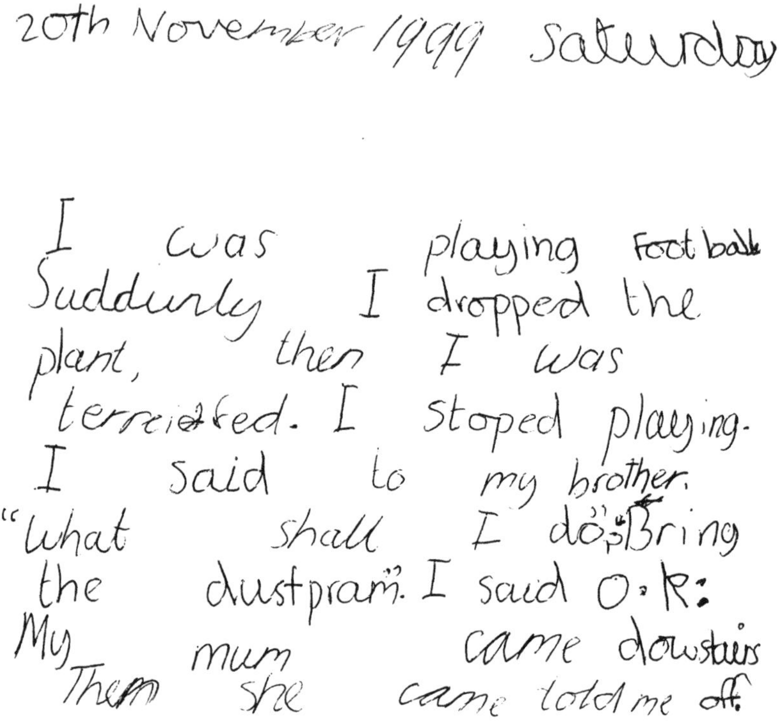

20th November 1999 Saturday

I was playing Football
Suddenly I dropped the
plant, then I was
terrieafed. I stoped playing.
I said to my brother.
"What shall I do?;Bring
the dustpram". I said O.R:
My mum came dowstairs
Them she came told me off.

Plates 27 and 28 Wasif's writing, at age 7, in English and Bengali, practised with his parents at home

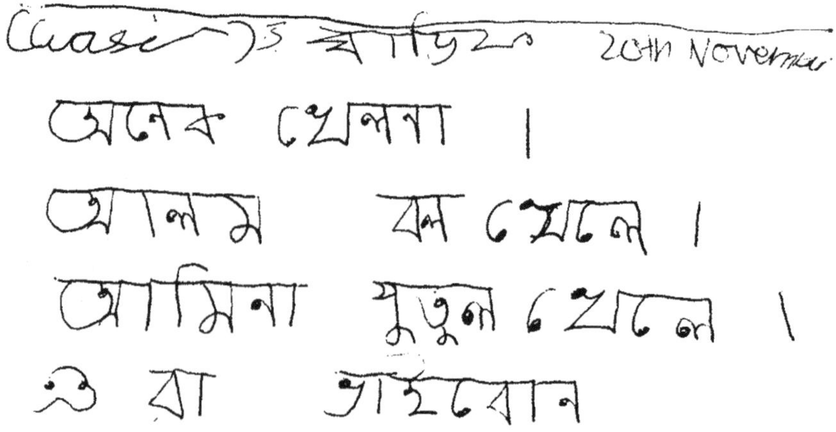

Cuasi)5 ২০th November

অনেক খেলনা ।

আলম বল খেলে ।

আমিনা ফুটল খেলে ।

ও বা গাইবান

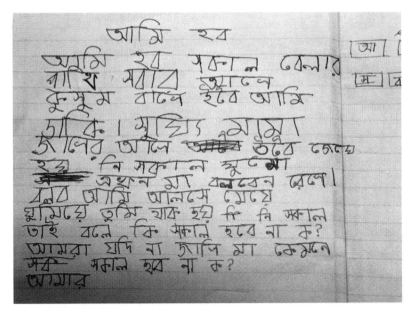

Plate 29 Waseq's writing in Bengali, with English translation below

I want to be the morning bird

I'll sing out in the flower garden before everyone else

I'll wake up before Uncle Sun rises

Mother will say crossly, 'Go back to sleep, it's not
   morning yet'

I'll reply, 'Lazybones, you're still sleeping.

Morning is on its way.

If we don't wake up, how can morning come?

Morning is coming and only your son is awake.'

From 'The Morning Bird', a poem for children
by Kazi Nazrul Islam (1899–1976), the
'Rebel Poet of Bengal'

Table 10 Community class attendance: Bangladeshi-British children

Child	Mon	Tues	Wed	Thurs	Fri	Sat	Sun
M	B	B	B	B	B	A	A
A	A	A	A	A	A	B	B
Sh	B	B	B	B	A	A	
H	A	A	A	A	B	B	
S	A	A	A	A	B	B	
U	A	A	A	A	A	B	B

B = Bengali class
A = Arabic (Qur'anic class)
Duration of lessons: 2 hrs

consists of younger children who are in a different part of the room with the second teacher, grappling with sounds and letters and oral verse. Everyone sits on the mat swaying to the sound of his/her own voice. Although on initial appraisal the noise level seems high, little of this is idle chatter. It is the expressed wish of the teachers that children read aloud, partly to assist their learning, but more importantly so that Allah can hear. Children are encouraged to develop a harmonious recitation in unison with the gentle rocking to and fro which accompanies the reading. They are told that Allah listens to his servants and is pleased if they take time to make their reading meaningful . . . 'Now, repeat after me', the teacher requests, 'Kalimah Tayyabh, la ilaha ilallaho, mohammadan rasolallahe'. He tells them to look at him as they repeat. I leave the room on the third recitation of the prayer and notice that the children have not wavered: all remain seated on the floor as they have done for the last hour and a half.[13]

Teaching methods are traditional: the teacher reads a phrase and the children repeat after him until they are word-perfect and the process continues with the next phrase. The pattern of listen, practise and repeat is shown clearly in the following extract, also taken from Rashid:

The teacher stands in the centre and calls upon each child in turn to recite the passage which they have reached in their reading of the religious primer or the Qur'an.

Teacher: *Read this, Shuma.*
Shuma: *Alif, bah, tah, sayh . . .* [14]
Teacher: *What was that? Say it again.*
Shuma: *Alif, bah, tah, sayh, jim . . .*
Teacher: *Yes, that's it, now carry on.*

Plate 30 Wasif and Waseq practising their reading together

Plate 31 Work from the Bengali community class

Shuma: *jim – jim, hae, kae, d- (hesitates) . . .*
Teacher: *Dal – dal, remember it and repeat.*
Shuma: *dal, zal, rae, zae, sin, shin, swad, dwad . . .*
Teacher: *(nods) What's next? Thoy, zoy.*
Shuma: *zoy, thoy . . .*
Teacher: *No, no, listen carefully. Thoy, zoy.*
Shuma: *(repeats)*
Teacher: *Fine. Now say it again from the beginning . . .* [15]

The Bengali classes take place in a variety of locations. Some are held in teachers' houses, some in the children's homes and some in community centres as the one described by Rashid below:

> Situated behind Petticoat Lane Market, this Bengali school is funded through the voluntary sector. It comprises two mobile rooms, the walls bare except for a few information posters made by the children. The room I enter has several rows of desks at which children sit quietly – some writing, others practising words under their breath. At the beginning, the teacher sits in front of the room, then starts to walk around. The children who are mumbling are practising the previous day's work and as the teacher passes around, the voice of the child he is listening to is momentarily amplified so that the teacher can correct if necessary before moving on to the next.
>
> Later the children read, some at a fast pace whilst others read with careful deliberation. When the teacher reaches the child I have come to observe, she reads confidently and eloquently and the few mistakes she makes are firmly corrected. Parts that are not understood are explained briefly in Sylheti . . . and the lesson continues in this way to the end.[16]

Teaching methods in the Bengali classes are equally traditional: children work on one primer at a time, progressing gradually through the series. As the following conversation indicates, learning Bengali, even if it takes place in someone's front room with a friend's mum as the teacher, is also a serious undertaking:

AW: *Tell me what you do, then, on Saturdays and Sundays.*
Maruf: *I don't come to school.*
AW: *You don't come to school but what do you do?.*
Maruf: *I go to Bengali school then I come home.*
AW: *What time do you go to Bengali school?*
Maruf: *11 o'clock to 1 o'clock.*
AW: *And what do you do there?*

Maruf: *We read Bengali.*

AW: *And how do you do . . . how do you learn that, then? And do you just have one book or do you have a lot of books?*

Maruf: *There's book two, book three, book four, book five . . . there's lots of books.*

AW: *Lots of books, and which book are you on?*

Maruf: *Book one.*

AW: *Book one. Is it hard?*

Maruf: *Easy!*

AW: *What do you have to do? Do you have to write in the book?*

Maruf: *You've got to read it. And sometimes they say, 'You've got to write it without looking'.*

AW: *Write it without looking and then what do you do?*

Maruf: *Then if I'm right . . . she . . . they tell us.*

AW: *And who is your teacher?*

Maruf: *There's two, Meli's dad and Jahanara's dad.*

AW: *Jahanara's dad! Is he the teacher?*

Maruf: *Jahanara's dad, and Tania . . . do you know Tania in Class One?*

AW: *No.*

Maruf: *Her mum.*

AW: *Her mum. And are they strict?*

Maruf: *They give us . . .*

AW: *Give you what?*

Maruf: *Punishment.*

AW: *What do they do? What punishment do they give you?*

Maruf: *They talk to us and do you know what Meli's dad does . . . says to pull our ear.*

AW: *He's going to pull your ear?*

Maruf: *No, you've got to pull it like that.*

AW: *You've got to pull your own ear. Have you ever had to do that?*

Maruf: *Never.*

Although Maruf is only 6 years old, he spends two hours every day in addition to his mainstream school, in such classes (see Table 10). In contrast with the monolingual group, who engaged mostly in informal literacy practices outside school, the Bangladeshi-British children spent on average thirteen hours per week receiving formal instruction in organised classes. Thus their home literacy differs from that of the monolingual children in many respects. First, it is conducted as group rather than individual or paired activities, and an individual's progress (towards the completion of the Qur'an, for example) is often marked by the whole group sharing sweets or other treats. Second, the notion of 'pleasure' in terms of 'immediate enjoyment' gained from a story read at home is not applicable to the kind of out-of-school reading practised by the Bangladeshi children: learning to read and write in Bengali is seen as entering a cultural world and acquiring a language which was fought over during the violent struggle for independence from Pakistan in 1971: learning to read the Qur'an is necessary for being accepted into the Islamic faith and therefore an adult and serious occupation. Finally, even the task of reading at home in English is quite different for Bangladeshi-British children. In this community where some parents are literate in Bengali but not necessarily in English, home reading usually means children reading their school texts not with mum or dad nor even with grandma or grandpa, but with those members of the family who are already fully proficient in English – that is, the older sisters and brothers.

Booksharing at home

It was 'booksharing' with older siblings that provided some of the most interesting insights into the young Bangladeshi-British children's acquisition of literacy. The combination of cultures and learning styles the bilingual children were exposed to in their daily lives resulted in a unique method of tackling the school reading books at home. When the home reading sessions were analysed, it became clear that the children were blending strategies learned in both their mainstream English school and in their Bengali and Arabic classes. This resulted in what we have termed 'syncretic literacy',[17] with the repetitions and fast-flowing pace characteristic of the Qur'anic reading grafted on to strategies such as echoing, 'chunking' of expressions and predicting, adopted from lessons in the English school. The transcriptions also revealed that the older siblings employed a series of intricate and finely tuned strategies to support the young readers as they struggled with the text. In the early stages, when reading with a child who was just beginning to read, the supportive 'scaffolding' was almost total, with the older siblings providing almost every word for the beginning reader. As the younger child's proficiency increased however, the scaffolding was gradually removed until the child was able to read alone. We were able to identify the following stages in the scaffolding of the young children's reading:

1   *Listen and repeat*: the child repeats word by word after the older sibling.
2   *Tandem reading*: the child echoes the sibling's reading, sometimes managing telegraphic speech.
3   *Chained reading*: the sibling begins to read and the child continues, reading the next few words until he/she needs help again.
4   *Almost alone*: the child initiates reading and reads until a word is unknown; the sibling corrects the error or supplies the word; the child repeats the word correctly and continues.
5   *The recital*: the child recites the complete piece.

The following two extracts illustrate Stages 1, Listen and repeat, and 3. Chained reading:

Stage 1

Child	Sibling
	1 *The postman*
2 *The postman*	
	3 *It was Tum's birthday*
4 *was . . . birthday*	
	5 *Ram made*
6 *Ram made*	
	7 *him a birthday card*
8 *him a birthday card*	

Stage 3

Child	Sibling
	34 *Okhta* [This one]
	35 *It's*
36 *It's a whobber. Meg . . .*	
	37 *Mog*
38 *Mog catched a fish*	
	39 *caught*
40 *caught a fish*	
. . .	
44 *They cook*	
	45 *cooked*
46 *cooked a fish*	
	47 *and*
48 *and Owl had a rest. Meg was looking*	
	49 *looked out*

In Stage 3, we see Akhlak and his sister practising 'chained reading': the sister starts and Akhlak continues reading the next few words until he needs help again; the sister then either corrects or provides the word. Akhlak repeats the correction and continues, a process very similar to the 'listen, practise and repeat' that the children are already familiar with from their community classes. These home reading sessions have a very high number of turns and a fast-flowing pace, also characteristic of the Qur'anic classes. It is notable that in spite of the child's young age, the focus is on print rather than on any illustrations. Furthermore, the older sibling's insistence on accuracy from the outset indicates that this is not play but serious work in which the roles of learner and teacher are clearly defined and not negotiable.

The mothers

In the Bangladeshi-British families therefore, we found that reading was a serious activity associated with school work or religion. This respect for books and reading was no doubt inherited from the parent generation, most of whom had been educated in Bangladesh, and who had often had to struggle to become literate against difficult circumstances:

> *I finished Class Five and then my mother died just after my engagement, leaving me and my five brothers and two sisters, so I had a lot of responsibilities.*
>
> (Mrs Choudry)

> *The trouble was there was no legal requirement for school attendance and also you had to provide books and stationery. On top of that, parents had to pay 10 per cent of teachers' salaries, so it was an expensive business sending your children to school, especially for the poor folk, of whom there were many . . .*
>
> (Mrs Bibi)

The Bangladeshi-British mothers had learned to read in Sylhet following traditional methods:

> *In the classroom all the children would sit in rows. The master would call out the alphabet, or words, or sentences, depending on the level, and then the class would repeat in unison . . . It was successful because there was a cane* [laughter] *you couldn't go far with the master's cane . . . from what I can remember, everything was taught with a lot of testing and memorising.*
>
> (Mrs Begum)

Moreover, as Muslims, they were also obliged to read the Qur'an and had to attend Qur'anic class before normal school:

> *Arabic learning took place before school started very early in the morning . . . we would have breakfast and go and read for several hours not far from home. Then we would return home, have something to eat and go off to school.*
>
> (Mrs Bibi)

There was little room in their lives for reading for pleasure. Learning to read in Arabic at the Qur'anic school had a strictly religious purpose. The only pleasure gained was the satisfaction of pleasing Allah. Reading Bengali literature for pleasure at home was not an option open to these young women either, since, just as in the lives of the older English Londoners, home reading was viewed as an inappropriate activity for a girl. Although one of the mothers now borrows Bengali books from the library, *reading* for most of the Bangladeshi-British mothers means simply '*reading the Qur'an*'.[18] An alternative entertainment to reading books is a practice labelled 'newstelling' by Nasima Rashid.[19] In Spitalfields where they live far from their extended families, the mothers meet regularly to chat and exchange news. This recounting of events and stories is a group activity and might be regarded as a continuation of the oral tradition practised back home in Bangladesh.

A new paradigm of early literacy?

The children and their families introduced in this chapter reveal the multiple home literacy activities of two communities living within one square mile in the centre of London. They also show the syncretism or 'hybridisation' referred to by Luke and Kale[20] as they mix and blend practices from home and school into unique new patterns and forms. Yet few of these activities fall within the officially recognised paradigm of preparation for school literacy, which is storyreading with the parent using a 'good book'. The extensive and intensive nature of these 'unofficial' literacy practices in both communities provides a strong argument for a shift in paradigms in the twenty-first century towards one which rethinks the way it authorises the literate and recognises strength in diversity. Fortunately, however, there are some school classrooms where teachers are already building upon the varied literacy experiences of their young pupils, as we shall see in the next chapter.

7

LEARNING THE LITERACY OF SCHOOL

Nadia, the 7-year-old whom we met in Chapter 6, is 'teaching' Aisha, aged 5, to read her schoolbook:

Aisha: *It's Monday again. You'd . . .*
Nadia: *Look. See that says bet.*
Aisha: *bet . . .*
Nadia: *and that says 'er'. Put them together and they make . . . ?*
Aisha: *better play nicely George so . . .*
Nadia: *says.*
Aisha: *says his mum.*
Nadia: *Reme . . . mber – remember . . .*[1]

In this chapter, we examine ways in which young children at our two schools in the 1990s go about learning the literacy of the classroom. Like those of past generations whose voices were heard in Part II of the book, these children do not enter school possessing the cultural capital of 'bedtime stories' or familiarity with the language of the books used in school. Although Nadia's mother has provided her with an encyclopaedia, writing paper and other literacy materials, Nadia generally practises her schoolbook alone at home. In other cases, parents may be unable to read English. Nor are they children whose parents have time to spend many hours reading with them or preparing other school tasks once they have started formal lessons. The questions tackled in this chapter, therefore, are: To what extent have these young children learned the literacy of school after one or two years and how do they come to know what they do? To what extent do they syncretise home and school learning patterns? How similar or different are they from past generations? The group's primary school learning spans the last five years of the twentieth century, and is taking place at a time of immense change in school literacy tuition.[2] The chapter concludes with a glimpse of Wahida, an 11-year-old in the same class as some of the children we met in Chapter 6. Like these children, Wahida entered school at the age of 5 speaking very little English. The way in which she now 'teaches' her younger sister highlights dramatically how children can take hold of school learning and make it their own in ways that few teachers would dream possible.

Nadia and her friends: the early syncretism of home and school learning

Playing school at age 7

The extent of Nadia's knowledge about reading is revealed more clearly when we eavesdrop further on her 'teaching' of a younger child. In the extracts below we see her at work again with 5-year-old Aisha:

Nadia: *Do you want this or this?* [Offering two books]
Aisha: *This* [starting to read]. *Snow is falling* . . .
Nadia: *Shall we read who it's by?* [Expecting Aisha to join in] *By Franklin M. Bradley. Illustrated by Holly Keller.*
Aisha: *Snow is falling.* [Aisha hesitates, Nadia points to the pictures.]
Nadia: *What is it there* [picture of night scene]?
Nadia: *It's night, isn't it? Night* . . .
Aisha: Night has come and . . .
Nadia: *snow* . . .
Aisha: *snow it* . . .
Nadia: *is* . . .
Aisha: *is falling. It* . . .
Nadia: *It* . . .
Aisha: *It* . . .
Nadia: *It falls* . . .
Nadia: *Try and do this one.*
Aisha: *Er, er* . . .
Nadia: *This . . . What's that say? You know snow, don't you? So what does that say? Look at this* [pointing to picture].
Aisha: *snow . . . snow . . . snowflake.*
Nadia: *Good!*

This short extract reveals Nadia's interpretation of what the teacher of reading should do. Importantly, she expects to be the 'expert' when reading with a novice or younger child. In other words, she does not count on the younger child automatically being able to read, nor does she as the teacher simply listen, and allow the child to continue without correcting her errors and assisting her. At the same time, she gives very few evaluative comments. On one occasion she says 'Good!' but this is rare. As she starts, Nadia allows Aisha a choice of book, while at the same time making it clear that the choice is restricted to those she feels are suitable for a beginner reader. She also knows about ways to get the younger child interested in the book. She introduces Aisha to understanding how books work by insisting on reading the title and the name of the illustrator. She uses picture cues to help Aisha to decipher the text and prompts and encourages her. At the same time, she pays close attention to the text itself. On other occasions, we see her providing words and phrases when necessary, breaking down words, and reminding Aisha of words that have already occurred in the story.

If Nadia is not accustomed to reading with her mother at home, where might she have learned these skills? Is it possible that she might be using her teacher as a role model – or are her strategies from some other source? To find out, we need to enter the classroom where Nadia, Susie and their classmates are spending their second year in school.

Into Nadia's classroom: learning the strategies of reading

Ch: *Gobble, gobble, glub, glub . . .*

Mrs K: *I was thinking, before we . . .*

Ch: *Gobbley gobbley glob glob . . .*

Mrs K: *Listen, before we start, cross your legs. Before we start, let's get the rules sorted out. Wait till I ask you a question. Sometimes I'll say you can all answer or read or sometimes put your hand up. Don't just call out when I'm trying to get another child looking for words. So . . . it's a lovely book. The title. You can all call out the title.*

Ch: *Gobbley gobbley glob glob.*

Mrs K: *Right now. What do you think that says?*

Ch: *Glob?*

Mrs K: *Have a look at it. Look at it carefully because it doesn't actually say glob. You've got the gl . . . part.*

Ch: *Gla . . . glo . . . glub . . .*

Mrs K: *Aha! What's the difference between gl . . . ub and gl . . . ob?*

Ch: *One is U [ju:] It's a U [ju:] instead of an O.*

Mrs K: *That's right. I wonder why you thought there was an O? Now look at this word very carefully: look at it carefully.*

Ch: *Gobbley gobble.*

Teacher and Children: *Gobble gobble glub glub.*

Mrs K: *Gobble gobble glub glub. And it looks a really nice book. It's all rhymes. And it's by Judith Swift. There used to be a teacher in this school called Judith Swift, but I don't think it's her.*

This short excerpt from Nadia's class reading lesson reveals one way that her teacher begins reading lessons. The 'rules' of turn taking are made very explicit; what 'counts' as successful participation (put your hand up) and what is not permitted. At the same time, her teacher draws attention to individual letters and words, tells the children what type of book to expect, talks about the title and the author and relates these to aspects within the children's own lives. We might say that she is teaching the children how to situate themselves in both the social (knowing how to participate successfully in reading lessons) and mental (learning how to use phonic and other cognitive strategies) contexts of reading.[3]

Mrs Kelly, Nadia's teacher in her second school year, was considered to be 'brilliant' by all the parents of our group. Her methods were not based on any current orthodoxy,[4] but rather on her own enthusiasm for reading, her high expectations of the children and on twenty years' experience of observing children learning to read. Her stated aims in teaching reading were wide ranging: to instil a love of books in the child (she believed that children should see adults reading and enjoying books); to make the child feel happy and secure in the reading environment; to promote the idea that reading can be done in a variety of contexts, for different purposes and across the curriculum; to engender text-to-life and life-to-text experiences and to provide a vehicle for children to talk about their own lives; to teach the child 'the language of books', that is, how books work; and to persuade the children to become confident and discriminating readers by encouraging them to talk about the books they read. She felt strongly that the teacher should have a knowledge of the words each child knows at any one time so that she can say, 'Look, there's "and", the word we looked at yesterday', or point to the word when it occurs 'in other contexts such as on posters and wall charts'. The teacher, she maintained, should also know when to intervene in the child's reading and when to let the child try to work things out for herself.

Observations of Mrs Kelly at work show how skilfully she puts her theories into practice. In the following extract she is reading with a small group of children. The school practice was for all children to read for thirty minutes every morning in graded reading groups. The class teacher, the English-language teacher,[5] the headteacher and the deputy headteacher each worked with a group of children in the class.

Mrs Kelly: *What made me think I might like to choose this book?*
Tope: *Maybe because Tony's in this school.*
Mrs Kelly: *No, no . . . Why Tony Ross? Why did I think that this might be a good book? I'm not sure. But why did I think it might be?*
Tope: *'Cos he's writ some nice stories.*
Mrs Kelly: *I think he has. I've read some books of his before . . . some books that he has re-told and I've really enjoyed them.*
Chris: *I think I've got a book at home by him.*
Mrs Kelly: *Have a look at the title when you go home. See if you can notice it. Do you remember Mr . . . Oh I can't remember his name . . . he was working with the juniors. He used to love books by Tony Ross.*
Nadia: *Oh I remember . . . I think his name was . . .*
Mrs Kelly: *He went back to New Zealand . . . or Australia.*
Tope: *Oh yes.*

Plates 32–35 Children at school in the East End

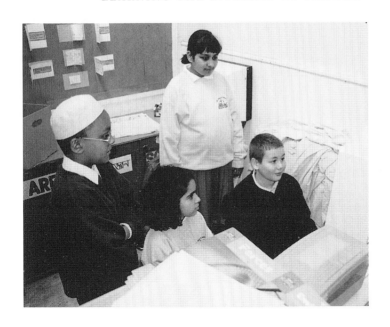

Nadia: *I think his name was Ross.*

Mrs Kelly: *Oh it was Ross! It was! Well remembered!* [laughter all round] *That was good . . . So before we read the story that he's re-telling who can remember the story of* Little Red Riding Hood*? Let's start with Susie.*

Susie: *Well, the mum made some cakes for her Nan . . .*

(Williams 1997: 98–9)

At the beginning of this reading lesson, we see Mrs Kelly mentioning her own and other teachers' enjoyment of books, using the 'language of books' by referring to the author and title of the book and conveying her excitement about the book the group is about to read together. The request 'Do you remember . . . ?' recurs frequently in Mrs Kelly's lessons in a number of different contexts. Here, she calls upon the children's collective memory of school life by referring to a teacher who used to work in the school and thus promotes a feeling of security in the group. She then gives the children an opportunity to express themselves in their own words by retelling the story before turning to the author's text.

The following extracts show ways in which she guides the children through the text. Her detailed knowledge of the reading process coupled with an understanding of the children's repertoire, their strengths and weaknesses, enables her to prompt them into remembering what has been taught. It is Susie's turn to read and Mrs Kelly reminds her of some phonic work they have recently done together (words in square brackets are unread):

Susie: [*She*] *tickled the wolf on the nose. He opened one* [*beady eye*] . . .

Mrs Kelly: [to the others] *Now, don't actually tell her this because I taught you. Do you remember? If you see the letter 'e' and the letter 'a' together . . . can you remember the sound?*

On other occasions, she calls upon a common understanding of the task, pointing out where the actual text appears to contradict expectations and quite explicitly models the skilled reader:

Mrs Kelly: *This is quite a hard one actually and just to show you* [pointing to the picture] *and it has to rhyme with peeling.*

Fatima: *Ceiling . . . ceiling.*

Mrs Kelly: *I didn't know whether you knew that word or not. I'm sorry I gave you a clue now. And do you know what it begins with?*

Fatima: *C.*

Mrs Kelly: *Oh you do know. Well done. What did I think you were going to say?*

Fatima: *S.*

Although children read in turn, the group-reading session is a joint, rather than an individual, reading activity, with a high number of turns per pupil.

Plates 36 and 37 Children at school in the East End

The children listen carefully to each other and are able to offer solutions to their friends' miscues within the safety of the group. It is the children themselves, then, rather than the teacher, who carefully scaffold each other's learning, while she 'orchestrates' the whole process,[6] offering praise and encouragement, prompting when necessary and providing words when no one has a solution. The whole interaction is fast flowing, ensuring that continuity and the meaning of the text are maintained. The extract below is typical of group-reading sessions that have the quality of a 'reciprocal dialogue' (Ninio and Bruner 1978).[7] Notice, too, how similar this reading is to the fast 'chained' reading we saw taking place between Bangladeshi-British siblings in Chapter 6:

Susie: *Once upon a time, a little girl lived on the . . .*
Chris and Nadia: *Edge! Edge . . .*
Susie: *of the forest. Her dad was a . . .*
Tope: *woodcutter . . .*
Susie: *woodcutter . . .*
Nadia: *whose . . .*
Susie: *whose . . .*
Tope: *job . . .*
Susie: *job it was to . . .*
Nadia: *hack . . .*
Susie: *hack down trees so that all sorts of things like houses . . . sorts . . .*
Tope: *sometimes . . .*
Susie: *sometimes little . . .*
Mrs Kelly: *Just a minute . . . sorry to interrupt you Susie* [reading] *. . . like houses . . . ?*
Mrs Kelly: *Go on two lines.*
Nadia: *comics . . .*
Susie: *comics could be made from the wood.*
Mrs Kelly: *Good girl.*

The whole activity is collaborative and the children have the opportunity not only to practise their own reading but also to listen to others and observe how Mrs Kelly tackles the teaching of reading.

From school to home and home to school

Might Nadia's observations of her teacher have informed her own 'teaching' strategies as she reads with Aisha? The excerpts from her classroom above would certainly suggest this might be so. In order to examine similarities and differences between Nadia and Mrs Kelly's reading sessions, a list of the strategies used by the 'teachers' to respond to their 'pupils' miscues and guide them through the text was compiled.[8] Twelve different strategies were

Plate 38 Children at school in the East End

Plate 39 Wahida and her younger sister Sayeeda, with two of their elder brothers

identified, which seemed to fall into two groups: 'modelling' strategies, which aimed to initiate the learner into behaving like a good reader but were not directly text based, and 'scaffolding' strategies, which aimed to help the child decode the text and are directly based on the text itself. 'Modelling' strategies included opening and closing moves (I like this book . . . I chose this book because . . .), imparting knowledge about books (the author of this book is . . .), relating the text to the reader's real life experiences (do you ever do that?) and providing positive or negative feedback to the learner (good girl! wrong!).

'Scaffolding' strategies included using phonics ('e' plus 'a' make . . . ?), breaking down words (gl – ub?), establishing meaning (how do you know 'head'? – points to picture), pausing and prompting (give Susie a chance to think . . . p – [pink]) and insisting on accuracy ('blue' what? 'blue branches'). The moves made by the 'teachers' in response to the learner's hesitations and miscues were allocated to one of the twelve categories of strategies and the number of moves in each category was expressed as a percentage of the total moves.

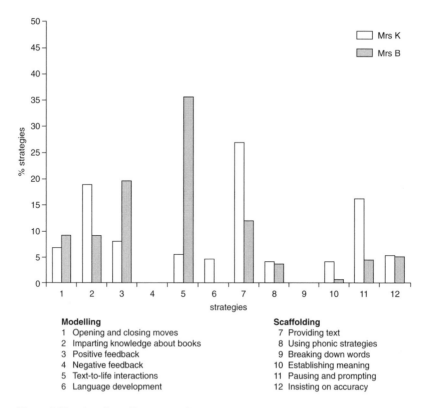

Modelling
1 Opening and closing moves
2 Imparting knowledge about books
3 Positive feedback
4 Negative feedback
5 Text-to-life interactions
6 Language development

Scaffolding
7 Providing text
8 Using phonic strategies
9 Breaking down words
10 Establishing meaning
11 Pausing and prompting
12 Insisting on accuracy

Figure 3 Teachers' reading strategies

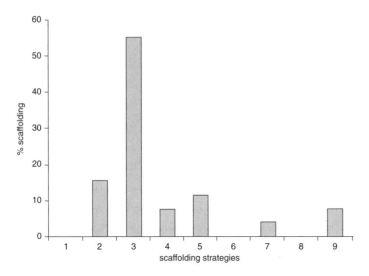

Figure 4 Mrs Kelly reading with group
Source: after Hannon *et al.* (1986)

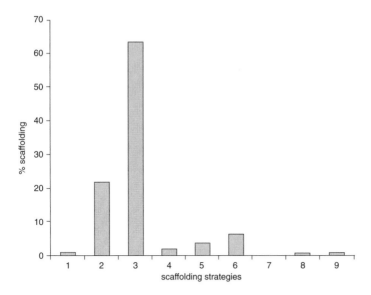

Figure 5 Nadia reading with Aisha
Source: after Hannon *et al.* (1986)

Key to Figures 4 and 5

1 Negative comment	5 Prompting
2 Insisting on accuracy	6 Splitting words
3 Providing whole words	7 Providing initial sounds
4 Pausing	8 Providing auditory clues
	9 Identifying phonic elements

191

We see from Figure 3 that Mrs Kelly uses a balance of modelling and scaffolding strategies, with the seventh strategy, 'Providing text', the most common (27 per cent of all moves). When Mrs Kelly's and Nadia's scaffolding strategies were broken down still further using principally scaffolding strategies (see Hannon *et al.* 1986), the resulting graphs (see Figures 4 and 5) were strikingly similar. It appears that Nadia has observed her teacher so accurately that not only is she now able to read well herself, but she can also reproduce Mrs Kelly's teaching skills in order to teach other children.

It would be wrong, however, to interpret Nadia's learning as a one-way process taking place only from school to home. During silent-reading sessions in her classroom, when Nadia is allowed to read books of her own choosing, she often goes to information books of all kinds. Her teacher noticed how she spent one thirty-minute silent-reading session in school poring over *Flags of the World*, a reference book clearly written for adults. We are reminded of her knowledge of and interest in adult books on nature, plants and birds, which she shares with her grandfather as well as the textbook *Language, Maths and Science Activities* and the *Collins Dictionary* and *Children's Encyclopedia* provided by her mother. The strong desire of Nadia's mother for her daughter to succeed in school may well have predetermined this choice of 'serious' books – a desire fuelled by her belief that her own parents should have put more pressure upon her to work in school. Thus we see that the histories of other family members as well as the strong role model of her teacher, Mrs Kelly, are already influencing Nadia's literacy history. None of this, however, is a passive process. Nadia successfully syncretises home and school learning in a way that shows her confident as a 'reader' at school, at home and with a treasured collection of books in her grandfather's house.

Maruf and his friends: the later syncretism of home and school learning

The early years: learning to learn differently at school

Teacher: *Do you think it was a surprise – the jellybean tree?*
Maruf: *Yeah.*
Teacher: *Do you think he's happy?*
Maruf: *Yeah he had a jellybean tree.*
Teacher: *Do you like jellybeans?*
Maruf: [Shakes his head]
Teacher: *No? Have you had them before?*
Maruf: [Pause . . . nods his head]
Teacher: *You don't like them. Well I do.*

(Rashid and Gregory 1997: 115–16)

How might 6-year-old Maruf and our other Bangladeshi-British children fare as they enter school? How easy do they find it to syncretise home and school learning? Is the process as unproblematic for them as it is for Nadia and her friends? There can be little doubt that the Qur'anic and Bengali classes described in Chapter 6 presented children with a very different type of teaching and learning from that seen in the excerpt from Maruf's classroom taking place above. In contrast with the pattern of 'listen, repeat, practise, test' of both kinds of community class, Maruf's teacher is asking him to reflect upon the text he has just read, interpret the feelings of the character in the story and relate them to his own experience. Whether or not he has ever eaten a jellybean, he soon realises that his response is not appropriate, since Mrs Brown, his teacher, makes it clear that these are something he should know about and like. Nor has this pattern of reading entered into the work between siblings, where comprehension questions remain firmly confined to the text itself. Given such differences in approach, what does happen when home and community learning meet that which is sanctioned by school? Do children participate in parallel but separate ways of learning – or do they find ways in which syncretism is possible?

Mrs Brown, Maruf's teacher, completed her education degree during the 1980s when research in linguistics was highlighting the importance of a knowledge of 'book language' in early literacy tuition.[9] She believed firmly that children learned to read best through meaningful texts that were of 'high quality'. Hence her reading tuition from the very start focused on *meaning*. Books were read to the children and taken home with the aim that parents could read and discuss texts before children were able to read for themselves. However, during the early 1990s, she and other teachers in her school were beginning to rethink their initial literacy programme. They were becoming aware that, paradoxically, 'meaningful' high quality books, especially those with a very colloquial or culturally specific text, might have little meaning for the children with whom they were working, or, indeed, for their parents with whom children were expected to work. For, in their infant classrooms, the children were all still at the beginning stages of learning English and were unfamiliar with both the experiences and the English assumed to be familiar by authors of books. Accompanying the teachers' own rethinking was a fierce debate in the national press by extremists from both the 'phonics' and 'real books'[10] camps of school psychologists and teacher educators as to which approach should best prevail.[11] The teachers were thus beginning to feel pressurised into including both reading schemes as well as more explicit phonics teaching in their early literacy provision. Consequently, the first half of the 1990s had gradually seen the reintroduction of simple reading scheme books into the school and a greater emphasis on the use of phonics to run alongside the policy of 'reading for meaning' using high quality books.

Young teachers like Mrs Brown were caught in uncertainty. How far should they question ideas and ideals learned during own training, in which they had invested much hope, effort and time? Some felt that they were 'betraying' their own beliefs if they used reading schemes at all. Others, like Mrs Brown, adopted the use of schemes and phonics but grafted these on to their existing approach of teaching children to find meaning in the text and relate this to life. Such hasty grafts, however, did not 'take' easily. The excerpts below show us that Maruf and his peers found themselves faced with a number of challenges, different 'rules' they needed to learn in order to participate successfully in the reading lesson. What is the nature of these and how do the children fare during their first two years at school?

In Chapter 6, we saw how the prevalent pattern of interaction in community classes was the child repeating after the teacher. Interestingly, we see how this pattern is actually reversed in this English classroom. Note how Mrs Brown repeats the child's response and the child immediately repeats the last word of the teacher as if it were a correction. Maruf and his peers at first find it difficult to learn that *teachers frequently repeat a child's response* instead of allowing the child to repeat after the 'expert' and then simply continuing. The teacher's aim here is to acknowledge the correctness of the child's response, but time after time we see a truncated interaction occurring whereby the child automatically repeats the teacher's last word even though he/she has already read it correctly.

Mrs B: *OK. Point to the words like you did last time.*
Sh: [*There*] *String.*
Mrs B: *String.*
Sh: *String. . . . on the . . . upstairs.*
Mrs B: *upstairs.*

In the extract below, Mrs Brown is trying to encourage Shima to use phonics to try to read a word. However, phonics have not yet been taught systematically and Shima is unsure of what to do. Mrs Brown also subtly changes her question from 'What letter does that start with?' to 'What does that say?' Shima appears not to understand that on one occasion the letter, and on another the whole word, is required. The pattern also denies Shima the opportunity first to repeat after the adult and is very different from home and community class reading sessions.

Mrs B: *What letter does that word start with?*
U: *F.*
Mrs B: *What does that start with?*
U: *M.*
Mrs B: *What is that?* [Child does not respond.] . . . *M-ma . . .*
U: *Mat.*

Mrs B: *What does that say? Last page.*
    [Child does not respond.] *Go on.*
U: *String on the cat.*

Another task that must be learned is to *interpret* texts. Below, we see how Uzma has to learn that Mrs Brown is encouraging her to interpret the text, using the illustration, and to interpret *why* someone might be doing something. Uzma is asked to identify with the character in the story and to try to predict what he might do – an approach very alien to her community classes. Again, the child must take the initiative to recommence reading.

Mrs B: *Why did he put flour on the car? Why do you think he put flour on the car?*
Sh: *He was playing.*
Mrs B: *Why do you think he was playing? Pretending that the flour is . . .*
Sh: [Does not respond.]
Sh: *Snow?*
Mrs B: *Snow! I think you're right.*

The question posed below, 'How many times did you read this book?', is not familiar to Shima either from her home or community classes. Mrs Brown expects Shima to understand and take responsibility for the choice of 'little or lot' and tries again to repeat the child's response after her.

Mrs B: *OK. How many times did you read this book?*
Sh: *I don't know.*
Mrs B: *Little bit or a lot?*
Sh: *Last.*
Mrs B: *Hm?*
Sh: *Last.*
Mrs B: *Lots? OK, Shima, thank you.*
Sh: *Little.*
Mrs B: *Only little? Thank you.*

It is, perhaps, hardly surprising that the children have difficulty in 'situating' themselves in the task. Mrs Brown is not familiar with the children's home and community learning and does not realise the contrasts in style they face. Maruf, in Chapter 6, explained seriously how 'gaining meaning' was separate from 'reading' or decoding the text in his Qur'anic class. In their English class, it is assumed that these beginner readers can use 'meaning' to help them to decode a text. We might conclude that children are expected to reverse the rules they are learning elsewhere. We see from Figures 3 and 6 how different Mrs Brown's (teacher 2) strategies are from those of both the children's siblings and Mrs Kelly (teacher 1).

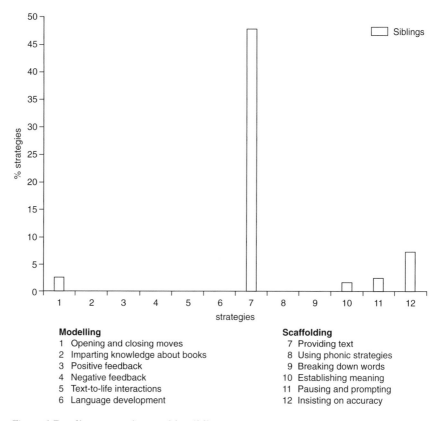

Modelling

1 Opening and closing moves
2 Imparting knowledge about books
3 Positive feedback
4 Negative feedback
5 Text-to-life interactions
6 Language development

Scaffolding

7 Providing text
8 Using phonic strategies
9 Breaking down words
10 Establishing meaning
11 Pausing and prompting
12 Insisting on accuracy

Figure 6 Reading strategies used by siblings

Mrs Brown felt that her most important task was to enable these children to make personal sense of the text by relating events to their own experiences in life and Figure 3 shows that she feels most confident with this approach. In contrast to Mrs Kelly, Mrs Brown had less experience in using text-directed strategies and was not quite sure how far to prompt children towards an accurate reading of the text.

But differences emerging from the graphs take us only one step in understanding what is happening in the classroom. There was also a major difference in the reading programmes used by the two teachers that may have facilitated teaching and learning in Mrs Kelly's class (where the majority of children were also emergent bilinguals). Mrs Kelly worked almost entirely through class and small-group reading sessions, whereas Mrs Brown felt she needed to listen to children read individually. However, as we saw in Chapter 6, Mrs Brown's children were accustomed to see reading largely as a group activity in their Qur'anic and Bengali classes. Indeed, in these community classes, individual reading was associated with being 'tested'. In contrast, the group reading sessions in Mrs Kelly's class gave children an excellent opportunity to scaffold each other's learning by providing answers, by correcting each other, allowing repetitions as well as echoing, and all in a non-threatening way. The group reading sessions also allowed phonics to be used as a collaborative way of making sense of a text, rather than remaining an isolated piece of teaching used by a teacher with an individual child. Mrs Brown was, in fact, surprised to hear that her children were all confident users of phonics in two other languages, but in their English classroom were confused as to what, precisely, they were meant to do. But there are other factors contributing to children's misunderstandings that were beyond Mrs Brown's control. Not only did the text of this particular reading scheme hold as little meaning and less interest for the children as that of a more difficult but higher quality text but Mrs Brown also found it boring. Putting flour on a car is an unlikely activity and one that is impossible to predict for most children, not least those where every penny is important in a household budget.

And so, at the end of their first year together in school, Mrs Brown and her children appeared to be using very different strategies as they set about the teaching and learning of reading. The children were bringing with them an expectation of 'listen and repeat' that focused on the text itself; Mrs Brown expected an ability to reflect upon and question the text. It would be easy at this stage to diagnose a clash of expectations and learning practices between home or community classes and school, resulting in parallel approaches to learning by the children and little chance of syncretism.[12] However, a very different and more optimistic picture can be found by returning to the children five years later, just before they proceed to their secondary school. Here we experience rather different patterns of teaching and learning taking place.

The shared world of home and school: playing school at 11

Five years later, 11-year-old Wahida, a classmate of Maruf, Shima and Uzma,[13] is 'playing school' with Sayeeda, her 8-year-old sister. Wahida's friend Kadija joins her during the maths 'lesson' as a classroom helper. Different 'lessons' follow the pattern of the school day: reading is followed by maths, then a spelling test, a session on homophones, assembly, science, geography and art. The children have a blackboard and chalk on which she demonstrates and writes questions and Sayeeda has an exercise book in which she writes answers.[14] We eavesdrop first on the maths lesson:

Wahida: *Good morning class.*
Sayeeda: *Good morning Miss Wahida, good morning everyone.*
Wahida: *I want to do the register. So, Sayeeda.*

Sayeeda: *Good morning Miss Wahida.*
Wahida: *Good morning Sayeeda.*
Wahida: *OK. We've done your reading today. Now we are going to do maths. OK. What's 24 × 4? If you can't do it, there is another easier way to do 'times'. Do you know what that is? Yes, Sayeeda, good girl for putting your hand up.*
Sayeeda: *I can't do lattice . . .*
Wahida: *OK. We'll do one together. OK. We'll do 24 × 4. First we draw a box . Then we do a line across and then we do two lines that way – diagonal way – yes, well done. Now you write 24 on the top and then on the side you write 4. Well done. So what's 4 times 4? What's 4 × 4?*
Sayeeda: *Sixteen.*

The maths 'lesson' continues, increasing gradually in difficulty:

Wahida: *So, I'm going to put some sums on the board for you, OK? Ready?*
Sayeeda: *Yes.*
Wahida: *The first sum's going to be – OK, Sayeeda, do you remember to write the date first?*
Sayeeda: *Yes, Miss.*
Wahida: *Well done! Now I'm going to write the sums. The first sum is 30 × 5 equals? If you want to do lattice, you can. Or you can do your own way, you can, or you can do in your mind, but I would love to see some working out. Yes, Sayeeda?*
Sayeeda: *Can I do lattice?*
Wahida: *Yes, you can. That's what I said. The next sum is number two is 15 × 6 equals? 20 × 4 equals? The last one is 25 × 4. OK, I'm going to give you some time to do it. OK, Sayeeda, ready?*
Sayeeda: *Yes.*
Wahida: *You can start now.*

The opening session of Wahida's maths lesson illustrates how skilfully she teaches her younger sister to participate in both the social and the cognitive demands of school learning. How does she go about this? We see clearly her mastery of the procedural rules[15] of the English classroom that she practises with Sayeeda. More precisely, she initiates the session with 'Good morning class . . . ', praises Sayeeda's good behaviour, 'good girl for putting your hand up', 'Well done!') and later tells her 'I'm going to give you a sticker . . . a headteacher's sticker . . . '. She reminds her sister of school rituals: 'do you remember to write the date first?'; 'We've only got another five minutes until assembly', and later, after assembly, 'Welcome back, children', 'OK, children, it's lunchtime now and I am going to have to do choir', 'We've got a new helper here called Miss Kadija. Say "Good morning" to her'. She reminds her sister of the marking routine: 'Put a tick near it if you got it right, put a cross if you got it wrong. What's your mark, Sayeeda?' Finally, she reminds

198

her of the need to be polite, shown by her frequent use of 'please'; 'Can you tell me some, please?; Can you only give me three, please?'.

Her sophisticated knowledge of the sociocultural rules and corresponding language of successful participation in lessons parallels ways in which she structures the cognitive demands made by her different 'lessons'. A very explicit opening move or interval marker introduces each new section of a session. Consequently, new expectations are announced clearly: 'We've done your reading. Now we're going to do maths . . . ; I'm going to give you some sums . . . ; And then we'll do English. OK?; You can start now . . . ; Now we're going to do spelling test. Are you ready?; I'm going to give you at least twenty seconds for each of them . . . ; OK, Sayeeda, I want your results now, please; Now we're going to do homophones. Who knows what a homophone is?; Now we're going to do science. We're going to do electricity. Now we're going to investigate. Are you ready? . . .' After announcing what is expected, Wahida carefully confines the task to what she knows the child is capable of with just a little help. At the same time, she 'scaffolds' the child's learning, through finely tuned tuition, giving the younger child hints and encouragement.

What might this scaffolding look like? The following strategies stand out clearly:

1 Scaffolding through demonstration, providing a model

In the extract below, Wahida pitches the task at just above Sayeeda's ability level and carefully puts words into sentences. In this way, Sayeeda will learn not just the word and how to spell it but the context in which it is appropriate, i.e. the English meaning of the word.

Wahida: *Now we're going to do spelling test. Are you ready Sayeeda?*
Sayeeda: *Yes, Miss.*
Wahida: *I'm going to give you at least twenty seconds for each of them, OK? The first one is 'tricycle', 'tricycle'. Tricycle has three wheels, 'tricycle'. The next one is 'commandment', 'commandment'. I **command** you to do as quickly as you can, Sayeeda. Otherwise you're going to get in **big** trouble. 'Commandment'.*

Next one is 'technology'. Technology is a subject. Once you're grown up, Sayeeda, you're going to do hard technology. The next one is 'polydron'. Polydron is something you play with or do maths with. 'Polydron'. Don't look at each other's work, Sayeeda especially. The next one is 'cuboid'. A cuboid is a box that you play with or make during maths. A cuboid. The last one is 'capacity'. Capacity is what you measure in water with. Capacity. That was the final one, children. Now you're going to mark it yourselves. Then you're going to tell me how – what your results are.

2 Scaffolding through direct instruction and checking up on past learning

It would appear that these homophones have been 'taught' on a previous occasion.

Wahida: *Now we're going to do homophones. Who knows what a homophone is? No one? OK. I'll tell you one and then you're going to do some by yourselves. Like 'watch' – one watch is your time watch, like 'What's the time?' watch. And another watch is 'I'm watching you. I can see you'. OK? So Sayeeda, you wrote some in your book, haven't you? Can you tell me some, please, Sayeeda? Can you only give me three, please?*

Sayeeda: *Oh, I want to give five.*

Wahida: *No, Sayeeda, we haven't got enough time. We've only another five minutes to assembly. And guess who's going to do assembly – Miss Kadija.*

Sayeeda: *OK.*

Wahida: *OK. So tell me one.*

Sayeeda: *'Son' is the opposite of 'daughter' . . .*

Wahida: *Yeah.*

Sayeeda: *and 'sun' is . . . um . . . it shines on the sky so bright.*

Wahida: *Well done! That's one correct one. The next one?*

Sayeeda: *The 'cell' means you go . . . to jail . . . in prison . . . you're going to prison and another 'sell' means the selling money . . . they are giving money.*

Wahida: *The last one is?*

Sayeeda: *Hear. 'Hear' is you're hearing something . . . people are telling you something and 'here' is 'come here'.*

Wahida: *Well done! Now you can go to assembly. Sayeeda, line up in order. Otherwise, you'll come back and do lines. So remember your order, OK?*

3 Scaffolding through providing alternatives if the younger child is in difficulty

Wahida: *If you can't do it, there is another easier way to do 'times'. Do you know what that is? . . . We'll do one together . . .*

Wahida: *Or you can do your own way, you can, or you can do in your mind, but I would love to see some working out . . .*

4 Scaffolding through giving her sister confidence to complete the task successfully

This comprises frequent use of 'Well done!' followed by 'put a tick beside it', 'only two wrong', 'I'm going to give you a sticker', etc.

There can be little doubt that Wahida, like most of her classmates, now has an intimate knowledge of many of the social and cognitive 'rules' of successful classroom learning. Gone is the confusion of five years earlier, replaced now by a confidence in which she uses appropriately whole 'chunks' of teacher language pronounced with the exact accent and intonation of her teacher. While playing school neither child slips out of role to use Sylheti for explanations or corrections. She is also confident in understanding the content and structure of both her sister's and her own lessons. Unlike her parents (or, indeed, most other people outside the teaching profession), she is able to use the appropriate lexis of different subjects (lattice, homophones, circuit, etc.) as well as the appropriate method of teaching, sectioning her lessons, announcing clearly the task in hand and how it will be completed.

Would this knowledge and ability have developed automatically over time, or could particular factors have contributed to her confidence? Teachers and parents familiar with the new National Literacy and Numeracy Strategies introduced into schools in 1998 and 1999 will immediately recognise many of Wahida's strategies as well as whole chunks of her lessons. The division of her lessons into sections accompanied by a clear announcement of what will be taught is reminiscent of recommendations in the strategy (the division of lessons into a whole-class section, followed by group work, followed by a reporting back by groups to the class). With extraordinary accuracy, Wahida's literacy 'lessons' on spelling and homophones fit into the 'word level work' recommended for children of her sister's age. At the same time, the content and strategies she uses fit well into the Bengali lessons that she and her sisters still attend. We may assume that it is not coincidental that Wahida's 'lessons' proficiently cover the 'word level' rather than either the 'sentence level' or the 'text level' work, both of which demand a more intimate knowledge of English grammar and comprehension as well as the ability to relate the text to one's own life. Nevertheless, it may be the case that the clarity of the new literacy hour structure does indeed enable her to draw upon existing knowledge and understandings and successfully use these as an entry point to the literacy of school.

Let us, then, allow Wahida, one of our youngest generation, to conclude this chapter with optimism, showing through play-acting today what she will be capable of achieving tomorrow:

Welcome back, children. Now we're going to do science. We're going to do electricity – about circuits because tomorrow or the next day we're going to make circuits of our own. So I'm going to show you how to make a circuit and then you're going to do it by yourselves. You always need wires, battery, bulb, switch – you can always make a switch by yourselves so it doesn't matter . . . and if so you need a crocodile clip. When you make a circuit, you always need a good battery for your bulb to light, obviously. You need the two wires to touch the two sides of the battery. And the bulb needs a bulb holder to sit up . . . the wire has a . . . a metal stuff so it can touch the bulb's screw for it to light . . . the metal. So that's when it lights up. Then you can make your own switch whenever you want. If you want to make one switch you can do . . . That's how I know to make a switch. You need a card with two pins and you wrap . . . and you wrap the paper clip around the one pin and then when you want the bulb to light up easily you need the wire's, erm, er silver bits to touch the pin so it . . . for the paper clip to go with the wire and then you wrap it . . . when you touch the paper clip to the other pin it lights up. So you're going to make your own circuit today. So you can start now. OK?

EPILOGUE

The aim of *City Literacies* has been to highlight the wealth of literacy practices in the lives of those often considered by the educational establishment to be 'deprived' of literacy. Throughout the twentieth century, these practices contrasted not just with the 'official' ways of the school, but between groups and individuals living and learning side by side in the same class. Thus in Part I we gave a historical perspective, revealing some of the contrasts both between and within the City and Spitalfields, as well as the different educational and literacy provision for the poorer members of each community. In Part II, these contrasts were embodied in the memories of different generations of pupils living and learning in both communities. Our pre-war generation looked back on the contrasts between 'Jewishness' and 'Englishness' portrayed through different lives and literacies; our post-war generation contrasted grammar and secondary modern education and the different ways of life provided by each, and our group of young Bangladeshi British women contrasted literacy practices across English and community schools and across generations. Finally, Part III raced to the end of the twentieth century and revealed some of the contrasts in literacy practices taking place in the monolingual English and Bangladeshi Londoners' lives as well as between both groups and the literacy of the school. Throughout the book, we have argued that access to *contrasting literacies* gives children strength, not weakness; that our children have a treasure trove upon which to draw as they go about understanding the literacy demands of the school.

However, our aim in this book has been not only to celebrate a diversity of literacy practices in children's lives. Although important, this diversity might not convince educators and policy-makers of the need to recognise as valid what takes place outside school. Rather, our intention has been to stress the ways in which each generation has syncretised home and school learning, drawing upon one to inform and change the other into a dynamic whole. This has been especially true for children entering school with a different home language and very different cultural practices from those of the school. In Chapter 3, Aumie told us how he brought aspects of his classical Hebrew

203

grammar learning into his English classroom and how this home knowledge gave him a greater awareness of English grammar. Norma and Gloria lived for their library books to learn about 'English culture'; it was their teachers in school who had first introduced them to these books. Abby remembered newspapers, atlases and visits to Kew Gardens as important literacy practices in her school; she later became a horticulturalist and took her old atlas as a gift to the school. Stanley read the classics at home with his mother and later recalled his love of these in school. The syncretism of home and school literacies continued to our younger generation of Bangladeshi-British women. We saw in Chapter 5 how Nina's work with her children reflected a combination of her memories of the English school and her community class learning. Ros retained vivid memories of her Bengali classes and how these informed her English school learning. Finally, we saw in Chapter 7 the extraordinary skill with which Wahida blended the teaching from her English and community schools as she worked with her younger sister.

What do participants in this book tell us about the teaching of literacy, and above all reading, in multilingual and inner-city classrooms? Throughout the twentieth century, we saw a whole variety of teaching approaches in use. However, each generation of pupils made it perfectly clear that *method* as such has not been the only factor in their successful acquisition of literacy but that the teacher's knowledge, her/his love of teaching and learning, high expectations and a respect for the child also played an important role. The two teachers in the study were differentiated, not so much by their teaching methods, but by the extent to which they presumed 'shared knowledge' with their pupils. Mrs Brown assumed that her pupils shared her culture and interpretation of the reading task, whereas Mrs Kelly adapted her approach to her pupils and worked to build up a shared classroom culture in which all the children participated.

So what might be the implications of this study for the future generation of learners and their teachers in Spitalfields? We cannot yet tell whether or in what ways the National Literacy Strategy introduced in Britain in 1998 will facilitate the literacy learning of children in the twenty-first century. Certainly, their teachers have become increasingly aware of their children's strengths in terms of vocabulary learning, spelling, phonics and grammar work. All this defies notions of cognitive or language deficit that previously may have prevailed, and in that respect the new strategy could be hailed as a success. As yet, however, teachers are still unsure whether or how these undoubted strengths can be built upon to increase comprehension, a love of English literature and an ability to relate school literacy to their own lives. Norma, Gloria and our other Jewish participants in Chapter 3 would probably remind us here of the importance of wishing to become part of the new culture in order for this kind of learning to begin. However, even they admit that such a wish is not so simple for the latest generation of migrants to Spitalfields at the start of the twenty-first century.

At this time, the 'gentrification' of Spitalfields is progressing fast. From one week to the next, its narrow lanes are filling up with wine bars, restaurants, health shops and, above all, with expensive accommodation for City workers. Every possible opportunity – even a bomb-blast in Brick Lane in spring 1999 – was seized upon to restore and transform simple shopfronts to a Georgian or Victorian splendour they may not have originally possessed.[1] Our older participants in the study reflect with astonishment that they could no longer afford to live in the very places they fled over thirty years ago. It seems, indeed, that the more a building can be transformed from its original purpose, the more sought-after it becomes and the higher is the asking price. Particularly fashionable are the original Soup Kitchen for the Jewish Poor and the old warehouses with ornate brickwork and large windows facing directly on to the City. One of the most recent transformations has been the old brewery that now houses chic fashion and art boutiques. A nightclub has finally broken the evening and weekend 'curfew' that hitherto allowed the Bangladeshi-British exclusive 'rights' to the streets. Does this mean a completely new era for Spitalfields? Will Canon Barnett School simply be demolished, or turned into desirable loft accommodation?

Spitalfields has not yet lost its other, darker face and contrasts still abound. In spite of its new rich, white population, local schools still have 99–100 per cent Bangladeshi-British pupils. In spite of the chic studios and health shops, the homeless and destitute still gather at Christ Church Spitalfields for a hot meal in the evenings, as they have done for the last three hundred years. Despite the large sums of money being invested in the area, Bangladeshi-British families are still refusing pay-outs to leave their 'desirable' houses and flats. Might, therefore, the present invasion of wealth simply mirror what happened in the nineteenth century when the upper classes from West London came East at weekends to find excitement in noisy pubs and bawdy houses? We do not know. But if Spitalfields is now to become a satellite of the City, a playground for its wealth, then existing and new immigrants will be found further east where accommodation is cheaper. East Ham, just five miles eastwards, now bears a striking resemblance to the Spitalfields of ten years ago.

Whether Spitalfields will remain on the cusp of change, embracing both rich and poor, or, whether, in the twenty-first century, it will actively exclude its poorer population and be overtaken by the City, we cannot know. This book, however, serves as a document of the twentieth century as it was. Its purpose is to give a voice to those families and teachers from local schools whose voices might otherwise have been submerged in the panic to raise standards in inner-city areas. It is, finally, a celebration of the remarkable versatility of Spitalfields children as, throughout life and against all odds, they have excelled in facing the challenge of new and increasingly complex worlds.

NOTES

Prologue

1 Padmore (1994).
2 Programmes for economically disadvantaged children set up during the 1960s and still continuing.
3 See Greenhaigh and Hughes (1999) for recent research in the British context, and Gallimore and Goldenberg (1993) for work in the USA.

Introduction: poverty and illiteracy – the deficit myth

1 Moll, Amanti, Neff, and Gonzalez (1992).
2 After an unhappy school career, Raymond enrolled for adult literacy classes and is now an avid reader.
3 Exceptional to this are children of first-generation immigrants who speak of leaving school because of family responsibilities, and place their hopes in their children.
4 Bereiter and Engelmann (1966).
5 Work in psychology was positing the interdependence of thought and language: 'Thought is not merely expressed in words; it comes into existence through them' (Vygotsky 1962: 125). Consequently, a child's intellectual growth was seen as contingent upon mastering language, which enabled the systematising of direct experiences, the categorisation of experiences and the formation of hypotheses.
6 The argument that different linguistic and cultural groups had access to certain modes of thought and observation was emerging from studies in anthropology. Language was said to predetermine certain modes of observation and, since the 'real' world was said to a large extent to be 'built up' upon the language habits of the group, no two groups would view reality in the same way (Sapir, 1949; Whorf, 1956).
7 Work during the 1950s by Bernstein (1958 in 1973: 54) had claimed that working-class boys used a significantly lower number of uncommon verbs, adjectives and conjunctions as well as cognitive verbs and phrases such as 'I think' and showed that 'the emotional and cognitive differentiation of the working-class child is comparatively less developed'.
8 'Children who are brought up in a home background where the forms of speech are restricted are at a considerable disadvantage when they first go to school and may need to have considerable compensatory opportunities for talking if they are to develop verbal skills and form concepts' (para. 55). The Report goes on to claim that children must understand 3,000 words before reading tuition can successfully begin.

9 Studies of early language development at this time were emphasising the importance of the home environment in terms of the quality and quantity of verbal interactions given by the adult in making 'rich interpretations' of children's speech (Brown 1973). The adult was seen to act as a model of conventional interpretations of intentions which were signalled by vocalisations given (Newson and Newson 1975; Bruner 1975).

10 Halliday (1973), particularly proposed a functional model of language development; that is, as the child learned the functions of language, he/she learned a system of meaningful behaviour or a semiotic system. The ways in which the child used the functions and patterns of meaning were determined by the child's family within the culture and subculture. In other words, the child constructed a semiotic or meaning system through interaction within the family and subculture.

11 Studies in psychology argued that experience with written language enabled children to gain a detached relationship with language rather than a personal interactive one. This would involve learning to converse with an unknown audience, where the text would be autonomous, presenting 'integrity' and 'detachment' rather than the 'fragmentation' and 'involvement' of spoken texts (Olson 1977). At the same time, linguists argued that children needed to see that written language involves carrying paralinguistic features into syntax as well as using an elaborate syntax (Halliday and Hasan 1976). Dombey (1983) showed convincingly how infants discussing familiar storybooks were able to use more complex syntax and lexis than in everyday speech.

12 Wells (1985); Wells (1987).

13 Ibid. (1987) p. 146.

14 Packets of Persil washing powder currently show a mother reading a bedtime story to her child with the caption: 'Bedtime Story: Brilliant non-bio cleaning for people who want things comfortable next to their family's skin'.

15 See Hannon (1995) for an overview of schemes currently taking place in Britain.

16 By September 1999, all schools must have set up official contracts with parents whereby specific homework tasks must be overseen.

17 See Jespersen (1923); Saer (1924); Goodenough (1926). In 1917, Goddard, in the USA, wrote of a huge increase of 'aliens' being deported because of 'feeble-mindedness'; it was later generally recognised that the aim behind this was a socio-political one – to restrict entry to foreigners while still maintaining that they were being given a 'fair' test (Goddard 1917).

18 Already in the 1930s, Vygotsky was claiming that bilingualism enabled a child 'to see his language as one particular system amongst many, to view its phenomena under more general categories ... which leads to awareness of linguistic operations'; see also Feldman and Shen (1971), Ianco-Worrall (1972), Ben-Zeev (1977), Hakuta (1986), among others.

19 Aramaic: the language of Jesus and the Apostles. Aramaic dialects are still spoken by some small groups in the Middle East.

20 The word for 'read' in classical Arabic is 'qara'a', which means 'recite by heart' (Baynham 1995: 28).

21 Although Cummins (1979) does not refer to this type of support within the definition of 'additive' (the reference is to bilingual education in Canadian schools), the scope and structure of community classes in Britain means they should be included in this frame.

22 Although the British Education Reform Act (1988) promised that the National Curriculum Council would be 'taking account of ethnic and cultural diversity and ensuring that the curriculum provides equal opportunities for all pupils regardless of ethnic origin or gender' (NCC 1988: 4), a promise which has been

reiterated until the end of the twentieth century, 'equality of opportunity' is interpreted as meaning 'the same provision for all' and bilingualism or biculturalism is mentioned in the National Curriculum and accompanying documents only in the context of children needing additional assistance in learning English. Although a task force was set up by the NCC in 1989 to investigate the provision for equality of opportunity, the government decided not to publish its findings and the group was disbanded in 1991. Tomlinson provides its obituary in 'The multicultural task group: the group that never was' (1993: 21).

23 A regional dialect of Bengali spoken in Sylhet.

24 Hamers and Blanc (1989: 7) stress the need to distinguish between the 'bilinguality' of an individual and the 'bilingualism' existing within a community. 'Bilinguality' must be viewed as a multidimensional phenomenon, including not just linguistic but social, psychological and cultural competence or 'at homeness' by the individual.

25 Differences between the Huguenots, Jews and Bangladeshis in Spitalfields are examined in Kershen (1997: Ch. 5).

26 From the reports given by our group. No generalisations can be made here.

27 Since the Education Act in 1988, parents have been able to choose a school for their child which may not refuse them unless full. For a full discussion on the implications of this policy, see Tomlinson (1997), 'Diversity, choice and ethnicity: the effects of educational markets on ethnic minorities', *Oxford Review of Education*, Vol. 23, No.1: 63–76.

28 Work by Thorndike (1874–1949) was influential at this time. Thorndike maintained that learning to read involved forming as many bonds between neurons in the brain as possible.

29 See Piaget (1926), Chomsky (1965) and Kelly (1955).

30 Important pioneers in this field were Sylvia Ashton-Warner, who worked using 'One Sight' words or an 'organic vocabulary' as early reading material with Maori children; and Paolo Freire's work (1973) in adult literacy in Brazil where reading sessions started with a discussion of key or generative words in people's lives before breaking words into patterns and sounds (see also Gregory 1996 for a summary of the impact of both practitioners on reading tuition for children in Britain).

31 Smith (1978); Wells (1985).

32 Waterland (1985).

33 Holdaway (1979).

34 Baynham (1995).

35 Barton and Hamilton (1998).

36 Rummelhart (1977).

37 This is particularly interesting, since the change to each new approach in the past was made for a specific reason: from letter names to phonics to enable children to build up words independently; from phonics to 'look-and-say' to help children to avoid irregularities and frustrations in blending sounds and to build up a large sight vocabulary; from whole word to language experience to enable children to predict chunks of text from their own experiences; and from language experience to story in order to help children to master the special nature of written story language. The arrival of the literacy hour has not so much signalled a change of method as a shift from individual to whole class and group work.

38 Introduced by David Blunkett under the Labour government in 1998.

39 Bourdieu (1977) refers to this as sharing the 'cultural capital' of the school, which he sees as an absolute requirement of early school success.

40 Street (1993).

41 See Goody and Watt (1968) and Olson (1977) for examples of this argument for 'autonomous' literacy as well as Street's (1984) response.
42 Street (1984); Barton and Hamilton (1998); Baynham (1995).
43 Barton and Hamilton (1998).
44 Baynham (1995: 39).
45 Padmore (1994).
46 Padmore (1994); Luke and Kale (1997); Williams (1997).
47 Volk (1997); Gregory (1998).
48 Bourdieu (1997).
49 Cole (1996: 273, 183).
50 Bateson (1979: 13).
51 Bruner (1986).
52 Vygotsky (1978).
53 Dunn (1989).
54 Rogoff (1990).
55 Duranti and Ochs (1996).
56 The work continued during 1999: the focus moved to siblings and children's literacy development in Bangladeshi-British and monolingual English families living in the Whitechapel area.
57 Ochs and Schiefflin (1979); Heath (1983); Duranti and Ochs (1996).
58 Anderson and Stokes (1984).
59 Barton and Hamilton (1998).
60 Cole (1996).
61 In addition, the relevant chapters of the book were returned to participants for their comments, which were then incorporated into the text.
62 Geertz (1973).
63 Bloome and Theodorou (1987).
64 Baynham (1995); Barton and Hamilton (1998).
65 Plenary paper presented at the Ethnography and Education Conference, University of Pennsylvania, Philadelphia, March 1999.

Part I: Living and learning east of the Aldgate pump

1 Places and peoples

1 District under a particular jurisdiction and administration.
2 Stow (1598: 97).
3 Porter (1994: 54).
4 Stow (1598: 116).
5 Tenter: device used for stretching and drying cloth.
6 Stow (1598: 116).
7 Laystalls: refuse heaps.
8 Stow (1598: 376).
9 Porter (1994: 91).
10 Inwood (1998: 187).
11 Ibid. p. 68.
12 Ibid. p. 71.
13 Ibid. p. 157.
14 Cited in Inwood (1998: 159).
15 Ibid.
16 Earle, P. (1994) *A City Full of People: Men, Women of London*, cited in Inwood (1998: 272).

17 Arthur Young, cited in Porter (1994: 133).
18 An activity conducted when there was fog on the line. When a train was in danger, an explosive clip was put on the line so that the driver would be warned of danger.
19 By 1700 there were approximately 20,000 Jews in London, most of whom were Sephardic Jews from Spain and Portugal, but the Ashkenazim from Poland and Germany were beginning to arrive and settle in Whitechapel. In addition, it has been estimated that there were between 5,000 and 10,000 black men and women, who had come as seamen or as slaves (Porter 1994: 132).
20 Cox (1994: 117).
21 Many of these elegant houses survive in the streets around Christ Church, Spitalfields. At the beginning of the twenty-first century, they are some of the most expensive houses in the capital and are very much sought after by lovers of Georgian architecture.
22 Defoe cited in Porter (1994: 116).
23 Throwsters: spinners.
24 Charles Greville, politician, cited in Porter (1994: 195).
25 Inwood (1998: 413).
26 Coster-monger: street seller of fruit or fish.
27 Mayhew (1851–62: 1949 edn, P. Quennell (ed.), p. 30).
28 Ibid. p. 278.
29 Ibid. p. 213.
30 Charles Booth (1892–7) *Life and Labour of the People of London*: vol 1, cited in Fishman, W. (1979), *The Streets of East London*, London: Duckworth p. 76.
31 Mayhew (1851–62: 1949, edn, P. Quennell (ed.), p. 273).
32 Harkness (1889) *In Darkest London*, cited in Fishman (1988).
33 Mayhew (1851–62: 1949 edn, P. Quennell (ed.), p. 275).
34 Ibid. p. 287.
35 White (1980: 250).
36 Felling: hand-stitching which attached the lining to main body of the garment.
37 Masher: fop.
38 Webb (1926: Pelican edn, 1938: 362).
39 Inwood (1998: 450).
40 Webb (1926: Pelican edn, 1938: 360)
41 Quotation taken from Mearns (1883).
42 Harkness (1889) *In Darkest London*, quoted in Fishman (1988: 83).
43 Porter (1994: 257).
44 *East London Advertiser*, Nov. 1888, cited in Fishman (1988: 21).
45 Fishman (1988: 18).
46 London (1903: 249).
47 Ibid. p. 117.
48 Morrison (1896: 138).
49 Whitechapel Board of Guardians: Minutes 21 December 1875, cited in White (1980).
50 Webb (1926: Pelican edn, 1938: 311).
51 White (1980: 35).
52 Ibid. p. 35.
53 Ibid. p. 70.
54 Sokoloff (1987: 59).
55 Published in *The Link*, 24 June 1888.
56 White (1980: 208).
57 Ibid. p. 255.
58 Greeners: new Jewish immigrants.

59 18.1 per cent, Asghar, M.A. (1996) B*angladeshi Community Organisations in East London*, London: Bangla Heritage Ltd, p. 60.
60 Ibid.
61 Eade (1997: 95).
62 Adams (1987).
63 Alam (1988).
64 Eade (1997: 92).
65 Alam (1988).
66 Adams (1987: 39).
67 Ibid. p. 46.
68 Alam (1988: 21).
69 Ibid. p. 15.
70 Adams (1987: 52).
71 Eade (1997: 104).
72 Ibid.

2 Schooling the City

 1 Stow (1598).
 2 The school attended by Cass girls who passed the eleven-plus. Joy, whom we meet in Chapter 4 started here at age 11.
 3 Stow (1598: 66).
 4 Barron (1996) 'The expansion of education in fifteenth century London', in J. Blair and B. Golding (eds) *The Cloister and the World*, cited in Inwood, (1988: 138).
 5 Briggs (1983: 118).
 6 Stow (1598: 68).
 7 Porter (1994: Penguin edn, 1996: 59).
 8 In London, women's literacy rates were much higher than the national level (Graff 1987).
 9 Langford (1984: 391).
10 Defoe (1724).
11 Langford (1984: 392).
12 Ibid.
13 Inwood (1998: 288).
14 Glynn (1998).
15 Ibid.
16 Education inspector cited in Knox (1960: Ch 3, n. 13).
17 Knox (1960).
18 Ibid.
19 Glynn (1998: 36).
20 Ragged schools were set up by philanthropic individuals for homeless and destitute children. The Ragged School Union was established in 1844 to manage the schools.
21 Booth (1892–7) *Life and Labour of the Poor of London*: Poverty Series vol 3. 202, cited in Inwood (1998: 690).
22 Webb (1926: Penguin edn, 1938: 301).
23 White (1980: 170).
24 Ibid.
25 Ibid. p. 175.
26 Ibid. p. 176.
27 Bermant (1969: 23).
28 Cited in Fishman (1988: 173).

29 Zangwill (1892: 512).
30 Ibid. p. 95.
31 Webb cited in Fishman (1979: 78).
32 Fishman (1979: 78).
33 Zangwill (1892: 182).
34 Ibid.
35 Webb cited in Fishman (1979).
36 Zangwill (1892: 182).
37 Bermant (1969: 127).
38 Madrassah: a Muslim college.
39 We are grateful to Caroline Adams and Ali Asghar for information compiled on Qur'anic and Bengali classes taking place in Spitalfields.
40 Robert in Chapter 3 of this book refers to the City libraries provided by each ward.
41 Keating (1976).
42 Cited in Keating (1976).
43 Keating (1976: 108).
44 Briggs and Macartney (1984: 4).
45 Lord Asquith cited in Briggs and Macartney (1984: 30).
46 Briggs and Macartney (1984: 5).
47 Inwood (1998: 510).
48 Ibid. p. 511.
49 Briggs and Macartney (1984: 5).
50 Ibid. p. 53.
51 Ibid. p. 31.
52 Ibid. p. 62.
53 Ibid. p. 67.

Part II: Childhood memories of literacy and learning

Introduction

1 Paid according to the amount of work completed.
2 See refs in Fishman (1988: 289) for more information on the great dock strike of 1889.
3 Bourdieu's (1977) ideas on 'social, economic and cultural capital' and schooling are helpful here: see Carrington and Luke (1997) for a detailed analysis of these.
4 We are grateful to Marilyn Martin-Jones and Jenny Cook-Gumperz for helpful comments on an earlier version of part of this chapter in Gregory (1999: 89–111).

3 Literacy for survival

1 The outbreak of World War II was chosen as the dividing point between the generations since it marks clearly the end of an era in the twentieth century. All the participants in this chapter share crucially important memories of learning in the pre-war and war years; all were born too early to reap the benefits of post-war prosperity during their childhood and the educational advantages this was to bring.
2 See Introduction to this book for a detailed outline of this.
3 Interviews with members of this group took place in 1998.

4 Vividly described in Charles Dickens' *Dombey and Son* (1867) and later referred to as having a 'decivilising influence' on the population by cutting off back-streets from main roads; quoted in Fishman (1988).

5 The first Ripper victim was found in Gunthorpe Street in 1888, just thirteen years before Commercial Street School was built almost on this spot (Fishman 1988). The slaughter of animals often took place in full view of children at this time.

6 During World War II, 164 of the City's 460 acres of buildings were devastated; 18 City Churches (14 of which were designed by Wren) were destroyed. There was complete devastation around St Paul's as well as the area around the Tower of London, close to which one member of our group was living.

7 1947.

8 This was partly due to children whose families did not return to London from evacuation during the war. Many classes had fallen to thirty in post-war London.

9 The Hadow Report (1931) had already stated the importance of promoting more 'child-centred' education in infant schools.

10 Inwood (1998: 811).

11 The term 'East End' was first used around 1880 and rapidly caught on. 'A shabby man from Paddington, St. Marylebone or Battersea might pass muster as one of the respectable poor. But the same man coming from Bethnal Green, Shadwell or Wapping was an "East Ender", the box of Keating's bug-powder must be reached for, and the spoons locked up'; quoted in Fishman (1988: 1).

12 The term 'English Londoner' has been chosen by the participants in question.

13 The total income-tax assessment on the City during 1879–80 was £41 million, more than half the combined assessment of Britain's twenty-eight major provincial cities. Of the forty richest men dying between 1809 and 1914, at least fourteen were City merchants, bankers or brokers.

14 Inwood (1998: 494).

15 These figures are from the City's own census. See Inwood (1998: 105).

16 Booth (15,4) industry series, vol. 3, 277–8, in Inwood (1998: 496).

17 Stanley was born in the ward of St George's-in-the-East, south of Spitalfields, described by Booth (1892–7) as having 49 per cent of its population living in extreme poverty and the poorest parish in the area. Eric was born in Bethnal Green, to the east of Spitalfields, referred to by Booth as a parish so poor that it vied with St George's in the 'unenviable race' of being the poorest in the area (Fishman 1988: 33).

18 Even here, the City retained its power and exclusivity. A special licence was given to those born in the City entitling them to trade in City markets such as Billingsgate.

19 Minnie refers to children who had these illnesses, but they were not unknown in the Christian children's lives. One of Robert's aunts had died of diphtheria as an infant, another of TB and an uncle had suffered from rickets as a child.

20 Speaking books on to audiotapes.

21 The Yeshiva at Aldgate was regarded as the Jewish equivalent of the grammar school where boys would attend five evenings a week to become learned in the Talmud, the book of Jewish law. This was written in Aramaic and classical Hebrew.

22 Dutch Jews were well established in London, anglicised and often indistinguishable from their gentile Cockney neighbours (Fishman 1988: 132).

23 Chain of cafes and restaurants, popular in the pre- and early-post war years.

24 This term is used by Moll *et al.* (1992) See Introduction to this book, p. 1.

25 Sir Basil Henriques, an ex-resident of Toynbee Hall, established the Oxford and St Georges Club for youngsters in the East End.

26 A reference section stocked with daily and weekly newspapers.
27 Norma's favourite was Angela Brazil.
28 The Central Foundation School where he was a pupil from age 11 to 14.

4 Literacy for equality

1 Sokoloff (1987).
2 Lowe (1988: 5).
3 Inwood (1998: 812).
4 Lowe (1988: Introduction).
5 Sokoloff (1987: 77).
6 Ibid. p. 89.
7 Dent (1968: 1).
8 Lowe (1988: 79).
9 *Report of the Secondary Examinations Council on Curriculum and Examinations in Secondary Schools* (The Norwood Report).
10 Lowe (1988: 37).
11 Cited in Gordon *et al.* (1991).
12 Lowe (1988: 38).
13 Evans (1991: 25).
14 Ibid. p. 26.
15 Hoggart (1957: 296).
16 TES 24 June 1949, cited in Lowe (1988: 50).
17 Jackson and Marsdon (1962).
18 Hoggart (1957: 296).
19 TES 30 March 1946, cited in Lowe (1988: 45).
20 Sokoloff (1987: 88).

5 Literacy for choice

1 For example, Nulon, Samuel Lewis, London & Quadrant, Toynbee, Spitalfields Co-operative, etc. See Asghar (1996: 72); as Asghar points out, this did not occur without a struggle and a long campaign by the BHAG (Bengali Housing Action Group).
2 Although Tahmin and Ros's families live in this area, both women are still deciding where they eventually want to live.
3 The eleven-plus was abolished by the LCC in 1963.
4 See the Introduction to this book, pp. 4–5, for a fuller account of these reports.
5 See DES (1975: 5:1).
6 See DES (1988: 2.3).
7 This is the term chosen by the group of women and has, therefore, been used throughout the book.
8 See also Minns (1990), Gregory (1998) and Gregory and Williams (1998) for other examples of the complex and structured approach used in home reading sessions between parents and siblings with young children in linguistic-minority homes.
9 The *Peter and Jane* books were part of a comprehensive series of structured readers known as the 'Happy Venture' series and widely used during the 1960s and 1970s in British schools. By the 1980s, they were rejected by many teachers in multicultural primary schools owing to their ethnocentric and middle-class suburban bias.
10 In current times, 'fun' in early reading in Britain is not generally considered to be compatible with a formal, structured approach at home.

11 See particularly Wells (1985) and Cochran-Smith (1984). The latter study of a middle-class kindergarten in Philadelphia showed how parents were concerned that their children should not be given any official literacy tuition at school (nevertheless, these children were found already to have acquired considerable literacy skills from home).

12 See particularly DES 1975; 1988); also the Introduction to this book on pp. 4–5.

13 At this time (the early 1980s) handwriting exercises for young children were virtually unknown in infant schools in London, as in many areas in Britain. Certainly, writing anything out a hundred times would have been uniformly frowned upon.

14 A number of research studies argue for the transference of literacy skills from one language to another, providing there is a threshold level of skill in both languages. For a summary, see Gregory (1994).

15 See the introduction to this book, pp. 7–13, for a brief historical account of change in approaches to teaching reading throughout the century.

16 See Waterland (1985) for a detailed description of the 'apprenticeship' approach to reading, and Gregory (1994) for an explanation of linguistic and psycholinguistic approaches.

17 The 'child-centred' curriculum, (see Blenkin and Kelly 1981), with its roots in Rousseau's work, was based on children's learning as an individual, not in competition with others. A child-centred orientation influenced the curriculum in most British state primary schools until the introduction of the National Curriculum in 1989, after which it was considerably weakened.

18 The examination taken in Britain at 18 years of age needed to qualify for entrance to university.

Part III: Looking ahead: young literacies, lives and learning

Introduction

1 See Kelly (1994: 1–23) for a discussion of discourse in relation to the Education Reform Act.

2 This power is rather in theory than reality, and has occurred very rarely.

3 The publication of exam results is national for ages 11 and 16 and local for ages 7 and 14. From 1999, children are also to be tested at age 5 as they enter official schooling.

4 See Tomlinson (1997) for a discussion on diversity, choice and ethnicity in the wake of the Education Reform Act.

5 See Tomlinson (1995) for a critical analysis of this procedure.

6 Information is drawn from Tower Hamlets Language Census (1994) and reported in London Borough of Tower Hamlets reports: *Pupil Language Census* (1994a) and *Education Statistics* (1994b), Policy and Performance Monitoring, Directorate of Education and Community Services.

7 The number 36,000 represents between 60.7 per cent (Decennial Census 1991) and 95 per cent (City Challenge) of the population of the community (information cited in Kershen 1997). It should also be noted that there is undoubtedly a considerable number of illegal immigrants as well as legal immigrants who were unwilling to declare themselves on the Census because of the poll tax then in operation (Kershen 1997).

8 GCSE (General Certificate of Secondary Education) is the examination taken at age 16.

6 Living literacies in homes and communities

1 Luke and Kale (1997: 16).
2 Office for Standards in Education.
3 Adult Literacy and Basic Skills Unit (1993) *Parents and their Children: the Intergenerational Effects of Poor Basic Skills*, London: ALBSU.
4 Wells (1985).
5 Snow and Ninio (1986: 136).
6 *Guardian*, 29 July 1997.
7 Heath (1983).
8 Street and Street (1995).
9 Dyson (1997).
10 Padmore (1994).
11 Luke (1992).
12 Luke (1992: 39).
13 Rashid, N. (1996) *Field Notes from Family Literacy History and Children's Learning Strategies*, Final Report to ESRC (R000221186).
14 The names of the graphic symbols on the page.
15 Rashid, N. (1996) *Field Notes from Family Literacy History and Children's Learning Strategies*, Final Report to ESRC (R000221186).
16 Ibid.
17 Gregory (1998).
18 A fuller explanation of reading in the Islamic world can be found in Wagner (1993).
19 Rashid, N. (1996) *Field Notes from Family Literacy History and Children's Learning Strategies*, Final Report to ESRC (R000221186).
20 Luke and Kale (1997).

7 Learning the literacy of school

1 Williams (1997).
2 See the Introduction to this book on p. 10.
3 See Cazden (1988) and Gregory (1996) for a fuller description of these categories and early reading.
4 The lessons cited here took place before the NLS was introduced in schools.
5 The teacher for children learning English as an additional language. In a school like Sir John Cass, where approximately 70 per cent of the pupils have English as an additional language, each teacher would have some additional help every week.
6 Mrs Kelly's role is reminiscent of that of a conductor at work with an orchestra, bringing in different instruments to complement each other at appropriate times.
7 This expression has been used to describe the pattern taking place between caregiver and infant during labelling in picture-book reading sessions.
8 The categories used were based originally on work by Hannon *et al.* (1986) and later adapted to suit our data.
9 See the Introduction to this book on p. 8, for a fuller explanation of this.
10 'Real books' was simply another term for non-reading-scheme books or books written for the value of their text and illustrations rather than with the express aim of teaching reading.
11 Lessons at this time were on the cusp of the introduction of the NLS in 1998 that was rumoured to want a stage-by-stage structured reading programme.
12 This is the most accepted finding in previous research studies. See, for example, Heath (1983); Michaels (1986).

13 Wahida is participating in the ESRC funded *Siblings as mediators of literacy in two east London communities* (R000222487) from 1998–9. The recordings were made by Ali Asghar.

14 The children often play school together and were left by the researcher Ali Asghar to tape the session on their own.

15 See Street and Street (1995) for an example of how procedural rules work in one US primary school context.

Epilogue

1 This was one of three bomb blasts occurring in London in the spring of 1999 (the others were in Brixton and Soho). They were originally thought to have been the work of organised right-wing extremists but were in fact caused by an individual acting independently.

BIBLIOGRAPHY

Adams, C. (1983) 'The East End community school', unpublished MS.

—— (1987) *Across Seven Seas and Thirteen Rivers*, London: THAP Books.

Ahlberg, J. and Ahlberg, A. (1978) *Each Peach, Pear, Plum*, London: Penguin.

Alam, F. (1988) *Salience of Homeland: Societal Polarisation within the Bangladeshi Population in Britain*, Research Papers in Ethnic Relations, ESRC publication.

Adult Literacy and Basic Skills Unit (1993) *Parents and their Children: the Intergenerational Effects of Poor Basic Skills*, London: ALBSU.

Anderson, A.B. and Stokes, S.J. (1984) 'Social and institutional influences on the development and practice of literacy', in H. Goelman, A. Oberg and F. Smith (eds) *Awakening to Literacy*, Portsmouth, NH: Heinemann Educational.

Asghar, M.A. (1996) *Bangladeshi Community Associations in East London*, London: Bangla Heritage Ltd.

Ashton-Warner, S. (1963) *Teacher*, London: Penguin.

Baker, C.D. and Freebody, P. (1989) 'Talk around text: construction of textual and teacher authority in classroom discourse', in S. Castell, A. Luke and C. Luke (eds) *Language, Authority and Criticism*, Lewes: Falmer Press.

Baker, K. (1987) Speech to annual Conservative Party Conference, Blackpool, 7 October 1987.

Barton, D. and Hamilton, M. (1998) *Local literacies. Reading and Writing in One Community*, London: Routledge.

Barton, D. and Ivanič, R. (1991) *Writing in the Community*, London: Sage.

Bateson, G. (1979) *Mind and Nature*, London: Wildwood House.

Baynham, M. (1995) *Literacy Practices. Investigating Literacy in Social Contexts*, London: Longman.

Ben-Zeev, S. (1977) 'The influence of bilingualism on cognitive strategy and cognitive development', *Child Development*, 48: 1009–18.

Bereiter, C. and Engelmann, S. (1966) *Teaching Disadvantaged Children in the Pre-School*, Englewood Cliffs, NJ: Prentice Hall.

Bermant, C. (1969) *Troubled Eden*, London: Valentine Mitchell & Co.

Bernstein, B. (1973) 'Social class, language and socialisation', in A.S. Abramson *et al.* (eds) *Current Trends in Linguistics*, 12, Amsterdam: Mouton Press.

Besant, A. (1893) *An Autobiography*, London.

Blenkin, G.A. and Kelly, A.V. (1981) *The Primary Curriculum*, London: Harper & Row.

Bloome, D. and Theodorou, E. (1987) 'Analysing teacher–student and student–

student discourse' in J. Green, J. Harker and C. Wallatt (eds) *Multiple Analysis of Classroom Discourse Practices*, Norwood, NJ: Ablex.

Booth, C. (1892–7) *Life and Labour of the People of London*, London: Macmillan.

Bourdieu, P. (1977) *Outline of a Theory of Practice*, Cambridge: Cambridge University Press.

Briggs, A. (1983) *A Social History of England*, London: Weidenfeld and Nicolson. (Penguin edn, 1985.)

Briggs, A. and Macartney, A. (1984) *Toynbee Hall: the First Hundred Years*, London: Routledge & Kegan Paul.

Brown, R. (1973) *A First Language in the Early Stages*, Cambridge, MA: Harvard University Press.

Bruner, J.S. (1975) 'The ontogenesis of speech acts', *Journal of Child Language*, 2: 1–20.

—— (1986) *Actual Minds, Possible Worlds*, Cambridge, MA: Harvard University Press.

Burt, C. (1955) 'The evidence for the concept of intelligence', *British Journal of Educational Psychology*, 25: 158–77.

Carrington, V. and Luke, A. (1997) 'Literacy and Bourdieu's sociological theory: a reframing', *Language and Education: An International Journal*, 11(2): 96–112.

Cazden, C.B. (1967) 'On individual differences in language competence and performance', *Journal of Special Education*, 1: 135–50.

—— (1988) *Classroom Discourse*, Portsmouth, NH: Heinemann Educational.

Chomsky, N. (1965) *Aspects of the Theory of Syntax*, Cambridge: MA: MIT Press.

Cochran-Smith, M. (1984) *The Making of a Reader*, Norwood, NJ: Ablex.

Cole, M. (1996) *Cultural Psychology: a Once and Future Discipline*, Cambridge, MA: Harvard University Press.

Cox, J. (1994) *London's East End*, London: Phoenix Illustrated.

Cullen, K. (1969) *School and Family*, London: Gill & Macmillan.

Cummins, J. (1979) 'Linguistic interdependence and the educational development of bilingual children', *Review of Educational Research*, 49: 225–51.

Defoe, D. (1724) *Tour through England and Wales*, London.

Dent, H.C. (1968) *The Education Act 1944*, London: University of London Press.

Department of Education and Science (1931) *The Hadow Report*, London: HMSO.

—— (1967) *Children and their Primary Schools* (The Plowden Report), London: HMSO.

—— (1975) *A Language for Life* (The Bullock Report), London: HMSO.

—— (1985) *An Education for all: The Report of the Committee of Inquiry into Education for Children from Ethnic Minority Groups* (The SWANN Report), London: HMSO.

—— (1987) *The National Curriculum 5–16. A Consultation Document*, London: HMSO.

—— (1988) *English for Ages 5–11. Proposals of the Secretary of State* (The Cox Report, November), London: NCC/HMSO.

Dombey, H. (1983) 'Learning the language of books' in M. Meek (ed.) *Opening Moves*, London: Bedford Way Papers, 17, Institute of Education.

Douglas, J.W.B. (1964) *The Home and the School*, London: Macgibbon & Kee.

Dunn, J. (1989) 'The family as an educational environment in the pre-school years' in C.W. Desforges (ed.) *Early Childhood Education, The British Journal of Educational Psychology: Monograph Series No. 4*. Scottish University Press.

Duquette, G. (1992) 'The home culture of minority children in the assessment and development of their first language', *Language, Culture and Curriculum*, 5(1): 11–22.

Duranti, A. and Ochs, E. (1996) *Syncretic Literacy: Multiculturalism in Samoan American Families*, University of California: National Center for Research on Cultural Diversity and Second Language Learning.

Dyson, A. H. (1997) *Writing Super Heroes*, New York: Teachers' College Press.

Eade, J. (1997) 'Keeping the options open: Bangladeshis in a global city' in A.J. Kershen (ed.) (1997).

Edwards, V. (1998) *The Power of Babel: Teaching and Learning in Multilingual Classrooms*, Stoke-on-Trent: Trentham Books.

Erikson, F. (1999) Plenary speech at Ethnography Forum, University of Pennsylvania, Philadelphia, 5–7 March.

Evans, M. (1991) *A Good School: Life at a Girls' Grammar School in the Fifties*, London: Women's Press.

Feldman, C. and Shen, M. (1971) 'Some language-related cognitive advantages of bilingual five year olds', *Journal of Genetic Psychology*, 118: 125–244.

Fishman, W.J. (1979) *The Streets of East London*, London: Duckworth.

—— (1988) *East End 1888*, London: Duckworth.

Freire, P. (1973) *Education: The Practice of Freedom*, London: Writers and Readers Publishing Co-operative.

Gallimore R. and Goldenberg, C. (1993) 'Activity settings of early literacy: home and school factors in children's emergent literacy' in E. Forman, E. Minick and C.A. Stone *Contexts for Learning*, New York: Oxford University Press.

Geertz, C. (1973) *The Interpretation of Cultures*, New York: Basic Books.

Glynn, S. (1998) *Sir John Cass and the Cass Foundation*, London: Sir John Cass Foundation Press.

Goddard, H.H. (1917) 'Mental tests and the immigrant', *Journal of Delinquency*, 2: 271.

Goodenough, F. (1926) 'Racial differences in the intelligence of school children', *Journal of Experimental Psychology*, 9: 388–97.

Goody, J. and Watt, I. (1968) 'The consequences of literacy' in J. Goody (ed.) *Literacy in Traditional Societies*, Cambridge: Cambridge University Press.

Gordon, P., Aldrich, R. and Dean, D. (1991) *Education Policy in England in the Twentieth Century*, London: Woburn Press.

Graff, J.J. (1987) *The Labyrinths of Literacy: Reflections on Literacy Past and Present*, London: Falmer Press.

Greenhaigh, P. and Hughes, M. (1999) 'Encouraging conversing: trying to change what parents do when their children read with them', *Reading* 33(3): 98–105.

Gregory, E. (1994) 'Cultural assumptions and early years' pedagogy: the effect of the home culture on minority children's interpretation of reading in school', *Language, Culture and Curriculum*, 7 (2): 111–24.

—— (1996) *Making Sense of a New World: Learning to Read in a Second Language*, London: Paul Chapman.

—— (1997) (ed.) *One Child, Many Worlds: Early Learning in Multi-Cultural Communities*, London: David Fulton Publishers.

—— (1998) 'Siblings as mediators of literacy in linguistic minority communities', *Language and Education: An International Journal*, 12(1): 33–55.

—— (1999) 'Myths of illiteracy: childhood memories of reading in London's East End', *Written Language and Literacy*, 2(1): 89–111.

Gregory, E. and Williams, A. (1998) 'Family literacy history and children's learning strategies at home and at school: perspectives from ethnography and ethnomethodology', in G. Walford and A. Massey (eds) *Children Learning in Context: Studies in Educational Ethnography*, vol. I, Stanford, CT: JAI Press.

—— (forthcoming) 'Work or play?: "unofficial" literacies in the lives of two East London communities', in K. Jones and M. Martin-Jones (eds) *Multilingual Literacies: Comparative Perspectives on Research and Practice*, New York: John Benjamins.

Gregory, E., Mace, J., Rashid, N. and Williams, A. (1996) *Family Literacy History and Children's Learning Strategies at Home and at School*, Final Report to the ESRC ref. R000 221186.

Hakuta, K. (1986) *Mirror of Language: The Debate on Bilingualism*, New York: Basic Books.

Halliday, M.A.K. (1973) *Explorations in the Function of Language*, London: Edward Arnold.

Halliday, M.A.K. and Hasan, K. (1976) *Cohesion in English: English Language Series*, London: Longman.

Hamers, J.F. and Blanc, M.H. (1989) *Bilinguality and Bilingualism*, Cambridge: Cambridge University Press.

Hamilton, M., Barton, D. and Ivanič, R. (eds) (1994), *Worlds of Literacy*, Clevedon: Multilingual Matters.

Hannon, P. (1995) *Literacy, Home and School*, London: Falmer Press.

Hannon, P., Jackson, P. and Weinberger, J. (1986) 'Parent and teacher strategies in hearing young children read', in *Research Papers in Education*, 1(1): 6–25.

Hayes, A.E. (1929) *Phonoscript First Primer*, London: G.P. Putnam's Sons Ltd.

Heap, J. (1985) 'Discourse in the introduction of classroom knowledge; reading lessons', *Curriculum Inquiry*, 16(1): 243–79.

Heath, S.B. (1983) *Ways with Words: Language and Life in Communities and Classrooms*, Cambridge: Cambridge University Press.

Heath, S.B. and Branscombe, C. (1984) 'The achievement of pre-school literacy for mother and child', in H. Goelman, A. Oberg and F. Smith (eds) *Awakening to Literacy*, Portsmouth, NH: Heinemann Educational.

Hoggart, R. (1957) *The Uses of Literacy*, London: Chatto & Windus. (Penguin edn, 1962.)

Holdaway, D. (1979) *The Foundations of Literacy*, New York: Ashton Scholastic.

Ianco-Worrall, A. (1972) 'Bilingualism and cognitive development', *Child Development*, 43: 1390–400.

Inwood, S. (1998) *A History of London*, London: Macmillan.

Jackson, B. and Marsden, D. (1962) *Education and the Working Class*, London: Routledge & Kegan Paul.

Jespersen, O. (1923) *Language*, London: George Allen & Unwin.

Keating, P.J. (1971) *The Working Classes in Victorian Fiction*, London: Routledge.

—— (1976) *Into Unknown England 1866–1913*, London: Fontana Collins.

Kelly, A.V. (1994) 'Beyond the rhetoric and the discourse', in G.M. Blenkin and A.V. Kelly (eds) *The National Curriculum and Early Learning: An Evaluation*, London: Paul Chapman.

Kelly, G. (1955) 'A theory of personality', MS, The Norton Library.

Kershen, A. J. (ed.) (1997) *London: The Promised Land? The Migrant Experience in a Capital City*, Aldershot: Avebury.

Knox, H.J. (1960) 'The Origin, Development and Present Day Function of a City of

London School', thesis presented for the Diploma of Fellow of the Royal College of Preceptors.

Labov, W. (1969) 'On the logic of non-standard English', *Georgetown Monographs on Language and Linguistics*, 22, Washington, DC: Georgetown University Press.

—— (1970) 'The study of language in its social context', *Studium Generale*, 23(1): 30–87.

Langford, P. (1984) 'The eighteenth century 1688–1789', in K. Morgan (ed.) (1984).

London Borough of Tower Hamlets (1994a) *Pupil Language Census 1994*, Policy and Performance Monitoring Unit.

—— (1994b) *Education Statistics 1994*, Policy and Performance Monitoring Unit.

London, J. (1903) *The People of the Abyss*, London.

Lowe, R. (1988) *Education in the Post War Years: a Social History*, London: Routledge.

Luke, A. (1992) 'The social construction of literacy in the primary school', in L. Unsworth (ed.) *Literacy, Learning and Teaching: Language as a Social Practice in the Classroom*, Melbourne: Macmillan.

Luke, A. and Kale, J. (1997) 'Learning through difference: cultural practices in early language socialisation' in E. Gregory (ed.) (1997).

Mayhew, H. (1851–62) *London Labour and the London Poor*, 4 vols, London: Griffin.

Mearns, A. (1883) 'The bitter cry of outcast London', in P. Keating (ed.) (1976), pp. 91–111.

Meek, M. (1988) *How Texts Teach What Readers Learn*, Stroud, Glos: Thimble Press.

Michaels, S. (1986) 'Narrative presentations: an oral preparation for literacy with 1st graders', in J. Cook-Gumperz (ed.) *The Social Construction of Literacy*, Cambridge: Cambridge University Press.

Minns, H. (1990) *Read it to Me Now!*, London: Virago Press.

Moll, L.C., Amanti, C., Neff, D. and Gonzalez, N. (1992) 'Funds of knowledge for teaching: using a qualitative approach to connect homes and classrooms', *Theory into Practice* 31(2): 133–41.

Morgan, K. (ed.) (1984) *The Oxford Illustrated History of Britain*, Oxford: Oxford University Press.

Morrison, A. (1896) *A Child of the Jago*, London: Nelson.

National Curriculum Council (1988) *Introducing the National Curriculum Council*, London: NCC.

—— (1992) *Starting out with the National Curriculum*, London: NCC.

Newson, E. and Newson, J. (1975) 'Intersubjectivity and the transmission of culture: on the social origins of symbolic functioning', *Bulletin of the British Psychological Society*, 218: 437–46.

Ninio, A. and Bruner, J.S. (1978) 'The achievement and antecedents of labelling', *Journal of Child Development*, 5: 5–15.

Ochs, E. and Schiefflin, B. (eds) (1979) *Developmental Pragmatics*, New York: Academic Press.

Ofsted (1996) *The Teaching of Reading in 45 Inner London Primary Schools* (Ref 27/96/D5), London: Ofsted.

—— (1998) *Requirements for Courses of Initial Teacher Training*, Circular number 4/98, London: DfEE/Ofsted.

Olson, D. (1977) 'From utterance to text: the bias of language in speech and writing', *Harvard Educational Review*, 47(3): 257–81.

Olson, D., Torrance, N. and Hildyard, (eds) (1985) *Literacy, Language and Learning*, Cambridge: Cambridge University Press.

Padmore, S. (1994) 'Guiding Lights', in M. Hamilton, D. Barton and R. Ivanič (eds) *Worlds of Literacy*, Clevedon: Multilingual Matters.

Piaget, J. (1926) *The Language and Thought of the Child*, London: Routledge & Kegan Paul.

Porter, R. (1994) *London: A Social History*, London: Hamish Hamilton. (Penguin edn 1996.)

Rashid, N. and Gregory, E. (1997) 'Learning to read, reading to learn: the importance of siblings in the language development of bilingual children', in E. Gregory (ed.) (1997).

Rogoff, B. (1990) *Apprenticeship in Thinking: Cognitive Development in Social Contexts*, Oxford: Oxford University Press.

Rogoff, B., Mistry. J., Goncu, A. and Mosier, C. (1993) 'Guided participation in cultural activity by toddlers and caregivers', *Monographs of the Society for Research in Child Development*, 58: (8) Serial No. 236.

Rummelhart, D.E. (1977) 'Toward an interactive model of reading', in H. Singer and R. Ruddell (eds) *Toward a Psychology of Reading*, Hillsdale, NJ: LEA.

Sacks, H., Schleghoff, E.A. and Jefferson, G. (1974) 'A simplest systematic for the organisation of turn-taking', *Language*, 50(4): 696–735.

Saer, D.J. (1924) 'An inquiry into the effect of bilingualism upon the intelligence of young children', *Journal of Experimental Pedagogy*, 6: 234–40, 266–74.

Sapir, E. (1949) 'Linguistics as a science', in G. Mandelbaum (ed.) *Language, Culture and Personality*, California: University of California Press.

School Curriculum and Assessment Authority (1996) *Desirable Outcomes for Children's Learning in Nurseries*, London: SCAA.

Schwarz, L.D. (1979) 'Income distribution and social structure in London in the late eighteenth century', *Economic History Review*, 32.

Searle, C. (1973) *Stepney Words I & II*, London: Centreprise Publications.

—— (1986) *All Our Words*, London: Young World Press.

Sims, G. (1889) How the poor live (extracts) in P.J. Keating (ed.) (1976), pp. 65–90.

Smith, F. (1978) *Understanding Reading*, 2nd edn, New York: Holt, Reinhart & Winston.

—— (1979) *Reading*, Cambridge: Cambridge University Press.

Snow, C. and Ninio, A. (1986) 'The contracts of literacy: what children learn from learning to read books', in W.H. Teale and E. Sulzby (eds) *Emergent Literacy: Reading and Writing*, Norwood, NJ: Ablex.

Sokoloff, B. (1987) *Edith and Stepney*, London: Stepney Books.

Stow, J. (1598) *A Survey of London*, Everyman edn, London: J.M. Dent & Sons.

Street, B.V. (1984) *Literacy in Theory and Practice*, Cambridge: Cambridge University Press.

—— (1993) *Cross-Cultural Approaches to Literacy*, Cambridge: Cambridge University Press.

Street, B.V. and Street, J. (1995) 'The schooling of literacy', in P. Murphy, M. Selinger, J. Bourne and M. Briggs (eds) *Subject Learning in the Primary Curriculum*, London: Routledge.

Tomlinson, S. (1993) 'The multicultural task group: the group that never was', in

A.S. King and M.J. Reiss (eds) *The Multicultural Dimension of the National Curriculum*, London: Falmer Press.

—— (1995) 'Hit squad needs new set of rules' *Times Educational Supplement*, 19 December: 12.

—— (1997) 'Diversity, choice and ethnicity: the effects of educational markets on ethnic minorities', *Oxford Review of Education*, 23(1): 63–76.

Verhoeven, L. (1987) *Ethnic Minority Children Acquiring Literacy*, Dordrecht: Foris.

Volk, D. (1997) 'Continuities and discontinuities: teaching and learning in the home and school of a Puerto Rican five year old', in E. Gregory (ed.) 1997.

Vygotsky, L. (1962) *Thought and Language*, Cambridge, MA: MIT Press.

—— (1978) *Mind in Society: The Development of Higher Psychological Processes*, Cambridge, MA: Harvard University Press.

Wagner, D. (1993) *Literacy, Culture and Development: Becoming Literate in Morocco*, Cambridge: Cambridge University Press.

Waterland, L. (1985) *Read with Me: An Apprenticeship Approach to Reading*, Bath: Thimble Press.

Webb, B. (1938) *My Apprenticeship*, 2 vols (Pelican edn), London: Penguin.

Wells, C.G. (1985) 'Pre-school literacy related activities and success in school', in D. Olson *et al.* (eds) (1985).

—— (1987) *The Meaning Makers: Children Learning Language and Using Language to Learn*, Portsmouth: NH: Heinemann.

White, J. (1980) *Rothschild Buildings*, London: Routledge & Kegan Paul.

Whorf, B.L. (1956) *Language, Thought and Reality*, Cambridge, MA: MIT Press.

Williams, A. (1997) 'Investigating literacy in London: three generations of readers in an East End family', in E. Gregory (ed.) (1997).

Williams, A. and Gregory, E. (1999) 'Home and school reading practices in two East End communities', in A. Tosi and C. Leung *Rethinking Language Education: from a Monolingual to a Multilingual Perspective*, London: Centre for Information on Language Teaching and Research.

Zangwill, I. (1892) *Children of the Ghetto*, 1998 edn, M.J. Rochelson (ed.), London: Heinemann.

INDEX

Numbers in *italic* refer to pages containing illustrations.